REAL TIME:
A TRIBUTE TO HASSO PLATTNER

REAL TIME:
A TRIBUTE TO HASSO PLATTNER

WILEY

Wiley Publishing, Inc.

Vice President & Executive Group Publisher: Richard Swadley
Vice President and Executive Publisher: Bob Ipsen
Publisher: Joe Wikert
Executive Editorial Director: Mary Bednarek
Acquisitions Editor: Katie Mohr
Senior Development Editor: Kevin Kent
Editorial Manager: Mary Beth Wakefield
Production Editor: Gabrielle Nabi
Project Coordinator: Bill Ramsey
Copy Editor: Foxxe Editorial Services
Text Design & Composition: Wiley Composition Services

Published by
Wiley Publishing, Inc.
10475 Crosspoint Boulevard
Indianapolis, IN 46256
www.wiley.com

Copyright © 2004 by Wiley Publishing, Inc., Indianapolis, Indiana

Published simultaneously in Canada

ISBN: 0-7645-7108-7

Manufactured in the United States of America

10 9 8 7 6 5 4 3 2 1

Preface

The Executive Board of SAP AG conceived of this book as a unique tribute to a unique individual. Hasso Plattner turning 60 is for all of us at SAP a time to reflect and say thanks. In 2003, Hasso took the helm as the chairman of the supervisory board of SAP, a position that, under German law, meant he could no longer be an employee of the company, ending a tenure that had lasted more than 30 years, since he helped create the firm. In 2004, Hasso turned 60, another milestone in a life crowded with activity and accomplishment.

All of us have sparred with Hasso through so many years of intellectual challenges in business and engineering that we felt strongly that any tribute had to reflect that experience. We chose the form of the *Festschrift*, a German word for a document that is produced at the end of a distinguished academic career. In the classic form, other academics in the field write original work that evaluates the contribution of the celebrated individual.

Accordingly, Hasso's *Festschrift* gathers the opinions of industry leaders from business, technology, and research and focuses their minds on the real-time enterprise, a concept that is at the very core of SAP's success. After all, the R in R/2® and R/3® stands for real time.

We focused on the real-time enterprise because, at SAP, we feel that it represents the highest form of value we can provide our customers. If our software and technology can assist in implementing the real-time enterprise that allows companies to anticipate and react with lightening speed to business conditions, then we are doing that job that SAP was founded to do.

What you will find in this book is a slow-motion version of a conversation with Hasso. Each commentator brings a career's worth of insight to the discourse, and a vast amount of ground is covered, from the early days of SAP to the way that web services will change corporate culture. The process of creating this book was a joy and a pleasure for the board. The quality of the thinking we gathered and the overwhelming response we received makes our tribute to Hasso all the more meaningful. We hope that readers find in this book their own path to the real-time enterprise and the success the fulfillment of that dream will bring.

ACKNOWLEDGMENTS

The SAP Executive Board is deeply thankful for the wisdom and generosity of the contributors to this book:

Pekka Ala-Pietilä	Claus Dieter Hoffman
Chris Anderson	Dietmar Hopp
Craig R. Barrett	Ravi Kalakota
Vinton Cerf	Alan Kay
Bruce Chizen	Vinod Khosla
Alan Cooper	Ulrich Kipper
Esther Dyson	Martin Klitten
Carly Fiorina	Anil Kumar
Michael Fleisher	Geoffrey Moore
Joe W. Forehand	Hubert Österle
Friedrich Fröschl	August-Wilhelm Scheer
Bill Gates	Ed Toben
Michael Hammer	Reinhold Würth
Bruce Harreld	

While the SAP Executive Board conceived of this project and helped assemble the contributors, we delegated most of the execution to Claudia Alsdorf, who, we are told, set new records in the publishing industry for one of the shortest publication cycles ever. She will be held to that standard in her new job leading SAP Inspire, the company's internal innovation and venturing initiative.

This book had many friends inside SAP. Herbert Heitmann, Head of Global Communications, and Oliver Christ, Board Assistant, helped to manage this project, assemble contributors, communicate with the board, and craft the deal with the publisher. Pascal Brosset provided valuable editing and commentary.

Dan Woods, author of several books about SAP technology, along with the team of writers from his firm, the Evolved Media Network, helped to bring many of the sections of the book to life and proved that writing could be a real-time activity. The writers who contributed to this book include Greg Lindsay, Charlie Rogers, John Verity, and Jerry Weinstein, all of whom have long careers writing about technology topics. Ronnie Peters created the graphics in the introduction. Deb Cameron, the author of several technical books including a guide to the Emacs editor, which sits on many shelves at SAP, was a masterful editor and distilled this book into the smooth form in which you find it.

Our partners in finishing the book were the publishing team at John Wiley & Sons. Katie Mohr and Kevin Kent helped in the trenches. Mary Bednarek provided excellent advice on how to structure this project. Jackie Smith made sure the deal got done. We are grateful for their efforts and professionalism.

Of course, we offer our most profound thanks to Hasso Plattner for bringing this grand enterprise to life.

The SAP Executive Board, January 2004
Henning Kagermann
Shai Agassi
Léo Apotheker
Werner Brandt
Claus E. Heinrich
Gerhard Oswald
Peter Zencke

Contents

Contents

Introduction

SAP Executive Board

In sports or in our work, most of us enjoy the thrill of the intense moment when conscious decision gives birth to effective action. On a soccer field, we are in the heat of the game. The ball tumbles toward us, and we move forward to kick it down field, partly conscious, but mostly instinctive. On the golf course, we think through our situation and plan a shot. As our backswing begins, we descend into our body. Instincts and training drive the club through the ball. It is in these moments that we are fully engaged. If the ball goes in the goal or the cup, we are flush with triumph.

This experience of our mind and body working together — partly conscious, partly automatic — is the essence of "real time" that we would like to explain in this book: Real time is a clear path from stimulus through decision to an effective response.

The enterprise now faces the possibility of getting closer to real time than at any previous moment. Senior management, the conscious brain of the enterprise, has better information provided by more systems and sources than ever before. The operational complex at most companies provides the instinct, in terms of a growing base of automated processes that can be set in motion to coordinate incredibly complex tasks. But from any perspective we are just at the beginning of fulfilling even the most conservative vision of what is possible.

The essence of the real-time enterprise is reducing the excise tax of inefficiency at all levels of a company. A simple example of an expense report, something we all have dealt with at one time or another, provides a clear illustration of the transformation (see Figure I-1).

In the traditional expense report, process delays are introduced as information is manually transferred from one form to another. The systems are not aware that they are playing a role in a larger process. In the real-time version of an expense report, a process has been designed for maximized efficiency and minimized delay, and each system knows what role it plays to maximize real-time automation.

Real time is the opposite of what used to be known as batch processing. Batch is still all too common today. When your Internet banking is slower than the ATM or the teller, you know that you're dealing with batch rather than real time. When a bank becomes real time, as the Postbank in Germany recently did using SAP technology, a new world of possibilities opens. The opposite of batch processing is posting all transactions as they happen. With its new systems, Postbank processes transactions twice as fast, dramatically increases its capacity, and can post transactions around the clock. This has enabled the firm to expand its business at a faster rate and bid on much larger contracts than ever before.

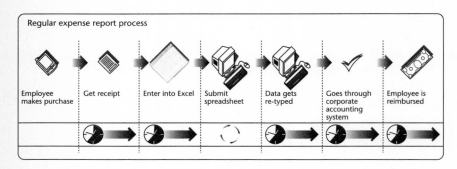

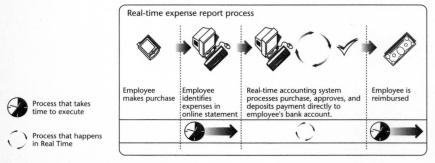

Figure I-1. Regular Versus Real-Time Processes

What is the barrier to real time? The infrastructure used to be the barrier. As we will explain in this introduction, the real-time potential of software was at first trapped inside the CPU and memory of a mainframe in its

> **" Real time is a clear path from stimulus through decision to an effective response. "**

glass house. But gradually the growth in power of the user interface and the evolution of a pervasive network removed structural barriers. Now the barriers to achieving real-time enterprise computing lie in the applications and how they are built, as well as in outmoded, inefficient business processes and the lack of globally accepted standards.

The challenge before us involves a radical evolution of software to meet the needs of the real-time enterprise. At every level, applications will be remade by this challenge: from the way data is stored to the way applications access and transform it to the processes that are embedded in the applications to the integration of powerful toolkits to the presentation of the user interface.

The world of enterprise software has become more relevant to the rest of society than at any previous point in time and will only gain in importance. The real-time enterprise is about making money, of course, but what enterprise applications do and how well they work is no longer just a question of shareholder value. Enterprise applications now reach far beyond the data center. Through the Internet, applications have spread throughout the company, across company boundaries, and have landed right in front of customers, partners, and also citizens, as real-time enterprise systems are being used increasingly by the public sector.

Our ability to protect our privacy, our ability to deal with spam, our ability to free ourselves of administrative straightjackets, and our ability to identify ourselves will all be determined by how well enterprise software works. The quality and ease of integration of enterprise applications will determine what sort of healthcare we get, how we pay taxes, how we interact with law enforcement, and how we cast our votes.

THE CHALLENGES OF THE REAL-TIME ENTERPRISE

In the last decade, the Internet proliferated real-time opportunities faster than we could execute and take advantage of them. An ocean of potential exists, and both companies and software vendors are racing to overcome

> " " *[B]oth companies and software vendors are racing to overcome the barriers to the real-time enterprise and to find the right way to exploit all of these possibilities.* " "

the barriers to the real-time enterprise and to find the right way to exploit all of these possibilities.

To lay the foundation for a detailed description of the challenges ahead, we take a brief look at how the notion of real time has expanded over the past 30 years.

GROWTH OF INFRASTRUCTURE

In the early mainframe era of R/1, real time existed only after a card reader had loaded a program, data, and any bits of the operating system into the memory of CPU. Data could be transformed and manipulated, only to be squeezed into static physical form again in the form of punch card or printer output (Figure I-2).

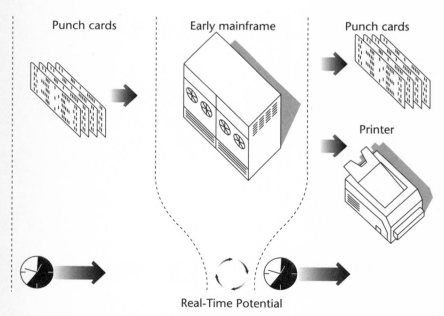

Punch cards   Early mainframe   Punch cards

Printer

Real-Time Potential

Figure I-2.   The Mainframe Era Part I: Punch Cards

In the era of SAP® R/2®, real time existed on the green and black text of the IBM 3270 terminal, which provided a window into what was happening with a program (see Figure I-3). Proprietary networks connected computers with limited bandwidth and allowed extension of the real-time interface through time-sharing.

In the era of SAP® R/3®, the arrival of the PC put real-time computing on the desktop, and the complex interaction between client and server greatly expanded the power of the user interface and the ability to provide instantaneous response. This architecture was so compelling that, as August-Wilhelm Scheer points out in Chapter 4, "software suppliers that started out with the two-level architecture later fell in line with the three-level model," confirming that SAP had made the right architectural choice in focusing on the three-tier model from the beginning (See Figure I-4).

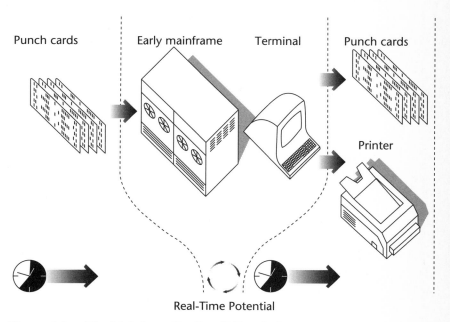

Figure I-3. The Mainframe Era Part II: Terminals

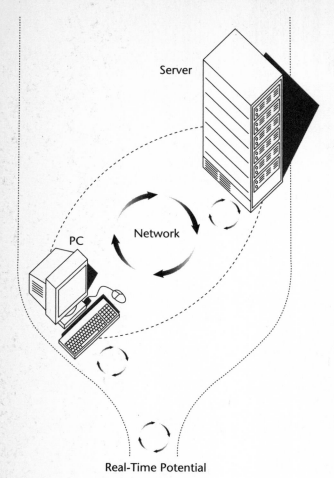

Figure I-4.   The Client/Server Era

The arrival of the Internet and the web browser expanded the availability of applications and increased their ability to talk to one another
(see Figure I-5). The scope of real-time interaction expanded beyond a
single application to a coordinated suite of applications communicating
using standard methods.

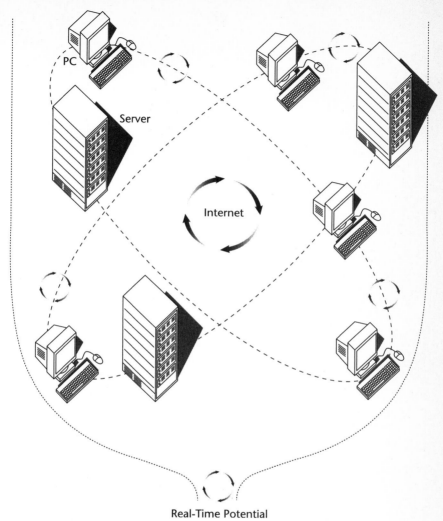

Figure I-5. The Internet Era

The age of wireless devices extends real-time processing to many new generations of devices with a range of processing capabilities and user interface paradigms (Figure I-6).

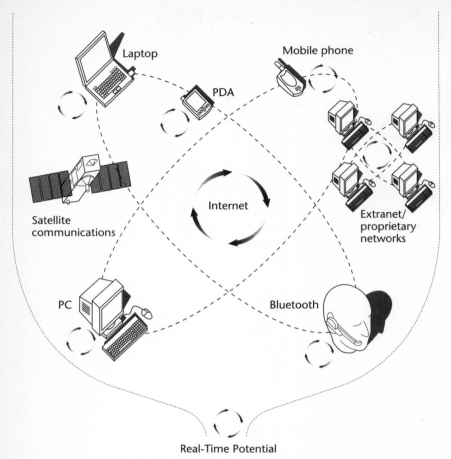

Figure I-6.   The Wireless Era

GROWTH OF APPLICATIONS

While the power of infrastructure was expanding, enterprise applications were like tigers in a tank, growling and ready to break free of the limits surrounding them. In the mainframe era, ornate workarounds such as complex memory overlay techniques and assembly language optimizations were created to overcome the limitations of memory capacity and operating system support. These helped developers push functionality up against the limits of the possible.

As the client/server era developed, the power of the personal computer as an interface was held back by the difficulty of upgrading thousands of client programs once they were installed.

In the Internet era, many of these problems were solved. The Internet provided ubiquitous connectivity. The web made a simple user interface instantly available on any PC. The result was an expansion during the Internet era of the footprint of enterprise applications. The core Enterprise Resource Planning applications that were aimed at automating finance and administrative processes spawned a bouquet of three-letter acronyms. Customer Relationship Management, Supply Chain Management, Supplier Relationship Management, and Product Lifecycle Management were all created or perfected in the Internet era, but never spelled out. Instead, they were known as CRM, SCM, SRM, and PLM. This alphabet soup achieved an important goal, however: The most common processes were automated from one end of a business to the other.

The problem with the rapid growth in the scope of enterprise applications was that each functional area was a silo of functionality unto itself, with only a limited and predetermined ability to interact with the other applications.

A TAXONOMY OF BARRIERS

The crash of the dot-com boom in 2000 put the brakes on the rapid expansion and deployment of applications. This allowed both companies and software vendors to take a breather as spending slowed and weak companies disappeared. The slowdown only disguised the fact that we had already reached a limit on several levels.

Some of the barriers that we face now are hard limits. Devices won't get smaller than our fingers' ability to manipulate them when needed or our ability to read information on a screen. Some barriers are significant but rapidly fading. Amazingly efficient markets drive down the cost

" [T]hese barriers must be overcome if we are to implement the real-time enterprise rather than merely talk about it. "

of computers and other devices. The network is not free but is trending that way and in any event seems to be priced within people's ability to pay.

The most significant barriers are those that we can do something about. To some extent, they are the legacy of how our infrastructure and applications developed. In other aspects, they are limits of our ability to master complexity through abstraction and design. In any event, these barriers must be overcome if we are to implement the real-time enterprise rather than merely talk about it. The following barriers are currently being attacked as companies and software vendors seek to catch up with the explosion of possibilities that the Internet created. The barriers include requirements to retool applications, simplify integration, manage data, create an effective interface, agree on real-world standards, reinvent the structure of the organization, and manage change itself more effectively.

- **Retooling applications** — The design and architecture of enterprise applications is one of the most significant obstacles to the real-time enterprise. The most commonly deployed applications from all vendors have monolithic architectures. Such architectures made sense at the time the applications were built but now stand in the way of managing complexity, enabling distributed computing, and supporting the service-oriented and event-driven architectures that provide the flexibility and reuse required by the real-time enterprise. Each enterprise application arrives as a set of services with associated user interfaces to enable the real-time enterprise.
- **Simplifying integration** — To support the real-time enterprise, integration between applications must be easy. On a semantic level, standards can put an end to the endless torture of mapping one trivial data format to another. Perhaps the most difficult level is process synchronization in which two applications each play a role in executing a larger process. The real-time enterprise demands seamless integration on all these levels.
- **Managing data** — Even if we had a full set of standards for all enterprise data, the question of distributed data management still represents a signifi-cant challenge. Key questions arise: Which layer owns the data? Does CRM own the customer record or does each application have its own record? How are distributed repositories synchronized? How would cen-tral repositories meet the performance demands of the real-time enter-prise? When collaboration beyond enterprise applications is attempted, heterogeneity of data always presents a stubborn problem.
- **Creating effective interfaces** — Perhaps the greatest challenge lies in pre-senting the power of the real-time enterprise to the user. Borders between the virtual world and the real world will blur. New ways of interaction between man and machine will proliferate in the real-time enterprise as

they come to support human behavior rather than reflecting the way the software was implemented. The number of devices on which a user interface is relevant is exploding.

- **Coalescing real-world standards** — An efficient process for setting standards is a bottom-line requirement for the real-time enterprise as processes and integrations routinely cross company boundaries and integrations between systems become the foundation for business relationships.
- **Implementing new forms of organization and leadership** — The real-time enterprise will challenge the command and control structures common to many companies. Managers will struggle to empower employees yet keep their actions aligned with corporate values and evolving processes.
- **Increasing the pace of change management** — The speed at which processes are executed has increased steadily over the past 20 years, but the pace at which the organizations are able to change to execute new processes and business models has improved little. Business conditions will demand ever more rapid adaptation, and the best vision of the real-time enterprise will not mean a thing unless it can be implemented quickly. Enterprise Services Architecture, which is explained in Chapter 25, is a blueprint for using web services and other technologies to remove IT as a bottleneck to change.

Vendors are attempting to meet these challenges by different means. But all vendors must address them to create software that meets the needs of the real-time enterprise.

For companies that use technology, the challenge of the real-time enterprise is to anticipate how the real-time enterprise will affect organizational structure, management, and operations, all of which are likely to be utterly transformed.

Perhaps the ultimate evidence of the real-time enterprise is that applications fade into the background. Today business leaders ask, "How do we make tools do what we need?" because the ideal process must be compromised to adapt to the capabilities of current IT tools. When the question becomes simply, "We know we can do anything, but what should we do?" we will know the real-time enterprise has been achieved.

> " When the question becomes simply, "We know we can do anything, but what should we do?" we will know the real-time enterprise has been achieved. "

THE STRUCTURE OF THIS BOOK

This book delves deeper into the issues facing the real-time enterprise in five parts:

- **Part I, "The Vision of the SAP Founders,"** examines the history of SAP's vision for the real-time enterprise from its seeds in the first months of the company to its realization in early client implementations.
- **Part II, "Client/Server and Open Communication,"** analyzes how client/server computing, the arrival of the Internet, the ability to manage distributed repositories of data, and the proliferation of web browsers and mobile devices set the stage for the realization of the real-time enterprise.
- **Part III, "The Real-Time Enterprise,"** examines the interaction between the organizational structure and the capabilities of the real-time enterprise to automate, reengineer, and rapidly optimize processes across corporate boundaries.
- **Part IV, "Real-Time Interfaces,"** looks at the history of user interfaces and human-computer interaction. Examining these interfaces critically will enable true innovation to support the real-time enterprise.
- **Part V, "Building Blocks for the Enterprise Nervous System,"** looks at the ways the real-time enterprise will take advantage of an emerging nervous system for information and computing that is arriving in the form of radio frequency identification (RFID), virtual collaborative environments, and other leading-edge technologies that promise to reshape our world.

REAL-TIME IN CONTEXT

This book is packed with ideas and commentary from different sources, none of whom were aware of what the others were writing. The variety of experts who brought this book to life is impressive. To help you tie together the important concepts in this book and get a feel how they relate to the real-time enterprise, take a look at sidebars like this one. They will give you perspective and help you find an interesting pathway through this book.

Why sidebars? In an ordinary *Festschrift*, the work of an individual acts as a unifying force. But the concept of the real-time enterprise is no such unifier. Many different perspectives are held about the notion of the real-time enterprise, and commentators vary widely about the implications of the concept for the world of business and information technology.

The information in these sidebars examines the flow of ideas in the book as a whole. You will find sidebars next to certain passages in the book. They explain the theme of nearby content and relate it to other passages.

Those who have met Hasso Plattner have found the experience exhilarating. His mind produces a steady stream of questions, ideas, and probing analysis. Most conversations begin with an invitation to attack and challenge the ideas he is setting forth. Doing battle with Hasso is a unique pleasure. The goal of this book is to recreate something of that experience for the reader.

HAPPY BIRTHDAY, HASSO!

This book is a celebration and a challenge. It celebrates Hasso Plattner's 60th birthday. Parts of this book look back and trace the notion of real-time applications to the excited minds of the group of German engineers who left IBM to form SAP. We will show how the essence of the real-time enterprise has always been inside the software products of SAP.

But we must do better than that. Anyone who knows Hasso Plattner knows that he won't stand for puffery or hero worship. To make this book a true Plattner-style tribute, we must reach for the stars and grapple with fundamental issues, which leads us to the challenge.

For 30 years, brilliant and inventive people at companies like SAP have dedicated their lives to making enterprise applications the best they can be. As we look forward to the next 30 years, we see a revolution of staggering proportions underway. Now, however, we are not held back by technology but by our imaginations and our ability to execute. So, as we tip our hats in birthday celebration to Hasso, we ask you to join us in mapping out how the real-time enterprise can be achieved.

Hasso Plattner: A Profile

This book was written without Hasso Plattner's knowledge. But the SAP Executive Board felt the book wouldn't really be complete without his participation. Being a crafty bunch, the Board decided to get Hasso's input for the book by indirect means. To that end, they asked Chris Anderson, Editor in Chief of Wired Magazine, to interview Hasso and provide a chapter for this book. The following provides some needed context and background information for those who are not part of the IT industry or the SAP family and who may not know much about Hasso and what he has achieved at SAP. For those who do know, it is a great version of the story of Hasso and SAP, in the style that Wired magazine has made famous.

Chris Anderson

Technology visionaries come in two types. The first embrace the name, fearlessly predicting the future in public and in their own boardrooms. Some of them get it right, but more get it wrong — the future is tricky that way. The second type of visionary, on the other hand, rarely gives Comdex keynotes or builds the home of tomorrow, but somehow when the future does arrive, often suddenly and in surprising form, they and their company are ready. This breed is more mysterious. How do they do it? Are they lucky? Fast-adapting? Or just well prepared?

For answers, look to the career of Hasso Plattner, SAP's chairman and co-founder. At first blush, enterprise software might not be where you'd look for futurology, the sector being somewhat light on nanotech and jetpacks. But the office is where computers started, and where they still have some of their most profound impact. We may not have personal robot-butlers yet, but our workplace has changed radically in the years since the computer arrived. Today, thanks mostly to the effect of enterprise software, a quarter of all Americans now work in jobs that weren't listed in the Census Bureau's occupation codes three decades ago.

As software has changed the world, so has the software world itself changed. It grew massively, of course, but also suffered regular upheavals that left many big companies on their knees while spurring even more small companies to form and dream of one day becoming big themselves. Plattner and four colleagues left IBM to form SAP in 1972, the pre-Cambrian era of software. The fact that the company not only exists today, unlike nearly any other IT company of that time other than IBM itself, but also is now the world's third-largest software company, is remarkable. The explanation has a lot to do with Plattner and his ability to anticipate change.

One of the advantages of a computing career that has spanned some 35 years (so far) is that it puts change in perspective. The latest distribution release of Linux is not a significant disruption; the introduction of the 3270 terminal in the early 1970s, which took computers from the punch card to the interactive terminal, was. It, along with the arrival of cheap mainframes, marked the beginning of widespread real-time systems, an opportunity Plattner spotted as a chance to do something different: he led the charge to recode SAP's first product, the batch-processed R/1, as the real-time R/2®. Obvious in hindsight, perhaps, but plenty of other companies missed that departure point. It would be just the first of many correct turns.

The next tectonic shift proved to be the crucial one. In the late 1980s, Plattner and his team were building next-generation enterprise software to follow on the heels of its success with R/2 in Germany. R/2 ran on mainframes (mostly IBM), and IBM had announced that it was coming out with a new System Application Architecture (SAA) architecture on the AS/400 minicomputers that was meant to usher in a new generation of computing. SAP, having its roots in IBM, was a loyal partner and promptly got on board with its next product, to be called R/3®, using all the tools IBM recommended. It was not until the early 1990s that it became clear that IBM had got it badly wrong — SAA wouldn't scale, potentially sinking SAP's great hope for the future.

At such moments, preparation, along with a bit of luck, saves the day. By 1988 SAP was already sensing trouble with SAA on the AS/400.

In combination with a clear trend towards cheaper computers, this suggested to Plattner that he shift development of the new software to Unix workstations using the C programming language. Initially, the assumption was that R/3 could be ported to SAA when IBM had the system ready. But once the porting began, the problems with SAA revealed themselves. Just weeks before the Hannover Fair, where SAP was due to introduce R/3, a four-processor mainframe choked on R/3's C code. One processor froze after another, leaving the machine virtually useless and bringing development to a standstill. "That was the day I stood with my back against the wall and thought, 'The R/3 project has actually failed,'" Plattner recalls.

But the engineers, who had been doing R/3 development on Unix workstations, realized that smaller machines were in some ways even more capable — perhaps even capable enough to run R/3 themselves. They wanted to try, and Plattner let them. Today this strategy seems entirely sensible, given what we know about the power of Unix boxes. At the time, it was somewhere between heretical and naïve: everyone knew that applications ran on mainframes and Unix workstation were little more than user terminals. But the balance of power was shifting — the engineers' DEC 5000 workstations were rated at the same 25 MIPS as their mainframe, and even taking into the account the difference between workstation MIPS and mainframe MIPS, this was worth taking seriously. Perhaps applications really could run on Unix machines after all, leaving data on the mainframe and PCs for the user interface.

Needless to say, on the day of the fair, the Unix-based system worked, or worked well enough. Plattner encouraged the presenter to tell the audience, who he thought wasn't yet ready to believe that Unix machines were so capable, that the system was running on a mainframe remotely. But he and the SAP engineers knew the truth and were ecstatic: a new era had been born. On a roll, Plattner then enthusiastically announced that the product would be available in 30 days, a risky move given the fear of both killing the existing R/2 and failing to deliver. Nevertheless, the SAP engineers pulled it off, and the rest is history.

Although it was not yet obvious in those initial days, the combination of using Unix development machines, spotting the problems in SAA, and having the courage to try to roll the product out in Unix, was a revolutionary moment. It marked the beginning of the three-tier client/server model and changed the world of enterprise computing.

From there came a host of trickle-down implications, SQL servers, TCP/IP, application servers, and even the Windows GUI, that would cement SAP's position in the next decade.

Plattner credits the moment to fortune and an almost innate recognition on the part of himself and his team of the underlying trends in technology. "It was probably just luck that IBM couldn't deliver on SAA," he says. "We were forced to looked outside, to Unix. The workstations started as a development device, but then they got better. First we needed multiple machines, but could soon work with just one."

Soon many other companies would come to adopt the three-tiered client/server model, making it the world standard. Companies of all sorts realized that the ability to tap services that aren't just data in a database but are instead applications talking to other applications on a network would enable a new level of complexity and flexibility. It created a new layer of apps that don't rely on databases — workflow. Indeed, three-tiered computing turned out to be such a powerful concept that Plattner's main regret is that SAP neglected to build a barricade of patents around it. "We were too busy!" he says.

On the back of R/3's success, SAP grew enormously through the 1990s. But the inflection points didn't stop coming. The next one arrived as a perfect storm: the arrival of the Internet at the same time as a swarm of best-of-breed enterprise applications, from CRM to HR, from companies with narrower focus than SAP. Five years after the previous challenge, SAP was under attack by a group of smaller application vendors building front office apps, leveraging the processes that were supplied by R/3. At the same time, the Internet boom hit the market, and SAP was perceived by the analysts and customers as "the company that didn't get the Internet."

This time Plattner dug into his strategy book and decided to create an integrated enterprise application suite to compete against the "best of breed." He also added two major Internet components: an enterprise portal "to dominate the corporate desktop" and marketplaces for cross-company integration. The suite is called mySAP.com in keeping with Internet bubble marketing. He again announces availability in 30 days and again sweeps the market. Today more than 80 percent of SAP license revenue comes from mySAP.com (now renamed mySAP Business Suite™ to disassociate it from the Internet dot-com bubble).

Most recently, the challenge for SAP has been to create its own integration platform. "For years, we tested other app platforms, IBM, Microsoft, and others," Plattner says. "We needed a 'superplatform' or we would have to build it ourselves. We couldn't find a platform that could accommodate both the Microsoft and anti-Microsoft camps."

In early 2001, SAP had to decide whether to adopt other platforms (such as WebSphere or WebLogic, or maybe even .NET) or build one on its own. Plattner pushed the decision and decided to build an integrated platform — called NetWeaver — and base all SAP apps on that platform. Today the product is taking off and is winning market share.

Looking forward, Plattner thinks the next leap will come when virtually every device has software inside and can provide a nonhuman interface: when devices can talk to devices. "We will be able to reach any object — they all have digital descriptions. A phone can provide a service. A shipment can identify itself and start talking. Everything can register on the Internet — here I am and here's what I can do." The result, he predicts, will be new generations of applications that are much closer to what's in the real world. "The whole transportation business was changed by the shipping container, and RFIDs will do the same. Fast networks and gigahertz computers can digest complex messages. Handheld devices, from GPS to phones, will be the interfaces. There are just cascades of opportunity."

And so there are. From batch processing to Bluetooth, Plattner's career has spanned the most extraordinary era in computing history, during which he has capitalized on more opportunities than almost anyone else in the business. Was it luck, fast reactions, or preparation? Plattner's lesson is clear: in the fast-changing tech world, you need all three.

PART I

THE VISION OF THE SAP FOUNDERS

When Dietmar Hopp quit IBM in 1972 to start SAP with Hasso Plattner, Hans-Werner Hector, Klaus E. Tschira, and Claus Wellenreuther, their first dream of "real-time" computing was a modest one. They wanted to create software that processed data when customers asked it to instead of saving questions to be answered later on a mainframe in the middle of the night.

Today, the idea of the real-time enterprise promises to transform corporate decisions into actions almost on instinct. Tomorrow's applications will find, process, and pass along data as demanded by the inner logic of a business rather than a user's request. We have arrived at this point thanks to powerful, compact hardware, universal standards for data and its transportation, and integrated applications that share this data effortlessly. Corporations that shared SAP's vision have long reaped the benefits, as the Würth Group's Reinhold Würth and Chevron's Martin Klitten will attest to in Chapters 2 and 3.

But none of these things existed when Hopp convened SAP's first meetings on his couch in Walldorf.

Their future customers struggled at the time with the tiny, punch-card fed memories of IBM mainframes, which were usually incapable of processing complicated instructions in one sitting, let alone in real time. Data was written to multiple cards and fed to the machines in the early morning after smaller, easier requests were answered during business hours. Asking questions and acting on their answers took days, and the questions' premises could change drastically in the meantime: inventories might run out before a program finished accounting for them. Today, these questions are answered before we ask.

SAP's first customer was the British chemical giant ICI, which wanted the new firm to finish a job that IBM had refused — an integrated software package that encompassed accounting, inventory management, and order processing, and performed all three in relative real time. Data would be processed and sorted immediately after input. ICI would lend them its computer — SAP didn't own one until 1980 — and the founders would keep the fruits of their labor. When they finished a year later, ICI had the programs in place and SAP had its first product, System R, the foundation of its mainframe successor SAP® R/2® and, later, the client/server-driven SAP® R/3®.

The principles of SAP's software and its culture were both forged during the founders' visits to ICI's mainframe. Lacking a way to pool data that could be shared by their applications, they created one. Working in an environment with no standards for moving and processing that data, they wrote them. And, faced with computers that often had no more than 512K of memory, they wrote applications that lacked even an ounce of fat, applications that snapped together but were not welded together, emphasizing performance, standardization, and modularity at every step. Working on behalf of the German office of a British multinational also drove home the need to solve the problems of global business from the beginning. While its American rivals would struggle years later to retrofit their native products for use abroad, SAP's applications had been prepared for multiple currencies and governments all along.

SAP celebrated its first birthday with nine employees and a small profit. Four years later, that number had swelled to 25, but the company still lacked an office that housed all of them under one roof. It was in many ways a virtual corporation, lacking a mainframe or any other hard assets. Its employees worked at the client site, adapting SAP's applications to the unique situations in which they would be needed. The founders still programmed themselves, and even though Hopp had assumed the chief executive role as the company grew, he and his partners considered hierarchies unnecessary and counterproductive. SAP's staff was as tightly integrated as its applications.

SAP rolled out the second iteration of its software in 1982. Dubbed R/2, it capitalized on the innovation of the dumb terminal. The screen became a window into the mainframes and replaced punch cards as a way of seeing, entering, and accessing data. The assumptions the founders had made when developing System R guaranteed that R/2 would blossom as IT became increasingly decentralized. Any worker sitting at a terminal became a part of the real-time process, extending its scope beyond executives and the technicians tending the machines. There were still many limits — primitive networks constrained the number of terminals and how far away from the mainframe they could be — but it proved that System R's architecture had been the right one.

Ten years later, after a steady decade of growth and profits while PCs swept mainframes out of power, SAP released a third version, R/3. Harnessing the processing muscle now present on every desktop, R/3 was a leap forward rather than a next step. By switching to a client/server model that connected networked PCs to database servers, R/3 took maximum advantage of the standards that had developed in the past 20 years — Windows, Ethernet, TCP/IP — with far-reaching results.

But R/3's early adopters first had to struggle with the infrastructural and organizational implications of the client/server approach. Though they were amply rewarded in the end with significant cost savings and heightened efficiency, to reap these benefits, clients like the Würth Group in Germany and Chevron (now ChevronTexaco) in the U.S. had to rethink the way they did business. Today, the Würth Group comprises 290 subsidiary companies, with over 39,000 employees in 80 companies selling products used in construction, all globally linked by R/3. Chevron was the first U.S. energy company to upgrade in the mid 90s, soon followed by its competitors.

Their respective leaps into the unknown may look like half-steps once the challenges and rewards of moving to real time are fully known.

CONTRIBUTORS TO PART I

- SAP co-founder **Dietmar Hopp** served as CEO from the company's founding in 1972 until 1998, at which time he became chairman and was succeeded as CEO by Hasso Plattner. Hopp oversaw SAP's expansion from roughly $200,000 in revenues in 1972 to $4.8 billion in 1998.
- **Martin Klitten** retired from Chevron at the completion of its merger with Texaco in 2001. In 31 years at the company, he held the posts of executive vice president, president of Chevron Information Technology Co., and CFO. At the latter post, Klitten began reengineering the company's approach to IT, saving Chevron hundreds of millions of dollars over a 15-year span.
- **Reinhold Würth** is the chairman and former CEO of the Würth Group, which sells materials used in construction and the assembly of products worldwide. He was the second employee of his father's wholesale screw business in Künzelsau, Germany, and became CEO in 1954 at the age of 19 after his father's death. He headed the company for 40 years before stepping down to become chairman in 1994, after expanding the business from a regional supplier to worldwide concern with €5.4 billion in revenue in 2002.

1

SAP: The First Years

SAP began in 1972 when five employees of IBM in Mannheim, Germany, launched a software revolution: off-the-shelf, integrated real-time applications. Today, SAP employs more than 29,000 people, and 12 million users throughout the world use SAP software. Dietmar Hopp, who had served at SAP AG as co-CEO and chairman of the Executive Board, became a member of the supervisory board in May 1998, 26 years after he quit his job at IBM to co-found what would become the third largest software company in the world.

Dietmar Hopp

SAP came about, primarily, because computers in the 1960s didn't allow integrated or real-time processing. Hasso Plattner and I were working as system consultants for IBM in those days. We were working on a project at ICI Fibres Europe, building a real-time order processing system using terminals instead of punch cards. In a world dominated by batch processing, Hasso and I were grateful for ICI's openness to trying something new. Even using terminals in business was very unusual at the time.

Working on this project, we quickly came to grips with the technical aspects of the application and started work on the design. To handle the issues facing us with the computer technology available at that time, we had to divide business operations into individual steps. At this point, a host of possibilities presented themselves. Once we moved beyond batch processing, we saw that it would be possible to instantly check whether a product was available, that stock levels could be tracked and constantly updated, that customer credit could be checked immediately when an order was placed, that express deliveries could be ordered at the touch of a button. The list went on and on.

We informed our counterparts at ICI that these options were sound and technically workable. Plenty of skeptics raised their voices, of course. Some of them, staunch Electronic Data Processing experts, mostly, thought we were crazy. However, we were given the go-ahead, and within 12 months we built a functioning system and handed it over to the client for live operation.

An integrated, real-time order processing system was born. It made quite an impression at IBM, since applications using screens, larger computers, and additional disk storage were welcomed there with open arms.

Many companies expressed an interest in this new form of data processing, which led us to leave IBM and concentrate on further development of the project. However, by the time we left, our work at ICI had allowed us to lay the groundwork for the fundamental technological direction — creating a clear separation between the various layers of an application, specifically:

- Separation of the terminal screen data from the application
- Separation of data management from the application
- Division of the application into many usable modules
- And later, separation of dialog program modules from database update modules

From the very beginning, our goal was to develop a comprehensive system allowing users to control functions throughout the entire company. It took some time to meet this goal. The limitations of available technology and the disparate requirements of the different industry sectors we served — retail, government, healthcare, and so on — meant that back in the 1980s, or even the early 1990s, it was not possible to offer the universal system that we have today. The basic technology, however, played a crucial role, allowing applications to be added as required. And the rapid development of computers has helped this process along considerably.

Although it's hard to believe in retrospect, the idea that off-the-shelf business software could be successfully developed and marketed met with strong opposition. It took a long time for our philosophy of integrated processing in real time to convince all the cynics.

Following the introduction of SAP® R/2® in 1980, our next phase of expansion saw the successful implementation of the first SAP® R/3® applications at customer sites. With SAP® R/3®, we achieved stability and reached extraordinary heights on the world software market.

Technological design and innovative software solutions alone have not determined the success of SAP; the corporate philosophy is equally important. SAP's considerate treatment of its employees has spurred them on to first-class performance. I think that our openness and willingness to discuss everything with the customer safeguarded us against development errors that plagued some other software companies. From the very beginning, our customers had a reliable partner who listened patiently to their needs. From the first, SAP has been interested in helping clients realize the real-time enterprise, even at a time when such an idea was unheard of.

2

Implementing SAP R/3 Financial Accounting

Adolf Würth founded his company in southern Germany in 1945 for the wholesale supply of screws, nuts, and bolts. After his death in 1954, Adolf's 19-year-old son, Reinhold Würth, took over the running of the business with two employees. A favorable post-war climate allowed the company to flourish, so much so that in 2003 the business generated worldwide sales of €5.4 billion at its 295 companies in 80 countries. Today, the Würth Group has a workforce of over 41,000 employees, more than half of whom are field service personnel.

Reinhold Würth

Würth is predominantly a traditional direct sales company that deals in connecting and assembly technology. The company uses a warehouse-based system to distribute its range of over 50,000 different materials for assembly, maintenance, and repairs (screws, nuts, dowels, chemical products, furniture fittings, and hand tools), and its products are sold under the Würth brand.

Würth's client base includes commercial customers as well as small and midsize businesses and numbers some two million clients worldwide. In addition to its headquarters in Künzelsau, Germany, Würth boasts a sales network of about 100 subsidiaries throughout the country.

The Würth Group has a decentralized organization, with each company responsible for its own sales revenues and income. In a decentralized

> ❝ In a decentralized structure . . ., timely and transparent reporting is vital if errors are to be detected early and appropriate action taken. ❞

structure such as this, timely and transparent reporting is vital if errors are to be detected early and appropriate action taken.

WHERE WE STARTED

After the fall of the Berlin Wall and the reunification of Germany, the number of customers of the German parent company Adolf Würth GmbH & Co. KG increased dramatically. Of course, this brought with it a huge increase in transaction data and longer processing times. Online sales order processing and retail management had recently been developed to handle the daily influx of transactions in this area. But the financial accounting system, on the other hand, was based on software that was almost 20 years old. This software had been enhanced, but fundamentally it still relied on batch processing. The high number of records to be processed was causing the parent company considerable delays. The nights simply weren't long enough to update all the data. Furthermore, organizational changes, involving restructuring of the business areas into divisions, could not immediately be mapped in the reporting system. Extra work was necessary to create the relevant reports, and this took time. By now, the group comprised 100 companies and was continuing to grow, largely owing to the purchase and founding of new companies. Therefore, effective controlling and a plan–actual comparison of the entire group became necessary. As the number of companies increased, so did the work involved in consolidating the group's data.

At the start of 1991, a project team consisting of members from the larger companies of the Würth Group was given the task of finding a new financial accounting system for the group.

The smaller companies in the Würth Group were already using the Comet financials package from Siemens Nixdorf. It was run on a local level, but the chart of accounts and development activities were controlled centrally.

Whereas a classic mainframe structure with the IBM operating system MVS was installed in the German parent company, by 1985 we had opted for a client/server architecture based on Unix for our small and midsize businesses. Based on this structure, a custom application was developed in-house for our sales order processing and retail management. Our core processes demand a streamlined and cost-efficient structure. Up to this point, Unix was largely unknown in commercial applications, but we saw great potential for the structure, especially in rapidly growing companies. Naturally, considerable risk was involved since no prior knowledge was available about how a Unix client/server system would behave in this environment with all types of transactions. In 1988, we were able to successfully install such a Unix-based client/server system with software developed at Würth Netherlands. In the years that followed, an average of four companies per year were equipped with this system.

The goal for the project team was to find an accounting system that offered worldwide availability, client capabilities, and room for growth. Moreover, the system had to support group reporting with business evaluations, contribution margin accounting, planned/actual comparisons, a wide range of analyses, and, of course, formulation of financial statements. Client/server operation was a prerequisite for the new system. It had to be hardware-independent, support distributed processing, and allow centralized maintenance of all tools, databases, and charts of accounts. Of course, this system also had to handle huge amounts of transaction data quickly and accurately.

THE DECISION

In 1988, SAP decided to develop its Unix-based system, SAP® R/3®. At Cebit in 1991, the first part of this system was available for inspection. In the second half of the year, we held extensive talks with SAP in Walldorf, Germany. After intense negotiation and risk assessment, performed by Gerhard Oswald and Hasso Plattner on behalf of SAP's Executive Board, SAP and the Würth Group signed a contract on January 23, 1992. It specified the implementation of the Financial Accounting (FI) module, followed by Human Resources (HR) and Asset Management (AM). FI was also to be implemented at additional companies outside of Germany.

The introduction of R/3 FI carried considerable risk both for Würth and for SAP. The Informix database had to be installed too, so

> ❝ The project was Hasso Plattner's baby. The SAP project team reported directly to him and Gerhard Oswald. This later proved to be an important factor in the project's success. ❞

this project was given top priority. The project was Hasso Plattner's baby. The SAP project team reported directly to him and Gerhard Oswald. This later proved to be an important factor in the project's success. The goal was to have the system up and running by January 1, 1993.

THE PROJECT

Employees from both SAP and Würth were assigned to project teams. All the employees of Würth, who had never worked with SAP software, needed quick and intensive training. Work began in March 1992 with the concept design, formulation of data, document types, charts of accounts, and balance sheet structure. Because Würth was dealing with some 380,000 transactions daily, the standard SAP dialogs for data entry could not be used. Instead, a batch input procedure had to be developed to transfer data to the SAP system very quickly and at low cost. All the interfaces to the order processing and retail management systems had to be created, and online data transfer was also required.

In April 1992, Release 1.1 was installed. The dunning procedure designed for the standard system could not be put into practice at our group. A new procedure needed to be developed, and it was at this point that the value of Hasso Plattner's support came to light. Decisions were made rapidly and SAP quickly put its developers at our disposal. By September 1992, it became clear that our plans to go live in January 1993 would have to be postponed. Processing of mass data was causing major problems and runtimes were unacceptable. SAP made some drastic changes to the standard FI module.

At the start of 1993, we could see light at the end of the tunnel. Tests were carried out and runtimes for the transfer of our four million data records were optimized. Easter 1993 was set as the target start date. It was now a question of building the entire infrastructure for live operation, providing intensive training to 120 employees, and integrating the optical archives. The data transfers were practiced many times and further

THE IMPORTANCE OF SCALABILITY

Würth addresses a central goal in designing real-time enterprise software: scalability. Scalability is vital to dealing with the ever-expanding volume of vital corporate data, a problem that the upcoming flood of data from radio frequency ID (RFID) tags and mobile devices will only exacerbate.

Würth and SAP managed the scalability challenges by attacking the problem as partners, concentrating their combined resources to develop a short-term and a long-term solution. Chevron (Chapter 3) and Colgate (Chapter 18) worked with SAP using the same techniques to handle the challenges of global implementation.

optimized so that within 3 days we were able to import all the necessary data into R/3. Again, this highlighted the importance of continuing support from the Executive Board of SAP. On April 8, 1993, during the Easter vacation, the final transfer began. Three days later, on April 11, the data transfer was successfully completed with the reconciliation of all accounts. On April 13, 1993, Würth was finally able to go live with SAP R/3 Financial Accounting.

THE RESULTS

As with the start-up of every new system, there was no expectation of increasing productivity in the short term. It took our employees 3 months to achieve the same processing rates that they had enjoyed with the legacy system over the years. Performance fell below expectations, so additional servers were installed to boost power. Furthermore, some processes were not designed for such a high volume of transactions. Then, in collaboration with SAP, MultiCash systems and electronic banking were introduced in 1994. Increased productivity was now an achievable goal.

Potential SAP users were so interested in this implementation that every week we had visitors from all over the world who wanted to see the SAP installation live. In June 1993, we held a joint conference in Künzelsau with SAP about the implementation of R/3 FI. In July 1993, Würth Denmark also installed SAP FI. We developed a template from

> *" Potential SAP users were so interested in this implementation that every week we had visitors from all over the world who wanted to see the SAP installation live. "*

these deployments and used it in subsequent years at the larger Würth companies. In January 1994, the larger German subsidiaries were transferred to the SAP system.

However, we weren't invincible, and in January 1994, the SAP system experienced a data crash. A hardware error prevented direct access to the databases and the data backup tapes. It took a painstaking effort in collaboration with experts from SAP to restore the dataset. The system was unavailable for 4 days, and it was a month before it was back up to date.

Did we achieve our goals? Well, our system administration is more time-consuming, and we need three times more memory space than before. However, additional optimizations have raised productivity and group reporting has been standardized. Online processing enables us to complete our monthly financial statements more quickly and safeguards our data. Quicker postings and improved dunning processes have reduced time spent on accounts receivable accounting by some 20 percent.

The organization of the project and our close relations with the Executive Board of SAP, and Hasso Plattner in particular, ensured that both SAP and the Würth Group were well-equipped to rise to the challenge of implementing R/3 FI in an environment with large amounts of transaction data.

3

R/3 Comes to the U.S.: The Chevron Story

ChevronTexaco is one of the world's largest energy companies, with business operations on 5 continents and in 180 countries. A Fortune 10 company, ChevronTexaco employs over 53,000 people worldwide. Martin Klitten, having joined Chevron in 1971 as a financial analyst, became president of Chevron Information Technology Company in 1986 and was promoted to CFO in 1989. At that post, Klitten began reengineering the company's financial sysytems.

Martin Klitten

Anew chairman arrived at Chevron in 1988, and one of his goals was to decentralize our business model to bring more decision-making and business autonomy to the individual business units. You can't run a decentralized business if you don't have good financial information, so, shortly after I became CFO, this became one of my goals — to update our financial system so the business units would have a lot more freedom to dive into their own unique data while still allowing corporate headquarters to gather and aggregate all information from the individual divisions and departments.

Up until the early 1990s, Chevron was operating with a financial mainframe system that dated back to the 1960s. It was a monolith. It was inflexible, the code was outdated, and we employed many people simply to service the existing system. Many of our programmers were retiring.

> ❝ We looked at several of SAP's competitors, but they didn't offer what I perceived to be the "drill-down" capability that SAP did. ❞

We had to move forward and explore other alternatives to support the new decentralized business model.

At this stage, the strengths of the client/server concept were becoming apparent. We looked at several of SAP's competitors, but they didn't offer what I perceived to be the "drill-down" capability that SAP did. If you had a question on a transaction with a particular customer, you could drill down into the invoice, tie it to a particular purchase order, and identify the individual transaction. And you could do it in real time. You could sit at your desk and say, "I don't understand this," and go into the individual databases to get the answers you needed. You didn't have to wait overnight for a printout from the mainframe facility.

INFORMATION IN REAL TIME

That was the vision — we wanted to put the information, as well as the power — on the desktop for the individual business managers to use. We weren't exactly sure what we were jumping into, but the whole SAP package intrigued me. At that time, SAP had no major U.S. clients. When we looked at SAP, we had to study what had been done in Germany. I thought that the end product, if we could get through the birthing pains, would be a great business system. We knew that there were risks, but we laid them out to our executive committee and made the decision to move forward with SAP.

It was a big gamble on our part and, in retrospect, we actually underestimated how much of a gamble it was. In talking to Henning Kagermann over the years, I learned that working with Chevron was an order of magnitude greater than what they had thought they were signing up for. Their U.S. target market was small to mid-sized companies, and the product had been designed with this in mind. We were the first Fortune 10 company to license SAP® R/3®. I believe that our license number was around 34 or 35.

It was a real growing experience. Chevron is so large and disparate that it challenged the SAP architecture, which, at that time, was designed for one central client system. Chevron, however, needed another level of magnitude because each of our operating companies had business units of its own. Each needed a client and those clients needed, in turn, to be able to communicate with a master client. Synchronization up and down the chain was vital — changes and corrections had to be reflected in the system every few minutes.

I was very fortunate to have a team of very smart and dedicated people who shared my vision. I gave them the authority to design an implementation plan. Chevron is segmented into operating companies, which are like divisions. Some are relatively small and some are 800-pound gorillas. In a smaller company, you could recover quickly. But, by the time we reached the 800-pound gorillas, we needed to be able to switch from the old mainframe system to the SAP system quickly, without any stumbles. It had to work.

One issue was the amount of training needed to implement SAP. Our previous system was like an old punch card. You had a certain number of characters to enter, and you just filled them in. SAP was completely different. It was powerful and robust, but the interface was unfamiliar — and, though it has gotten better over the years, initially it wasn't very intuitive for the casual user. You had to be a hardcore SAP user to really appreciate it. Another issue was that we had underestimated the rigor and the amount of detail that was required to configure the SAP system. SAP configuration is very detailed, and the configuration differed from one business unit to the next. It required an intensive effort.

The team decided to use two smaller companies as test cases — Warren Petroleum in Oklahoma and one of our Canadian companies — and implement SAP to validate the concept. We put a group of people to work developing a legacy interface program that was unofficially referred to as MOAP (Mother Of All Programs). It interfaced SAP with our legacy systems. As more and more of the business information was entered into SAP, the legacy systems atrophied and the SAP system became more robust. Eventually, you could just turn out the lights on the legacy side.

That was our methodology, and it worked. So, over our 3- to 4-year implementation horizon, we simply lined it up operating company by operating company, beginning with the smaller companies, and went to work. It took a lot of time and effort by some terrific people to get it done, but we kept getting better and better with each implementation. The first company took about 8 months; the second took 6 months. And we became more efficient from there.

It was a real challenge to create an architecture robust enough to handle the multiplicity of operating companies and diverse businesses of a company like Chevron, but it was in both SAP's and Chevron's best interests to make the whole thing work. We had excellent cooperation over the years from SAP. I made a number of trips to Waldorf to talk to Henning Kagermann and his whole team. Of course, we encountered some rough spots, but basically Henning understood our needs and was able to rally SAP's resources to make it happen.

We had a special relationship with SAP. Once, when we were having some real problems with synchronization of data, we were in Waldorf in a meeting with the chief programmer and his team. Henning walked in and asked a few questions, then went to the chalkboard and said, "This is what we are going to do. This. And this. And this." He turned to the chief programmer and said, "This is correct, yes?" Of course, they all said yes. I don't think any of them had a clue about how to do what he was asking, but within weeks we had a whole different design that moved us forward on the project. It was one of a number of times that Henning helped us get over hurdles. My hat is off to him.

FOCUS ON PROCESS

Perhaps the most interesting thing about implementing SAP was that to configure the system, the team had to spend a lot of time understanding the operating companies' processes. SAP forced us to become very process-oriented because you can't configure the system without really, really understanding your business — who does what and why — before you even start trying to implement SAP. We would have teams go to each of the companies and they would work for weeks, if not months, detailing the processes in place. On the one hand, it meant slow implementations, but on the other hand, you really knew what you were doing when you were done. In the old systems, you might have never understood why you did certain things. That's just the way they were done. But with SAP, you had to validate and document your processes.

PROCESS RULES

Klitten's experience in implementing R/3 illustrates two points. It shows how SAP's customer engagements improved the design of its products and how to handle new requirements. Chevron, for example, required the ability to manage many distributed instances of R/3. The Würth Group (Chapter 2) required that, as well as the ability to handle data on a massive scale. The theme of focusing on customer needs is mentioned in later chapters by Geoffrey Moore (Chapter 16), Michael Hammer (Chapter 10), and Esther Dyson (Chapter 27) from a service perspective and by Alan Kay and Alan Cooper from a user interface perspective (Chapters 19 and 20).

Klitten's experience also illustrates that one of the key benefits of implementing R/3 was an increased and detailed understanding of Chevron's processes. The rise in process as the key element to success is the theme of Hammer's chapter and is also driven home by Vinod Khosla in his vision for the real-time enterprise, detailed in Chapter 13.

You could see if there were changes you needed to make (which, undoubtedly, there were), and usually you became more efficient. When the team was finished, you could look at an entire business process clearly. On balance, I think that's a good thing.

The first stage took roughly 5 years. When it was over, we declared victory. Hasso came out to California, and we had a dinner, exchanged awards, and had a nice party. Once we implemented the financial systems, some of our operating companies added the sales and distribution module and the marketing module to complement the financial systems. Now, after more than 10 years, many of our operating companies have the entire SAP product suite. I think the benefits are still being realized.

Of course, many of our competitors followed in our footsteps, becoming SAP users, and many major U.S. industrial companies followed as well. For me, that confirmed the success of the effort. If you are an early adopter, one of the signs that you made the right decision is that the marketplace follows you.

PART II

CLIENT/SERVER AND OPEN COMMUNICATION

As the PC era dawned at the beginning of the 1980s, Hasso Plattner and his partners finally purchased their company's first computer: a standard-issue IBM mainframe. Ten years later, SAP's engineers had fully embraced the beige box. When SAP® R/3® debuted in 1992, customers discovered they had retooled the company's suite of applications for the desktop, which had changed radically since SAP had bought its first machine.

The dumb terminal had been replaced by IBM PCs, the Apple Macintosh, and Microsoft Windows. The speed of the first Intel Pentium chips a few years later far outstripped the mainframes of a decade earlier. At the same time, great strides in networking and the introduction of the client/server model radically altered the way information managers viewed technology, according to August-Wilhelm Scheer (Chapter 4). The explosive popularity of the Internet a few years later began the linking of entire networks and made the web browser the interface to everything, thanks to pioneers like TCP/IP cocreator Vinton Cerf (Chapter 6). The next step is wireless, as PDAs, cell phones, and other devices acquire the power and sophistication to access the enterprise from anywhere at anytime, says Ravi Kalakota (Chapter 5).

Connecting PCs to mainframes over ever-strengthening networks abolished the first and perhaps most significant barrier to the real-time enterprise — poor hardware performance. Servers relinquished the role of processing data to PCs, freeing them to store and sort databases or manage the networks themselves. A three-tiered model evolved with PCs at one end and databases at the other, while application servers that spoke to both stood in the middle. Growing ever stronger, PCs became the entry points and workhorses of the nascent real-time enterprise. Employees could enter and access data through rich, complex interfaces, communicate through emerging messaging systems (proprietary, intraoffice systems at first, then email) and work collaboratively via shared file servers.

It wasn't always smooth. The switch from a highly centralized approach to a widely decentralized one introduced many small problems for every large one that the client/server approach solved. Thousands of PCs, and many more thousands of applications, suddenly required continual maintenance while millions of employees had to adjust complicated and unfamiliar client interfaces.

The rise of the Internet and the simple web browser offered new solutions. The mass adoption of TCP/IP set a global networking standard on which the real-time enterprise could be built, while the Web gave a common look and feel to the Internet experience itself. Functionality was hobbled in the transition to the browser, as customized features were lost — at least temporarily — to its ubiquitous but underpowered HTML foundation. Later standards like Java and XML are proving to be adequate workarounds. It was undoubtedly worth the tradeoff; today, the standard browser can connect to the heart of an enterprise from anywhere in the world on its own.

But the next leap forward is already here. Wireless devices are proving they can assume the duties once handled by PCs, extending the network to anywhere the Internet can reach. While the latest generation of PDAs still lacks the general-purpose abilities of the PC, handheld devices are perfectly capable of entering and accessing data residing on any server via wireless Internet connections. Client/server has taken another turn — in the wireless age, the processing burden is slowly returning to the server, which becomes invisible and is everywhere there is open air. The enterprise is now not just always on but always present — freeing workers from the desktop and, more importantly, freeing up their time. As workers vacate the office to visit customers and make new sales, formerly dead time is suddenly productive. In the short run, ROI is accelerated as time and space collapses, while in the long run, wireless clients will cause us to forget about servers altogether.

CONTRIBUTORS TO PART II

- **Vinton Cerf** has been called one of the "Fathers of the Internet." He codesigned the TCP/IP protocol and original architecture of the Internet while working at the U.S. Department of Defense's Advanced Research

Projects Agency (ARPA) in the 1970s and early 1980s. Today, he is chairman of the Internet Corporation for Assigned Names and Numbers
(ICANN), which administers domain names on the Internet, and senior
vice president of technology strategy for MCI.

- **Ravi Kalakota** is CEO and cofounder of E-Business Strategies, a research
and consulting firm. An ecommerce pioneer and an early advocate of
wireless technology applied to business practices, he is a prolific speaker
and author.
- **August-Wilhelm Scheer** is chairman of the consultancy IDS Scheer.
A professor at Saarland University and a member of SAP's Supervisory
Board, Scheer has been an advocate for improving process and instilling
innovation in both the business sphere and academia. At IDS Scheer,
he developed the ARIS suite of applications to improve efficiency inside
corporations.

4

Power on the Desktop

August-Wilhelm Scheer is chairman of the consultancy IDS Scheer.
A professor at Saarland University and a member of SAP's Supervisory
Board, Scheer has been an advocate for improving processes and instilling
innovation in both the business sphere and academia. At IDS Scheer,
he developed the ARIS suite of applications to improve efficiency inside
corporations.

August-Wilhelm Scheer

A PARADIGM SHIFT IN ACCOUNTING

I first met Hasso Plattner in 1981 at the Saarbrücken Working Session for Accounting and Electronic Data Processing, which I was hosting with my late colleague Wolfgang Kilger. Plattner gave a presentation about dialog processing in cost accounting and outlined a system that later emerged as a module in SAP® R/2®. After his presentation, a heated discussion developed with Hans-Georg Plaut, the doyen of costing in Germany and an early pioneer in the use of data processing in accounting. Plaut argued that dialog processing had no place in accounting, and certainly not in cost accounting, since all business settlement procedures such as cost planning and target/actual comparisons are period-based. It should therefore be quite sufficient to perform these calculations — along with extensive product cost planning — in batch processing without user involvement. Dialog processing would, at best, be of use in updating

master data. Incidentally, the same would also be true of financial accounting, since financial statements are period-based and do not require continuous access by the user. Therefore, only data entry would be relevant
for dialogs. The examples cited by
Plattner in reply, such as real-time
product cost planning based on a
sudden rise in the price of an
important raw material, were
accepted as exceptional cases,
though this did not refute the
basic argument regarding period-
based processes. Hasso Plattner
concluded with a statement that I
have never forgotten, "We use
dialog processing in accounting
because we can." There is more to
this statement than meets the eye.
He showed that when assessing
the benefits of a particular technology, its improvement of current processes is not the only
factor that we should take into
account. Indeed, consideration must also be given to how the technology
will facilitate and advance the development of new processes.

> " " [W]hen assessing the bene-
> fits of a particular technology,
> its improvement of current
> processes is not the only factor
> that we should take into
> account. Indeed, consideration
> must also be given to how the
> technology will facilitate and
> advance the development of
> new processes. " "

Managers need access to information about company assets and costs
at all times, and not just at the end of the month, quarter, or year. Because
of the amount of manual work involved, however, business accounting
was traditionally restricted to certain financial reporting periods. "Pen
and paper" technology placed restrictions on the accounting process.
Data processing, however, has lifted these restrictions, making real-time
data about assets and profits available. Information technology has thus
opened the door to the development of new business processes and
strategies in accounting. Dialog applications for evaluation, simulation of
process changes, and real-time access to information are now taken for
granted in accounting.

Later, cooperation between the Plaut Consulting Group and SAP led
to the development of a modern accounting system, worldwide distribution of which contributed more to the internationalization of German

business administration than all the German academic literature about corporate accounting.

It is perhaps surprising that the success of SAP has been achieved through standard business software when there is not a single business administration expert among the founders and main system developers. Furthermore, Henning Kagermann, who was later responsible for developing the accounting systems, was formerly a professor of theoretical physics. It is possible, though, that their lack of experience in the subject was, in fact, the secret to their success because they were open to new IT-based business ideas and were not confined by strict academic rules. It is also rather telling that many researchers in business administration did not recognize the importance of the integration concept in the SAP software for some time. At first, many of my colleagues couldn't see the forest for the trees. It was simply easier to criticize a cost allocation process in cost center accounting or a lot size algorithm than to grasp the basic philosophy of a system that could interlock all the functions of a company.

After the working session in Saarbrücken, I invited Hasso Plattner to my institute to address my assistants in a presentation about the architecture of R/2. His commitment and expertise filled them with enthusiasm.

Thus began a close collaboration between Hasso Plattner and IWi, my institute for information systems. He has held lectures over many years, giving the students valuable insight into the technology involved in large data processing systems. Equally important, Hasso is a role model for successful entrepreneurship in the German high-tech industry. Later, his lecturing and scientific contribution to the development of the R/3® architecture earned him an honorary doctorate and the title of honorary professor at Saarland University.

I was immediately convinced by the integration concept of R/2, as it was in line with my own thoughts on information systems. I envisaged using information systems to analyze and manage entire companies. What interested me most about this was the design of the data structures required. A company-wide database, which R/2 already had as its foundation, is very important for integration. It ensures consistent use of data definitions, enabling the modules to be integrated by the standard database. The role played by the central database in the SAP system, therefore, is vital.

THE CLIENT/SERVER BREAKTHROUGH

If the success of R/2 can be attributed to dialog processing and integration between different functional applications, the client/server architecture of SAP® R/3® was responsible for the support of decentralized organizational areas. The success of client/server architectures was certainly not determined by cost alone. When costs were mentioned in debates about central systems, it was often purely political; the real reason for success was the desire of many companies to decentralize their information processing. It was difficult to argue that the head of a decentralized operation should be responsible for the efficiency of business processes if data processing support for these processes lay in the hands of a central data processing manager. The obvious thing to do was to demand that the operation be given an independent information system and allow the decentralized staff to configure it themselves. This development received a mixed response in central data processing areas, because some were reluctant to loosen their grip on the reins. Moreover, large companies still had serious reservations about the use of standard software. However, this attitude changed somewhat with the release of R/3 and the capacity bottlenecks of the central data processing areas for decentralized area-specific developments. I remember having many discussions with the central information managers of large companies to ascertain whether it made sense to introduce standard software "on a trial basis" at smaller (less important) decentralized plants or sales subsidiaries. Using standard software at the headquarters was not an option on account of the company's unique requirements.

> " Customers no longer wanted a hardware manufacturer and its affiliated software suppliers. Instead, they wanted freedom to define their information processing strategically by choosing their hardware and application software independently. "

In this respect, targeting R/3 at small and midsize businesses was the right approach, since decentralized units of a large group are also structured like small and midsize companies. There was another facet to the initial positioning of R/3. With its original platform choice, the IBM AS/400, SAP intended to reach predominantly small and midsize companies. But then something totally different occurred. During project development, instead of using the proprietary IBM platform SAP switched to open standards such as C, Unix, SQL, and TCP/IP. Hasso Plattner gave a comprehensive report (Plattner 2000) on the reasons for this change in strategy, which chiefly related to performance difficulties in software development in the IBM world. It was a stroke of luck for SAP to have recognized that the future did not lie in accomplished and efficient proprietary platform worlds, but in open standards. Customers no longer wanted a hardware manufacturer and its affiliated software suppliers. Instead, they wanted freedom to define their information processing strategically by choosing their hardware and application software independently. For SAP, this meant the difficult process of bringing in a leading partner in the field of open standards in addition to Siemens and IBM, previously its most important partners. A partnership with Hewlett-Packard was the result, facilitated in part by the personal relationships between Klaus-Dieter Laidig, who was General Manager of HP GmbH, and the Board of SAP, in particular, Hasso Plattner. It is still rumored that some of the Unix machines making their way from the HP production plant in Böblingen to customers in the north of Germany were

" Unlike SAP, they didn't see the signs of the times and instead basked in the success of their central systems, ignoring opportunities for reorientation. Remaining successful in high-tech requires a nose for new developments. "

"diverted" to Walldorf to meet the rapidly increasing demand in the SAP's development department, jumping ahead of other customer orders.

When SAP decided to develop R/3, it was not simply following a trend but was compelled by a much stronger force within the company — its corporate culture. Only this can explain how, at the peak of its success with R/2, SAP found the courage to make such a dramatic change in the direction of its development strategy.

At the time of R/2's success, there were other successful competitors in Germany with comparable integrated business application software, such as ADV-ORGA. Today, however, these software companies are no longer represented on the market. Unlike SAP, they didn't see the signs of the times and instead basked in the success of their central systems, ignoring opportunities for reorientation. Remaining successful in high-tech requires a nose for new developments. The founder of Intel hit the nail on the head with his book *Only the Paranoid Survive* (Grove 1996). Only high-tech companies that foresee new developments can quickly take appropriate measures to avoid falling behind. In this respect, the decision to develop a new system while enjoying the success of R/2 and thereby also risk conflict with previously important partners was a real entrepreneurial decision and one that was not taken lightly within the company. Many R/2 experts scoffed at R/3's initial performance tests. In Plattner's keynote speech at Sapphire 1992 in Orlando, his announcement that R/3 was available in the United States (I can still remember his tone of voice as he said, "You can buy R/3 *now*") was received rather apprehensively by some of his own employees. After all, R/2 expertise was just taking off in the States, and now people were expected to run a new system. It was in these situations that Hasso Plattner's true leadership skills came to the fore.

The importance of R/3 for SAP was demonstrated by the fact that the status of R/3 development became a regular item on the Supervisory Board's agenda. Throughout the entire development process, Hasso Plattner personally reported on all new developments in the application architecture and the processing progress.

A major factor in the success of R/3's development was that nobody dwelt too much on concepts that were of academic interest but had not yet been tested in real situations. Whereas some software manufacturers wasted time discussing concepts of distributed database systems that sounded interesting in theory but were undeveloped in practice, SAP found a suitable practicable approach in the three-level architecture of R/3.

- Conceptually, many areas of R/2's architecture could be kept in place because a central database (database server in the first level) would still be used.
- The business solutions were then installed at the second level (application server).

- On the third level, the presentation level, the graphical interface to the user was created and additional independent analyses were supplied by the SAP application.

Alternative concepts like the two-level model pursued by other software suppliers would have made it considerably more difficult to transfer the knowledge gained from R/2's design. With the central database as the first level, the results would have been comparable. However, had the application level been moved to the PC, increased separation of the applications in the direction of distributed processing would have been necessary. It's true that in this architecture the user might have gained a seemingly simpler PC network structure, but synchronizing the distributed applications would have caused some insurmountable problems for the developers. The closeness of the three-level architecture to the architecture of R/2 made it an easier and ultimately more successful route to take. What's more, software suppliers that started out with the two-level architecture later fell in line with the three-level model.

An article in *Wirtschaftswoche* (Böndel 1995) maliciously compared SAP to lemmings, doubting that SAP used state-of-the-art technology in R/3. This accusation enraged the Executive Board, and rightly so. Apart from the fact that these criticisms were unfounded, professional development of application software is not about test-driving the great new features currently propagated by technology gurus at universities or research institutes. It is about developing a financially viable system that is accepted by the customer. With its R/3 architecture, SAP had set out on exactly the right route, and the success of R/3 has proved as much.

> " *[P]rofessional development of application software is not about test-driving the great new features currently propagated by technology gurus at universities or research institutes. It is about developing a financially viable system that is accepted by the customer.* "

The combination of the content of R/2 with the powerful three-level client/server architecture gave SAP the edge in the software development competition. In just a short time, a comprehensive integrated system was developed, the performance of which improved month by month owing to further development of hardware and system software. I recall Supervisory Board meetings in which performance tests were presented for the first time and R/3 was superimposed on R/2. Suddenly, there was the possibility of implementing R/3 not only as an enhancement to R/2 for decentralized applications, but also at company headquarters. Very quickly, attitudes about the use of standard software had changed.

> " Intellectual and entrepreneurial flexibility is a must. It is better not to chase an initial goal stubbornly but to adjust the development strategy to cater to advances in technology and the market environment. "

From the initial intention to develop an application system with the IBM AS/400 platform that would be suitable for small and midsize companies, a system finally emerged based on open standards that was implemented mainly in large companies and used both at headquarters and in decentralized areas. Intellectual and entrepreneurial flexibility is a must. It is better not to chase an initial goal stubbornly but to adjust the development strategy to cater to advances in technology and the market environment.

CONSULTANTS STEP IN

Partnerships also played a major role in the success of R/3. I have already mentioned the successful collaboration with Hewlett-Packard. At the same time integrated application software was being developed, consulting firms were emerging that focused on implementing these systems. The consulting market was created because the implementation of integrated business applications had become too complex for companies to cope with on their own. Specialization in business administration studies might also have played a part in this, since trained management experts were able to deal only with areas like accounting, human resources, production, and so on, but were not equipped to handle integrated business processes that crossed these functional areas. New knowledge of business processes was required, and the best way to obtain it was through consulting engagements. There is no other way to explain why consultants with astronomical rates were suddenly required to implement a procurement system dealing with one area that is viewed rather contemptuously in the academic world and is reduced to algorithms for optimum order quantities and the like. In the implementation of a procurement process, a huge amount of detailed logistical knowledge is required: knowledge of accounts payable accounting, bill of material organization, and knowledge of R/3 and its options for customization. At that time, no academic programs provided the kind of training required for this. Fortunately, things are much improved nowadays (also thanks to considerable support from SAP) and not only advocates of information systems but also many teachers of conventional business administration courses use SAP software in their lectures.

SAP's partnerships with large international consulting firms have primarily been fostered by the early availability of R/3. Consulting firms did not want to train their employees to work with several systems, as this would naturally have increased costs. R/3 therefore received preferential treatment and became a winner on the consulting scene too. Partnerships with other hardware producers, in particular Siemens and subsequently almost all Unix computer manufacturers, were another driving force. I can recall situations where large international hardware manufacturers got in line in hopes of joining SAP's inner circle of partners.

A DATA MODEL DEFINED

The key words *open standards* in the client/server discussion earlier in this chapter related to the liberation of hardware from the proprietary operating systems and operating system-specific software. With Unix, SQL, C, and TCP/IP as standards, software suppliers were no longer tied to individual hardware vendors, but suddenly discovered an open market. For example, with R/2, SAP was restricted to the Siemens and IBM mainframes. Open systems caused a rapid increase in the number of international software suppliers. Use of these technical standards alone did not serve to open the application logic for the user. In fact, the application logic was further hedged in the programming language. The user

handbooks described the application logic more from a system administration perspective. Because of this, at the end of the 1980s and start of the
1990s, I requested talks with the Executive Board of SAP, and particularly
Hasso Plattner, to convince them of the need for more formal logical documentation of the system that would be comprehensible to the user.

We embarked on a project to build the data model of the SAP software. This had already been started at the time of R/2, but was given an
extra push thanks to the debate about system openness in the R/3 environment. Since the database is the integration layer of the system, documentation of its content is a prerequisite for understanding the entire
system. The data model of the SAP software took several years to
develop and is surely one of the world's largest data models. At the start
of the project, it was impossible to estimate the dimensions of the
model. The immense size of the model demonstrates the highly sophisticated nature of R/3. There is not just a single data object for each business term, such as sales order, procurement order, or production order;
rather, there are a multitude of variants for these terms. In a procurement order, for example, there is an order for consignment stores, for
clearance items, for special production items, for goods with risk potential, and so on. Different logistical processes lie behind each variant of
this procurement order, and every variant must be modeled as a specialization of the generic "procurement order" object. This multitude of
variants gives rise to the complexity of business software, but it is also
where the value of an integrated business application system lies. The
data model revealed this complexity and displayed the basis of the integration that took place via the standardized database.

It became clear that the documentation of the data objects contained
only part of the application logic. Representation of the business processes

DRILL DOWN

The data model that Scheer describes is crucial to enabling real-time processing because it preserves the rich, vital relationships between any number of data elements. In Chapter 3, Martin Klitten states that, for Chevron,
one of the most important benefits of R/3 was the drill-down capability
facilitated by this data model. It greatly aided analysis and problem-solving.
Here, Scheer mentions that the model becomes the basis for a robust
product that, right out of the box, is able to handle many contingencies.

themselves was the next logical step in formally documenting the system. With the development of event-driven process chains (Keller, Nüttgens, and Scheer 1992), a method was developed in collaboration between SAP, my institute IWi, and IDS Scheer AG that, on the one hand, was comprehensible to the user, but on the other was sufficiently formalized to be used in configuring and customizing the system. Working with Executive Board member Dr. Peter Zencke on this project produced many positive results. Only now, with the development of more powerful business process–oriented architectures, such as the SAP NetWeaver™ technology platform, is the value of this model apparent. The workflow engine in the SAP NetWeaver architecture requires a formal description of the content of the business processes that are controlled by the workflow system. The exchange of data by enterprise application integration (EAI) between the application components within a system and between the systems of different users requires knowledge of the data structures and business processes. After all, the business processes are the reason why integration is needed within and between companies. The many years of collaboration between SAP AG and IDS Scheer AG on the modeling of complex business application systems (Scheer 2000) are only just bearing fruit and opening doors to many new possibilities.

HASSO PLATTNER, THE RESEARCHER

Without a doubt, had Hasso Plattner chosen a career as a professor, he would have been a highly innovative researcher and teacher. His course of study at the University of Karlsruhe and his contact at that time with the inspirational Dr. Karl Steinbuch would almost certainly have given him the motivation to follow such a career path. Thank goodness he didn't, however, or else SAP software, if it even existed, would certainly not have been so successful. His decision to found the company was a piece of good fortune for the future of information technology. Indeed, there are far fewer successful entrepreneurs than there are professors.

Nevertheless, Hasso Plattner has maintained his interest in the academic world. In addition to his lecturing activities at the University of Saarbrücken, which I mentioned earlier, he has supported project collaboration between SAP and colleges. His generous donation to the University of Potsdam to build the Hasso Plattner Institute for Software System Technology is certainly more than a gift to his hometown. It also

> " " *The complexity of a system is not determined by size alone, but also by change. Traditional informatics struggle to cope with such problems since no available information covers the multitude of variants in companies of different industries.* " "

relates to his experience in working with very complex large systems. One can well believe that the development and maintenance of such systems is comparable to that of airplanes, as he has been known to state. Just as after a few years an airplane contains hardly any of its original components, a software system constantly undergoes change too. The complexity of a system is not determined by size alone, but also by change. Traditional informatics struggle to cope with such problems since no available information covers the multitude of variants in companies of different industries. The real challenge of this institute is to bridge the gap between science, informatics, and practice and gain a competitive edge for Germany's software.

BIBLIOGRAPHY

Böndel, B.: SAP - Wie Lemminge. In: *Wirtschaftswoche* 49 (1995), no. 12, p. 108-118.

Grove, A. S.: *Only the Paranoid Survive: How to Exploit the Crisis Points that Challenge Every Company and Career.* New York [and others]: Currency Doubleday, 1996.

Keller, G.; Nüttgens, M.; Scheer, A.-W.: Semantische Prozeßmodellierung auf der Grundlage "Ereignisgesteuerter Prozeßketten (EPK)". In: Scheer, August-Wilhelm (Hrsg.): *Veröffentlichungen des Instituts für Wirtschaftsinformatik*, no. 89, Saarbrücken: Universität des Saarlandes, 1992. — URL http://www.iwi.uni-sb.de/Download/iwihefte/heft89.pdf [20.11.2003].

Plattner, H.: *Dem Wandel voraus : Hasso Plattner im Gespräch mit* August-Wilhelm Scheer, Siegfried Wendt, und Daniel S. Morrow. Bonn: Galileo Press, 2000.

Scheer, A.-W.: *ARIS — Modellierungsmethoden, Metamodelle, Anwendungen.* Fourth Edition Berlin [and others]: Springer, 2001.

Scheer, A.-W.: *ARIS — Vom Geschäftsprozess zum Anwendungssystem.* Fourth, Revised Edition Berlin [and others]: Springer, 2002.

Scheer, A.-W.: *Unternehmen gründen ist nicht schwer ...* Berlin [and others]: Springer, 2000.

5

Mobility Unleashed

Ravi Kalakota is CEO and cofounder of E-Business Strategies, a research and consulting firm. An e-commerce pioneer and an early advocate of wireless technology applied to business practices, he is a prolific speaker and author.

Ravi Kalakota

The founders of SAP AG envisioned a real-time enterprise three decades ago. Their vision is being taken to a whole new plateau with the emerging innovations around mobile technology, communication and integration infrastructure, and applications.

Mobile technology is rapidly dismantling some of the barriers and restrictions that limited the concept of the real-time enterprise. The foundation for the next generation of the real-time enterprise is slowly but surely being put in place.

The emergence of the mobile Internet capable of interconnecting numerous devices and multiple information webs represents a global megatrend. It represents a new phase in enabling the knowledge worker. As a result, a substantial new innovation cycle predicated on the marriage of the Internet, wireless technology, and e-commerce is upon us.

Sure, you're thinking, I've heard that before. Well, think again. It's true that in the late 1990s wireless networks burst onto the scene with promises of big payoffs that rarely materialized. But today, the industry is broader and healthier, thanks to five key developments: huge advances in handheld computers, advances in software, a more robust mobile broadband infrastructure, a more interested consumer, and the burgeoning demands of real-time business.

> " *Mobility means fully portable, real-time access to the same information resources and tools that, until recently, were accessible only from your desktop.* "

The most important development is not just related to technological advancements but to users and market demand. Mobile users are no longer just geeks and early adopters; they are mainstream users, such as field service and field sales employees, who are demanding mobility. Mobility means fully portable, real-time access to the same information resources and tools that, until recently, were accessible only from your desktop.

This chapter reveals the scale and scope of the mobile computing revolution. The structural changes taking place in computing are unveiled. We end by looking at the impact of mobile innovations in creating a new real-time organizational architecture representing the next practices for the enterprise software industry.

STRUCTURAL MIGRATION IN COMPUTING

In January 1975, *Popular Electronics* published a cover story on a computer kit called Altair 8800 that sold for less than $400. Microinstrumentation & Telemetry Systems (MITS) of Albuquerque, New Mexico, designed the Altair. It didn't look anything like the sleek machines of today. It had no monitor, no keyboard, and no mouse. The MITS Altair 8800 was a simple box with switches and small lights, designed for scientific calculations. It appealed mainly to hobbyists.

The MITS was typical of first-generation technology. Many industry executives did not see a need for it. In 1977, Ken Olson, founder, president, and chairman of Digital Equipment Corp., was quoted as saying, "There is no reason anyone would want a computer in their home." Even consumers did not see any need for it. If someone said, this would be great for calculations and accounting, people would laugh and say, "This would never replace the HP-35 four-function calculator." Or if someone said, this would be great for word processing, people would say, "This will never replace a typewriter." Clearly, the most troublesome aspect was not the technology per se but gauging the scale and speed of user acceptance.

Few could have foreseen what was to come. From that ordinary start in 1975, the PC industry has exploded into a $500-billion-a-year business. In a 25-year period, the PC has become an integral part of life — a word-processing tool, accounting tool, messaging device, and entertainment center. The PC industry's fortunes increasingly sway the direction of the global economy. How did this industry become so influential so fast? Four reasons stand out:

- Customers found creative uses for the PC.
- PC software steadily improved in its price/performance ratio.
- Processor speed followed Moore's Law, doubling roughly every 18 months or so.
- The Internet greatly increased PC use.

The evolution and adoption of mobile devices (wireless handhelds, smartphones, laptops, and tablets) is likely to follow a similar path — from toys to business tools. Although the dominance of tethered PC-based computing will remain in the short term, a shift of seismic proportions is underway. Facilitated by mobile technology, the next-generation vision has been referred to by a variety of labels — Evernet, Supranet, X Internet, and Hypernet.

> *" Although the dominance of tethered PC-based computing will remain in the short term, a shift of seismic proportions is underway. "*

MOVING STORY

The ability of wireless networks to reach virtually any point on the planet makes mobile computing one of the most important and challenging frontiers in enterprise computing right now. It demands new methods for managing information, distributing business processes, and creating compact but friendly devices. Yet, as Kalakota explains here, mobile access to real-time information has the potential to revolutionize how corporations interact with their customers, suppliers, and other business partners. In Chapter 22, Pekka Ala-Pietilä ponders the design of mobile devices and champions the advantages of extending business applications out to the field.

The development of mobile technology (handhelds, Wi-Fi networks, RFID tags, and 3G networks) coupled with the multi-channel customer revolution in its many manifestations is beginning to have a profound effect. No one is in any doubt about that. The uncertainty lies in precisely when and how a new order will be imposed and which applications will emerge as the winners and losers.

Gradually but relentlessly, the structure of computing is changing. Figure 5-1 illustrates the five cascading structural changes that have taken place over the last two decades. The first two structural shifts — mainframe and client/server — required a major internal retooling of the corporation. Since 1995, we have seen literally three major structural shifts in rapid succession: three-tier client/server, web-based distributed computing, and now mobile computing (also called nomadic computing).

Mobile computing architecture is quickly being put in place. The use of mobile devices has increased tremendously as handheld computers, mobile phones, pagers, and personal digital assistants have achieved popular acceptance and become more advanced and powerful. Improvements in mobile technology and wireless infrastructure are facilitating greater bandwidth, thereby enabling both data and voice transmission.

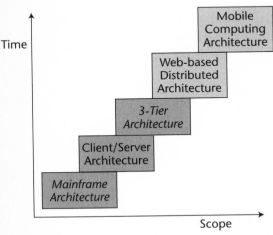

Figure 5-1. Structural Shifts in Computing

Interestingly, the structural changes caused by these shifts are not restricted to the computing architecture but also impact the boundaries of the enterprise. Mobile architecture has tremendous impact on how companies interact with their customers. It has similar impact on the supplier and employee side. Since it is too early to say definitely, one can only speculate that mobile computing will have even more impact since its tentacles spread everywhere. One reason for this is a shift in the user interaction paradigm:

- **Old paradigm** — the user going to the computer's location (PC–centric)
- **New paradigm** — the computer is wherever the user is (person–centric)

The most significant economic consequence of the new paradigm facilitated by mobile computing will be the increased real–time interaction between companies and their customers, employees, and suppliers.

So what does all this mean for leadership? Management everywhere must assess how the person–centric computing architecture will alter existing business models and develop proactive scenarios for deriving the greatest benefit from the technological changes taking place.

> " *The most significant economic consequence of the new paradigm facilitated by mobile computing will be the increased real-time interaction between companies and their customers, employees, and suppliers.* "

THE EVOLUTION OF MOBILE APPLICATIONS

Most customers don't buy technology. They buy applications to solve a problem. Customer value creation is occurring in five solution phases based on continuous improvements in mobile technology. These phases are Messaging, Info-Connectivity, Transactions, Transformation, and Infusion.

- **Phase 1 — Messaging.** The ability to interact with others. Short Message Services (SMS) have proven to be extremely popular on two-way pagers and mobile phones. Sources estimate that more than 80 percent of worldwide wireless data subscribers subscribe to SMS. The next stage in the development of messaging technology is direct access to corporate email accounts. However, significant improvements in the data rate, memory, and storage capacity of wireless devices need to occur before corporate email access displaces SMS as the messaging tool of preference.

- **Phase 2 — Info-Connectivity.** The ability to access and retrieve information from the web. Unlike messaging, this requires a mobile device to maintain a real-time connection to the Internet. While such a capability already exists, the quality of information currently available is poor. Much of the information is free and often trivial. At a minimum, wireless devices with easy-to-use browsers should become commonplace before this phase takes off.

- **Phase 3 — Transactions.** Business transactions begin to take place via the mobile channel. Rather than applying a quick-fix approach to achieve a wireless web presence, corporations develop a strategy for extending and growing revenue-generating wireless transactions. Growth in the third phase will occur in predictable ways. It is very much dependent on enabling various mission-critical back-office applications.

- **Phase 4 — Transformation.** The interconnection of business processes — inside the company and between organizations — takes place. For the notion of "business without boundaries" to prevail, back-end applications and data must be reengineered to take complete advantage of the features mobility offers. Implementing mobility-enhanced internal and external business processes will be the most difficult and challenging aspect of the m-business revolution. It is also where the largest gains in true economic and business value will be found.

- **Phase 5 — Infusion.** The enterprise absorbs mobility into its way of doing business. Mobility is no longer separated from the normal course of doing business. Infusion requires a shift from a culture in which technology is merely occasionally present to one in which technology is an accepted part of business. Infusion requires a company, its employees, its suppliers, and even its customers to once again reengineer their business processes and relationships to acclimate the company's culture to the technology's presence. It is a common occurrence in Phase 5 for strategies to evolve, morph, and mutate.

A significant portion of the mobile economy is engaged in messaging. However, the period when messaging and email applications will dominate wireless communications will be short-lived. As noted earlier, how quickly and completely the mobile Internet is adopted and used will be determined by how well the mobile software applications meet real enterprise needs.

THE MOBILE ENTERPRISE FRAMEWORK

Mobility is reshaping the enterprise. SAP AG and others in the enterprise software industry are anticipating that their customers in a variety of industries — beverage, consumer products, utilities, pharmaceutical, and manufacturing — will embrace mobility. They are paving the way for the future by demonstrating real-time applications and infrastructure useful to the customer.

Let's look at mobile application framework to understand the nature of applications that are being developed. The mobile applications fall under one of four general but distinct strategic opportunities, which capture literally every business activity taking place in the mobile landscape (see Figure 5-2). The four strategic opportunities are what we term innovation focus, customer focus, supply chain focus, and operational focus.

> " *SAP AG and others in the enterprise software industry are anticipating that their customers in a variety of industries . . . will embrace mobility. They are paving the way for the future by demonstrating real-time applications and infrastructure useful to the customer.* "

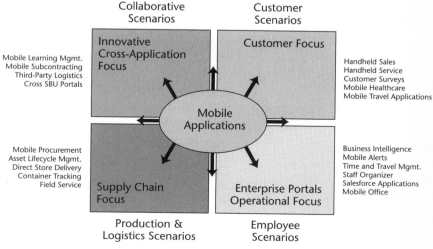

Figure 5-2. The Mobile Landscape

INNOVATION FOCUS

Companies use mobile technology to develop and deliver new products and collaborative services to customers, partners, and suppliers. For example, a wireless portal operator could create a new distribution channel and funnel customized content from publishers directly to readers. Wells Fargo, for example, decided to forego its wireless banking project and concentrate on using the wireless channel to project targeted customer alerts about mortgage rates and stock market activity.

PocketScript, a developer of wireless software applications for doctors, is another example. The company created mobile technology that allows physicians to use mobile handheld devices to write prescriptions while they are at the patient's bedside. The device can also enable billing entries, transcription, lab result viewing, email functions, and Internet access. Using this wireless technology, doctors can prevent prescription errors and decrease the amount of time the medical community, particularly pharmacists, spends tracking down doctors for help in deciphering sloppily written prescriptions.

CUSTOMER FOCUS

Companies use mobile technology to increase the scope of their interactions with existing customers from "brick and click" to "brick, click, and flick." They try to determine how mobile fits into customers' everyday tasks and lifestyle and then create multichannel interactions. Customer-facing m-business is becoming an important new complementary channel for commerce.

Companies can use the mobile Internet to establish direct links to customers, resellers, or distributors. For instance, Pepsi has created another way for thirsty customers to enjoy its beverages by experimenting with wireless point-of-sale vending machines that allow people to pay with credit cards. The vending machine's connection to the wireless network also allows the company to view the machine's real-time vending status.

SUPPLY CHAIN FOCUS

Companies use mobile technology to enhance supply chain and distribution operations by improving the flow of information, orders, products, and payments among the various participants. In many industries, business pace has accelerated so quickly that a company's fortunes can rise and fall on its ability to monitor and manage the volatile supply chain. RFID (radio frequency ID) has revolutionized how companies track products and material throughout the supply chain by emitting low-power wireless signals to read and update information on a "tagged" item.

Burlington Northern Santa Fe Corp., operator of North America's largest railway line, uses RFID tags to track its rail cars. Rather than employ hundreds of workers to physically walk up and down tracks to record individual car information and then wait for the data to be manually keyed into a computer, RFID tags automatically emit the necessary information along a train's route, resulting in 100,000 tags read each day with virtually no errors. The information is then transferred instantly to the company's mainframe system and made immediately available to Burlington and their customers. The system provides Burlington's customers more accurate data about their shipments, reduces track delays, and significantly cuts operational costs.

OPERATIONAL FOCUS

Companies use mobile technology to leverage their IT investments and increase the productivity of employees who are away from their desks. Productivity improvements occur when a company's employees, particularly the sales force, field service, and business partners, share and access information and perform transactions anytime, anywhere.

For the Progressive Corporation, a provider of auto insurance and other property and casualty policies, deploying mobile technology to its employees in the field has resulted in streamlined accident-to-claims processes and increased customer satisfaction. Using mobile technologies, Progressive's claims representatives can perform up to 20 different transactions in the field — everything from entering police-report information to downloading specific car part costs and repair estimates — on their own on a single site visit. The ability to instantly move information back and forth between a laptop and a mainframe and keep claims moving toward resolution gives Progressive a major marketplace advantage.

> " " *SAP AG is unique in the market because it offers customers an integrated mobile platform that mobilizes critical business applications from email to field service, sales force automation, and customer relationship management.* " "

It is quite evident from these different categories that the scale and scope of the mobile revolution will spawn a new wave of innovation. Clearly, the mobile application market is still developing. SAP AG is unique in the market because it offers customers an integrated mobile platform that mobilizes critical business applications from email to field service, sales force automation, and customer relationship management. The real-time vision of SAP's founder is being redefined yet again.

THE MOBILE ECONOMY

"Prediction is very difficult," wrote Nobel Laureate Niels Bohr. "Especially about the future."

Despite the difficulty in predicting the future, it is fairly clear that the mobile economy is both inevitable and imminent. Businesses are at the threshold of an innovation tidal wave offering unforeseen technical and process capabilities. This mobile economy is facilitated by the convergence of the Internet, e-business, and the wireless world where customers, employees, and suppliers can go online anytime, anywhere, and using any device.

As a result, the nature of customer interaction and speed of business is bound to change in the next decade. Businesses in the mobile economy will have to deliver existing and next-generation services and applications with greater speed, intelligence, interactivity, and personalization than ever before. To support this vision, a new computing value chain is emerging that focuses on the blending of mobile device types, wireless access, and content.

The early phases of the mobile economy will likely be chaotic. The adoption of technological innovation by the business world is seldom a neat, linear process. When a company first adopts an innovation, it can come as an abrupt shock. The period immediately following the adoption is often tumultuous and disruptive to the existing social and business processes. However, this period is typically short-lived and the technological and process changes soon diffuse throughout the organization in a steady and gradual manner. This is particularly true for larger firms. How technological and process diffusion occurs within companies will be a major issue as the rapid proliferation of mobile devices and new Internet appliances sets the stage for the mobile business boom.

Certain media spin doctors portray the transition to the mobile economy as nothing less than a total and complete upheaval in the way that every company and every industry currently conducts business. Other observers — those who lived through the roller-coaster years of the new economy or were burned by the Internet boom and bust — view the transition as a gradual evolution of existing business landscapes wherein corporate cultures steadily absorb the new innovations over time.

> " *The truth about the mobile economy . . . is a mix of revolution and evolution.* "

The truth about the mobile economy combines aspects of both perspectives — it is a mix of revolution and evolution. Add them all up, and you get an enterprise software landscape that'll look quite different going forward — and radically different from that of even 5 years ago.

6

Everything-to-Everything Connectivity

Vinton Cerf has been called one of the "Fathers of the Internet." He co-signed the TCP/IP protocol and original architecture of the Internet while working at the U.S. Department of Defense's Advanced Research Projects Agency (ARPA) in the 1970s and early 1980s. Today, he is chairman of the Internet Corporation for Assigned Names and Numbers (ICANN), which administers domain names on the Internet, and he is senior vice president of technology strategy for MCI.

Vinton Cerf

The evolution of networking and, in particular, of the Internet, followed the digital revolution made possible by computers and the invention of the transistor (in that order!). Without computers, there would be little motivation for the development of networks to connect them. Computers without software are inanimate devices, bereft of utility. It is the software contained within them and interpreted by them that makes computers and their progeny so remarkably flexible, adaptable, and useful.

It should come as no surprise that the Internet and its predecessors, such as the ARPANET, were developed primarily during the 1970s and 1980s by computer scientists interested in applying computers to a variety of tasks and in sharing these then–expensive devices through remote time-sharing. The ARPANET set the stage for the use of computers in military command-and-control. It is not a large intellectual leap to think of computers in use in civilian business settings, managing processes; exchanging ordering, production, and invoicing information; and generally automating much that was once purely manual labor.

These considerations help to explain the remarkable impact that SAP has had in the business and government sectors, where the management of information is a key element of successful operation. Standardizing the representation of information and standardizing the procedures by which it is transmitted, exchanged, and processed are important elements in the foundation of *information infrastructure*. As these standards spread and the networks and computers that support them proliferate, one can begin to see the outlines of a global information infrastructure emerging from many decades of work by many people.

FROM THE WEB TO THE SEMANTIC WEB

Much of the value of the Internet lies in the software that permits otherwise unstructured information to be searched, organized, analyzed, and displayed in near real time by hundreds of millions of users around the world. Tim Berners-Lee, whose work beginning in the late 1980s led to the World Wide Web, sees a future in which information will have more structure, permitting what he calls the *semantic web* to emerge from the seemingly undisciplined world of the Internet. In fact, the presence of standard markings to identify the meaning of data by reference to various standard descriptive terms makes the semantic web a nearly emergent property of networking.

Once software is capable of making inferences derived from its understanding of textual information that has been

> " *In some very basic sense, virtually every activity of mankind benefits from and relies upon information of one kind or another. . . .[T]hose who make tools for managing and analyzing information are increasingly important players in the global information infrastructure.* "

semantically marked, we have the beginnings of a powerful new tool in our never-ending battle to manage an increasingly large body of information that seemingly grows daily. As the business of information continues to evolve, the management and use of information will grow in importance. In some very basic sense, virtually every activity of mankind benefits from and relies upon information of one kind or another. It should therefore come as no surprise that those who make tools for managing and analyzing information are increasingly important players in the global information infrastructure.

EVERYTHING ONLINE

Equally important are the means by which information is accumulated. In the opening years of the twenty-first century, many are beginning to see and speculate on the effects of the RFID devices that respond to pulses of radio energy with bursts of information. On the Autobahn, one no longer needs to slow down when passing through a toll gate — the RFID chip tells the gate-keeping system which account to debit as you breeze by at 100 kilometers per hour (or faster!). These same chips can identify packages and pallets that are being shipped by air, rail, or truck, tracking them from start to finish and accumulating an audit trail of information.

Over the last decade, enterprises have made enormous investments in information technology, both in software and hardware. For these investments to produce long-term benefits, it will be essential that intra- *and* interenterprise standards evolve so as to permit the automatic processing of transactions between companies and between divisions within companies. The software needed to realize this promise is inescapably the business of SAP and its partners. International standards and conventions for the exchange and processing of information will be essential for the successful pursuit of these benefits.

It is becoming clear that literally billions of devices will find their way onto the Internet. Many will be simple devices such as Internet-enabled picture frames that can interact with web servers to download, store, and display images, sound, and text. Others will look like and behave like mobile telephones but will have a variety of additional functions resulting from the onboard software that permits mixed information streams to flow into and out of the device.

DATA POINT EXPLOSION

Vinton Cerf is not the only contributor to this book to note the coming explosion in the number of devices that will be connected "live" to the Internet. Countless billions of sensors, radio frequency identification devices (RFID), and mobile computers are about to increase by many orders of magnitude the volume of information that enterprise applications will be able to collect. In Chapter 17, Hubert Österle looks at how sensors and actuators, in everything from cars to washing machines, are directly reporting data that humans once entered into computers manually, if at all. In Chapter 14, Ulrich Kipper explores new uses of RFID tags at Frankfurt Airport. In Chapter 29, SAP Global Research & Innovation describes how SAP has been working closely with customers to explore the promise and challenges of RFID technology.

Sensor systems are evolving that will supply an endless stream of status information about mobile devices, about environmental conditions in key urban or agricultural or industrial areas, and about the functioning of complex mechanical and electronic systems. Making sense of all of this information is the challenge facing SAP as it reinvents itself for twenty-first century operation.

Only in the presence of organized and essentially consistently available information can one consider analysis leading to optimized operation. SAP has an opportunity to introduce a variety of tools that take advantage of this possibility.

More generally, the presence of billions of Internet-enabled sensors, devices, and systems will open up vast new opportunities to provide online services to businesses and consumers who want to use the power of intermediary devices to manage and control so many Internet endpoints. The many familiar remote controls that, today, populate our homes and offices and have to be in the same room and within view of the controlled device will be replaced by a single Internet-enabled device that can refer to the controlled system by a domain name or an IP address. Moreover, the controller need not be anywhere near the controlled object — it merely has to be on the net and able to authenticate itself to the system under control or the system through which the control is to be exercised. Intermediary devices will be configured to know about and track the status of myriad systems online at home, at work, in the car, and perhaps on our persons. All of this information will become grist for the SAP software mill — providing a new platform upon which to build new applications.

CHANGES IN THE SERVICE GRID

Familiar services such as telephony, videoconferencing, television, and radio broadcasting or cablecasting will migrate onto Internet platforms, creating their own new opportunities for software enhancement. Today's broadcast satellite will become tomorrow's broadcast Internet service, from which will be derived not only the familiar radio and television broadcast services but also a variety of data distribution services, inter-active group game applications, collaboration services, and logistics ser-vices, all evolving and enhancing the utility of software. Adding to this mix is the emergence of speech understanding as a new modality for interacting with computers, allowing spoken conversation to become a new means of controlling the devices that serve us. It will probably take a while to get used to chatting with the refrigerator and the television set, although most of us have gotten used to talking to our cars — but not so used to them talking back! Of course, the familiar global posi-tioning location systems have made our cars chattier than before as they advise us in which direction to go next in our journeys. Let us hope that the conversation remains just that and does not turn into a major debate while we are behind the wheel!

CONCLUSION

It is a privilege to take this opportunity to speculate a bit about the future of networking and computing. It is likely safe to predict that Hasso Plattner will see more changes in the next 10 years than he has seen or personally undertaken in the last 60. I offer to him and to SAP a personal wish for success in the years ahead.

PART III

THE REAL-TIME ENTERPRISE

W e are almost there. Hasso and his colleagues at SAP have strived for 30 years to arrive at our destination, when the IT chain finally closes its last loop and the real-time enterprise begins. Given virtuous cycles of decisions and feedback, beginning in the executive brain of organizations and becoming autonomous, continuous action in the organizations themselves will be instant and automatic. The real-time enterprise is just over the horizon.

Real-time computing — which has been SAP's vision and its promise to customers since its founding — is no longer the issue. The limits that SAP's engineers once struggled against — slow machines, tiny memory, low bandwidth, bottlenecks, latency, cost — are being struck from our list faster than new problems can replace them. Today, our networked computers can do almost anything we ask, but so far we haven't asked any new questions.

Part III's contributors have all played pivotal roles in building and understanding the enterprise as we know it and are working on finally bringing the real-time enterprise into being right now. Carly Fiorina, Joe Forehand, Bill Gates, and Bruce Harreld are grappling with the technical and infrastructural underpinnings at Hewlett-Packard, Accenture, Microsoft, and IBM, respectively. Meanwhile, Michael Hammer, Vinod Khosla, Anil Kumar, Geoffrey Moore, and Hubert Österle ponder how organizations and individuals must change to bring real time into being — dismantling hierarchies and discarding any activity, including managing itself, that distracts workers from fulfilling customers' needs.

Real-time organizations focus on process, says Michael Hammer, "performing work that is of value to their customers, work that takes into account the larger context, work that is directed toward achieving results rather than performed as an end in itself."

Traditionally, SAP has helped its customers optimize the processes common to every enterprise and invisible to consumers — accounting, logistics, and the like. SAP applications assumed the burden of streamlining the work of both routine tasks and advanced customized processes.

Geoffrey Moore says that by embedding best practices for common tasks in its enterprise applications, SAP rightly convinced customers to adopt proven methods for routine work. "Change your process, not the program," was the path taken by many SAP customers, says Moore. By commoditizing such work, companies can spend more time using technology to support unique processes for creating value.

Vinod Khosla says that in the real-time enterprise the technology will serve the process. The programs must be changed before we can even envision how process will follow. Companies have to adapt their business processes to take advantage of the technology, but the technology has to adapt easily to whatever those business processes are. The resulting applications will be business process applications. Most of what we've done so far are transaction systems. SAP has done those very well. But nobody has really focused on the business process itself, says Khosla. The contributors in Part III will.

While SAP and its rivals race to rebuild business applications, the infrastructure beneath them has already begun fading into invisibility, migrating from the desktop to a cloud of omnipresent resources presently thought of as "web services." Efforts like Microsoft's .NET and the rise of wireless devices force us to think about life after the desktop, when process becomes the focal point of the enterprise.

Once infrastructure ceases to be the limiting (and therefore defining) factor in how organizations use technology, how will organizations themselves change to seize this new advantage? When we have finished reengineering our software, it will become necessary to reengineer ourselves — the accepted virtues of proximity, hierarchy, and the paring away of noncore activities will all need reevaluation.

And this, in turn, will spark a wave of soul-searching at companies like SAP. How do we rewrite applications to make the switch from monolithic architectures to distributed computing? What data formats must be devised to operate in real time? And how will that data be stored, shared, transported, and synchronized once the real-time enterprise matures, mingling seamlessly with other companies — vendors, customers, outsourced services — and crosses national borders?

These are just the broadest implications. Parts IV and V will deal with the steps immediately following these — what interfaces will be needed to see process in real time, and how will the digital nervous system just beginning to evolve incorporate new data and devices? So much work still remains to be done.

CONTRIBUTORS TO PART III

- **Carly Fiorina** is chairman and CEO of Hewlett-Packard, one of the world's largest providers of computing and imaging solutions and services. She spearheaded the company's efforts to merge with Compaq, which was completed in 2002. Before joining HP in 1999, she held a number of senior positions at Lucent Technologies and AT&T.

- **Joe W. Forehand** is chairman and CEO of Accenture. Prior to becoming CEO, he led the company's global Communications & High Tech group, and in 30 years led 11 of Accenture's 18 industry groups.

- **Bill Gates** is chairman and chief software architect of Microsoft, the software giant he cofounded with Paul Allen in 1975. Gates stepped aside as CEO in 2000 to work more directly with product groups and to focus on the company's long-term technical strategy.

- **Michael Hammer** is president of Hammer and Company and the author of many books, including *Reengineering the Corporation, Beyond Reengineering,* and *The Agenda: What Every Business Must Do to Dominate the Decade.*

- **Bruce Harreld** is IBM's senior vice president for strategy, a role in which he oversees the company's business and investment strategies, examines emerging business opportunities, and manages its long-standing relationship with SAP.

- **Claus Dieter Hoffman** is chairman of the supervisory board of SupplyOn AG. SupplyOn is an Internet marketplace tailored to meet the needs of the automotive supplier industry. Prior to this, Hoffman held a variety of executive-level positions during his tenure of nearly 30 years at Bosch. Since his retirement in 2002, Hoffmann became Managing Partner of H + H Senior Advisors GmbH.

- **Vinod Khosla** has been a General Partner of Kleiner Perkins Caufield & Byers since 1986. He cofounded Daisy Systems and was founding CEO of Sun Microsystems, where he pioneered open systems and commercial RISC processors.

- **Ulrich Kipper** is Senior Executive Manager Application Development and Deputy CIO with Fraport AG, the owner and operator of Frankfurt Airport, and one of the leading companies in the international airport business.

- **Anil Kumar** is a director of McKinsey & Company, based in Silicon Valley. He is responsible for McKinsey's global business process outsourcing and offshoring practice, as well as its electronic business practice. In 1993, he moved to India to launch McKinsey's practice there before subsequently returning to the U.S.

- **Geoffrey Moore** is chairman and founder of The Chasm Group (TCG), a consulting practice in California named after his influential 1991 business strategy book *Crossing the Chasm.*

- **Hubert Österle** is the director of the Institute of Information Management at the University of St. Gallen, where he has taught since 1980. A frequent speaker and author on information management, business engineering, and process and system development, he is also founder and president of The Information Management Group (IMG).

- **Ed Toben** joined Colgate in 1990 as Vice President of Information Technology and was promoted to CIO in 1999. In 2000, he was named one of *Computerworld*'s Top 100 IT Leaders.

7

The Integration Story: How to Integrate People, Processes, Ideas, and Work

Carly Fiorina is chairman and CEO of Hewlett-Packard Company, a global technology solutions provider focused on making technology and its bene-fits accessible to all. Fiorina has returned HP to its roots of innovation and inventiveness while delivering the best customer exeprience. Fiorina led the successful acquisition of Compaq in May 2002 to accelerate HP's strategy, catalyze growth in a changing technology landscape, and increase long-term customer value. Prior to joining HP in 1999, Fiorina spent nearly 20 years at AT&T and Lucent Technologies, where she held a number of senior leadership positions. HP and SAP have enjoyed a long-standing partnership that included HP serving as the development partner and platform for SAP's R/3 client/server architecture.

Carly Fiorina

INTRODUCTION

I t is an honor to be asked to contribute to this book since it is a celebration of Hasso Plattner's 60th birthday and a tribute to his visionary thinking. The real-time enterprise is something HP knows a
great deal about and is a topic we continue to advance in collaboration
with the great people at SAP.

In fact, HP and SAP have established a long and storied partnership
over the last decade that has proven to be highly successful for both
companies. When SAP decided to enhance their product offering from
the SAP® R/2® mainframe application into the next era of computing,
HP became the development partner and computing platform for SAP's
R/3 client/server architecture. During that joint development, the first
SAP Competence Center at the SAP headquarters in Walldorf, Germany, was established with HP in 1990. In 1992, the first SAP® R/3®
customer installation was on an HP platform. It was with Compaq that
SAP established the Windows NT platform for SAP R/3. No other
company can claim to have completed more SAP installations than HP.
One out of every two SAP installations is running on an HP platform.
HP also has the largest SAP services organization in the world, delivering first-class consulting, support, and hosting services for SAP environments on all major platforms: Windows®, Unix®, and Linux®. HP
services became the market leader for SAP R/3 outsourcing services in
1997, and in 1999, HP was the first to deliver a joint SAP support solution map. These accomplishments are a direct result of the tight alignment of our two companies.

But as proud as we are of the capabilities that HP and SAP share, we
are equally proud of those things that define the character of our two
companies: the dedication of our people, our standards and values, and
the reach and depth of our commitment to innovation and global citi-
zenship. Thank you for your commitment to HP and to innovation.
Happy Birthday, Hasso.

IT CANNOT BE DONE

Few words can express the implicit finality of the statement: "It cannot
be done." Typically, this remark asserts that the potential to succeed in a
given endeavor simply does not exist.

In contrast, the statement can also represent a rallying cry of sorts for those charged with achieving a difficult objective. In that sense, it can encourage change in the midst of uncertainty, potential despite limitations, and confidence as opposed to skepticism. In many cases, meeting this challenge is not always easy — yet in equally many cases, meeting this challenge is a necessity. Imagine the world as we know it if Christopher Columbus never left the security of the Spanish coastline or if Sir Edmund Hillary remained at the base of Mount Everest. Risks are inherent in any venture; the key is to weigh the odds and use your instincts and abilities to tip the scale.

When we first announced plans to merge HP and Compaq, our words were met with a resounding chorus of skeptics who expressed doubt in our abilities to successfully execute. On the one hand, there was cause for apprehension — after all, a merger of the size of HP and Compaq combined had never been achieved, much less attempted, in the history of the industry.

On the other hand, for those of us within both companies who saw the wisdom and logic behind the merger, the very prospect of failure and surrendering to the echoes of "It cannot be done" became a proverbial call to arms for achieving the impossible. We knew it would not be easy and there would be seemingly insurmountable obstacles along the way, but our instincts also told us that it was the right thing to do and the right inflection point to do it. Perhaps more than anything, we knew we had the people, products, services, and partners that in themselves inspired confidence in our decision to accomplish the impossible.

FROM STABILITY TO AGILITY

The inflection point that I am referring to came about as the result of a shift in focus among IT executives from IT stability to speed and agility, thanks in large part to the exponential growth of the Internet. As a result, executives have increasingly found that for an enterprise to effectively compete in this new marketplace and respond to ever-changing business demands, the IT infrastructure must be fluid enough to quickly adapt to change and deploy systems in real time.

My good friend Bob Napier, HP's former CIO who passed away in October 2003, made perhaps one of the most compelling cases for why the real-time enterprise is vital when it comes to recognizing and adapting to change. He said, "IT is a pervasive and integral part of how every major corporation runs its business, and every business decision generates an IT event."

> " [F]or an enterprise to effectively compete in this new marketplace . . ., the IT infrastructure must be fluid enough to quickly adapt to change and deploy systems in real time. "

Today's businesses face unrelenting pressure to do more with less in an environment of constant change. As a result, businesses are demanding more from IT, and CIOs are facing new challenges. They are charged with balancing traditional IT requirements of managing costs, mitigating risks, and increasing the quality of service with the new dimension of increasing business agility — of being able to rapidly anticipate business opportunities and respond quickly to change. The scope of this change can also cover a wide swath, from evolving customer needs, economic turbulence, or mergers and acquisitions to technological innovation, supply chain interruptions, or aggressive competition.

The ability to manage change is important because as it impacts a company's IT systems, the change must be addressed as a challenge that is both predictable and controllable. The changes that are triggered in turn have to be predictable and controllable as well.

CASE IN POINT: THE HP-COMPAQ MERGER

To illustrate the amount of change a company can anticipate in today's operating environment, consider HP's own IT organization. On average, it addresses more than 500,000 business-driven IT events in a given week. These events are not the type of changes that result from extraordinary business events like a merger — they are everyday business decisions, such as changes in pricing, changes in the supply chain, changes in capital markets, or the addition of a new employee. IT events don't happen in a vacuum or in discrete silos; they trigger a series of changes across the entire IT infrastructure.

In that sense, technology has to support an infrastructure that requires constant tuning and updating to reflect real-time results. It also has to be structured to give an enterprise the ability not only to control the impact of change but also to use it as a competitive advantage.

The challenge that many enterprises experience is an inability to respond rapidly enough to benefit from change. In these cases, they have deployed proprietary, customized technologies to solve individual business problems, resulting in nonintegrated, complex, and expensive vertical IT silos that are slow to adapt to changes in business priorities. In a world where business and IT are inextricably linked — where every business decision triggers a ripple of IT events — these vertically integrated business processes and applications aren't flexible enough to adapt.

At a fundamental level, a real-time enterprise is one that enables a company's infrastructure to flex with the business whenever the business demands it. It is a platform for the efficient and effective operation of the business based on the real-time delivery of data, business applications, and processes.

HP's overall ability as a real-time enterprise is perhaps best demonstrated by the results we achieved in the merger with Compaq. By applying our own experience, people, products, services, and world-class partners like SAP, we were able to successfully execute the largest merger in the history of the IT industry, 1½ years ahead of schedule, saving $1 billion above the $2.5 billion that we promised to deliver. While these results reflect efforts that are relatively recent, the course leading HP to where it is today has been several years in the making.

> " *The challenge that many enterprises experience is an inability to respond rapidly enough to benefit from change.* "

As far back as 1999, it was becoming apparent that enterprise customers could no longer afford to simply tear out existing equipment and start over. Rather, they were becoming increasingly interested in how their entire IT infrastructure could support and enable change in real time — both inside and outside their organizations. The results find today's enterprise customers looking for fewer yet more capable technology partners who can enable them to compete and win in the changing marketplace. They want partners who can help them apply current data to minimize obstacles in their business-critical processes and help maximize the return on their investments in information technology. Ultimately, they want partners who can help them establish a real-time enterprise.

At the time I first began working at HP back in 1999, I felt confident that the company had the potential to deliver on these offerings to our enterprise customers. However, I also knew that some significant changes had to occur for us to realize that potential because the company had been losing ground.

This conclusion prompted an evaluation of every part of the business over the next 2 years, resulting in a cost reduction of more than $2 billion and the consolidation of 83 product lines into 16. We addressed the many process redundancies that had become entrenched across the company and refocused ourselves on invention, innovation, and customers. However, despite these efforts, it was not enough to achieve our true strategic intent to become the leading technology company in the world. At that point, the conclusion was reached that for HP to regain the leadership position it once held throughout the industry, it would require a radical step: to merge with our rival, Compaq Computer Corporation.

At the time, while the possibilities of the merger were certainly appealing and represented a one-of-a-kind opportunity, it was also apparent that it would be an enormous undertaking. To effectively leverage the vast scope and scale of the combined company, we would have to plan the merger in great detail. We also knew that success would hinge on integrating the best people, processes, ideas, and work, and, above all, the best technology from both companies — to make HP a real-time enterprise to be reckoned with throughout the industry on day one.

As is the case with any collaborative endeavor on a large scale, integrating people was one of the most vital tasks for ensuring the merger's success, and this in itself was no small feat. To put it in some perspective, the new combined company had more than 160,000 employees in 167 countries, with 232,632 user accounts and 229,000 mailboxes. On such a scale, it was obvious that the critical infrastructures had to be completely integrated to enable employees to communicate and collaborate on day one, making HP's IT infrastructure the glue that bonded people and processes.

The other people that we focused on throughout the integration process were our customers and partners. And on day one, we not only were able to announce comprehensive roadmaps and transition plans, but we also named the account team leaders for many of our top customers, the managers for our key partner relationships, and more than 800 senior managers.

One of the primary internal tools we used during the integration — and still use today — was an intranet portal. This vital tool enabled every employee of both companies to conduct day-to-day business. It was a 100 percent paperless self-service vehicle for standard global processes that centralized our policy and program information from business groups and goal functions, based on industry-standard software components. It also included the entire employee directory so anyone could reach anyone else on day one, which made people feel as though they were part of a single company immediately. Today, we regard the HP portal as one of the best proof points of our ability to synchronize an IT infrastructure with the needs of the business.

As for email and directory services, we created a new *hp.com* address for all employees involved in the merger, enabled full NT domain trusts between HP and Compaq, and cross-populated and synchronized directories.

THE ADAPTIVE ENTERPRISE

Today, we have applied the experiences we gained from the merger, combining them with our people, products, services, and partners, to provide a powerful strategy to help companies adapt to changing demands and evolve into real-time enterprises. We call this strategy the Adaptive Enterprise, and it provides exactly the kind of benefit its name suggests: to help enterprise customers synchronize business and IT to capitalize on — and adapt — to change.

A ready-made Adaptive Enterprise cannot be purchased as a single entity; rather, it is built based upon the unique requirements of a company's business over time. Instead of a vertical stack approach that assigns IT to individual applications, an Adaptive Enterprise is built horizontally, based on modular and well-managed systems that can support the entire business and flex as business needs change.

When it comes to addressing change, what makes the Adaptive Enterprise unique is that it is not only able to survive change, but also in fact, thrives in the face of change by driving business strategy and processes into the underlying applications and infrastructure to fuel business success.

> " Ultimately, the Adaptive Enterprise is designed to help customers predict and control the impact of change and to use it as a competitive advantage . . . "

Ultimately, the Adaptive Enterprise is designed to help customers predict and control the impact of change and to use it as a competitive advantage by leveraging many of the concepts that HP and our customers have used to manage change over the past several years.

- It's how we integrated the largest technology merger in history and how we are continuing to become a more agile company that is creating new business value from our IT investments.
- It's how GM can bring new vehicles to market in less than 24 months today versus 42 in the past.
- It's how Amazon.com is able to integrate a growing number of global merchants, ensure that systems can adapt to heavy loads, and simultaneously cut costs and lower prices.
- It's how Alcatel is succeeding in its IT consolidation efforts throughout its North American operations by eliminating regional data centers and shifting workloads to its Canadian data center, where HP 9000 servers will support 6,700 users of SAP® R/3® and other enterprise applications.
- It's how the New York Stock Exchange uses management software to respond to real-time business events, moving capacity on the fly when trade volumes skyrocket.

MEASURES OF BUSINESS AGILITY

For a business to become more adaptive, it's important to first benchmark its current capability for addressing change across three core measures of business agility:

- **Time** — How long does it take to make a change in the enterprise? If there is a change in price or the addition of a new supplier, how long before it ripples throughout the organization? (Example: It used to take HP 5 to 8 weeks to add a partner to our supply chain; we can now do it in less than 2 hours.)
- **Range** — How broadly across the enterprise can the change be implemented? Can the change in price or supplier be cascaded throughout the company? Can it be achieved across a hundred countries for all products, or one country for one product?
- **Ease** — How much effort is required to make the change in the enterprise? How many people and how much money does it take?

Once the strengths and weaknesses in addressing change have been assessed, projects can be prioritized based on business value and the unique needs of the given environment.

DESIGNING AN ADAPTIVE ENTERPRISE

HP has outlined four specific steps for designing an Adaptive Enterprise that call upon the lessons learned from best practices that have been developed with thousands of customers. These steps can be used consistently across business processes, applications, and infrastructure.

- **Simplify** — Remove complexity from the business and systems wherever possible by reducing the number of business processes, applications, and interfaces to help automate change. This leads to a more adaptive environment by reducing the number of elements the business has to deal with in the midst of change.
- **Standardize** — Drive standardization across enterprise architecture, technologies, and processes using standards-based components and best practices. This will eliminate silos, reduce planning and execution time, lower costs, and facilitate collaboration with partners, suppliers, and customers.
- **Modularize** — Convert monolithic structures such as applications into modular, reusable components and virtualize IT resources by sharing and pooling to dynamically balance IT supply and business demand.
- **Integrate** — Integrate business processes, applications, and infrastructure components to manage data and processes across the enterprise and beyond. This increases flexibility and makes it easier for change to ripple through the entire enterprise value chain.

We apply these steps at every stage of a customer's journey to becoming an Adaptive Enterprise, with each customer starting at a stage that best reflects particular corporate goals and accomplishments.

HP enables the Adaptive Enterprise with a broad portfolio of services, products, and solutions that can be integrated with a customer's existing systems and partner solutions. Companies can make choices at every level of the stack — from applications to middleware, from database vendors to messaging, from operating systems to processors. We then apply these capabilities to a customer's existing systems and partner solutions to provide a framework for thinking about an environment horizontally, and building more flexible connections among business processes, applications, and underlying IT infrastructure. We call this framework the Darwin Reference Architecture — and with good reason.

Over the past several years, I have frequently referenced a poignant remark by Charles Darwin — a man revered for his thoughts on change and adaptability — who said, "It is not the strongest of the species that survives, nor the most intelligent, but those most responsive to change." At HP today, we've taken the essence of Darwin's observations on change with respect to a species and applied it to the enterprise in the form of the Darwin Reference Architecture. For example, connecting inventory and pricing applications creates a dynamic system for increasing profits. Integrating information about the availability of products in the supply chain with customer-facing sales channels increases customer satisfaction and profits.

> " It is not the strongest of the species that survives, nor the most intelligent, but those most responsive to change. "

When applying the Darwin Reference Architecture, HP can help customers assess their current business agility across time, range, and ease. We then help architect and integrate heterogeneous technologies; manage and control business processes, applications, and IT environments; and extend and link resources across suppliers, partners, and customers.

Regardless of the starting point, HP's approach to building an Adaptive Enterprise enables a business to more quickly capitalize on change — improving agility and efficiency while maintaining a predictable, secure, and stable environment. And by simplifying, standardizing, modularizing, and integrating an IT environment at every level, we create a foundation that is more cost-effective, easier to manage, and ultimately more adaptable.

The American inventor and electrical engineer Charles Kettering once said, "The world hates change, yet it is the only thing that has brought progress." I think his words ring true — particularly when it comes to change and its effect on business. I say that because, without question, the ability for an enterprise to recognize change and adapt to it in real time represents a daunting challenge for most businesses in today's ever-changing operating environment. Fueling the fire of this challenge are budget constraints and limited capital investments that slam the door on the conventional approach to IT problem-solving — that of throwing money at it in the hopes of finding a solution.

Based on these challenges and others that make up the new rules for the real-time road in business today, one could almost succumb to the belief that "It cannot be done" — that the potential to succeed in creating a real-time enterprise simply does not exist. However, the very nature of business demands an element of risk, and, as a result, I think most businesses that succeed today in becoming real-time enterprises are of the type that view the statement "It cannot be done" as a rallying cry to achieving success.

They are the businesses that embrace change in the midst of uncertainty; they are the businesses that demonstrate potential and overcome their limitations; and they are the businesses that exude a level of confidence that silences the skeptics.

8

Preparing for the Real-Time Global Marketplace

Joe W. Forehand is the chairman and CEO of Accenture, a global management consulting, technology services, and outsourcing company with more than 83,000 people in 48 countries. As CEO, Forehand has led Accenture through one of the most groundbreaking periods of its history – including a redefinition of the company's strategy, an initial public offering, and a global rebranding campaign. In his 30 years with the company, he has led 11 of Accenture's 18 industry groups. Known for his collaborative, inclusive management style, Consulting Magazine named Forehand the most influential consultant for 2001 and credited him with leading Accenture "to the outer edges of consulting's frontier." Forehand is a member of the Business Roundtable and the G100. He is a frequent speaker and has been featured at several international business and technology conferences, including the World Economic Forum. Raised in Alabama, Forehand graduated from Auburn University in 1971 with a degree in industrial engineering. He earned his master of science degree in industrial administration from the Krannert School of Management at Purdue University in 1972.

Joe W. Forehand

S AP and its founders were true visionaries of real–time processing. Now, more than 30 years later, SAP has become the world's largest interenterprise software company, known for providing collaborative business solutions for all types of industries in every major market around the world.

The concept of the real-time enterprise has matured into a vision that is being pursued by the world's largest companies. And to help them, Accenture and SAP have teamed together for many years to develop cross-industry and industry-specific enterprise solutions that help organizations dramatically improve their business operations and drive rapid return on investment.

In honor of Hasso Plattner, it is my pleasure, on behalf of Accenture, to share our thoughts on the importance of real-time technology and how it has changed — and will continue to change — the way an enterprise generates value for its stakeholders.

A REAL-TIME BUSINESS ENVIRONMENT

Beginning with today's business environment, it is no secret that real-time information is in high demand. Not only is access to the right information at the right time essential to running an efficient and informed enterprise, but it is also a competitive differentiator.

As we move from global economic recession to recovery in the developed world, several factors such as management talent, access to information, new organizational models, innovation, and precision execution will further separate the leaders from the laggards. This stands in stark contrast to the safe and stable environment of the 1990s, when most players in an industry were lifted by good tides or were acquired. And it contrasts with the past few years, when companies were rewarded for cost management efforts and the strength of their balance sheets.

We are moving into a watershed era for global business. We can expect a dramatically altered business environment defined by fluid market and industry boundaries, shifting regional risk and opportunity, rapidly changing formulas for economic value, and disparate economic shocks. The combination of these factors requires companies to adapt their strategies and operations if they want to thrive and perform at their very best.

In this environment, each area of the business must be completely connected on the inside and outside in real time. More specifically, business leaders will need to grow revenue and market share by managing more things more precisely with a narrower margin for error than ever before: each customer, each product, each price, each unit cost, hour-by-hour supply chains, and the like. This "real-time" business environment will require quicker management teams with faster information flows than is often the case today.

The organizations that understand the environmental shifts that have shaped the landscape we see now and are recalibrating their strategies to meet the challenges that lie ahead will be winners, outperforming their competitors and the marketplace. Detailed, precise, real-time knowledge will drive that understanding.

> " *The organizations that understand the environmental shifts that have shaped the landscape we see now and are recalibrating their strategies to meet the challenges that lie ahead will be winners . . .* "

THE REAL-TIME ENTERPRISE OF THE FUTURE

Presuming that a real-time business environment is upon us, what effect will it have on corporate structure, strategy, and operations? What will define the winners in a given industry?

Essentially, the real-time enterprise of the future will operate as a high-performing business, consistently outperforming its industry peers. While this will vary somewhat by industry, all high-performance businesses share certain features, most notably a hierarchy of capabilities that reflect foresight rather than chance:

- First, high-performing organizations have the insight and ability to determine most important industry drivers of present and future value. High performers have an uncanny ability to sense and respond to major environmental shifts.
- Second, high-performance businesses are masters of action, turning real-time knowledge and information into action. They create adaptable and executable strategies that can weather uncertain environments. They have

leadership teams who adapt to rapid change and flexible organizations that learn quickly.

- Third, high-performance businesses understand which of their core competencies are critical to driving value. They master these core competencies and compete on them, yet they also know when and how to achieve extended mastery by partnering in areas outside their core. They are not obsessed with a "made here" mentality. They intelligently outsource or seek alliances and partnership opportunities. Industry by industry, companies and governments are looking at outsourcing as a strategic change weapon — one that provides performance and flexibility.
- Fourth, high-performance businesses are obsessive about winning the battle for the customer. They know that connecting with customers unlocks real business value. They use customer insight to create highly satisfied, lifetime customers who in turn drive significant economic benefits.
- Fifth, every high-performing business has something unique — a cultural bias toward winning, a genetic code that is difficult to replicate. Think of it as a predisposition to perform at the highest levels.
- Finally, high-performance businesses are extremely effective at managing paradoxes. They know how to balance present and future agendas and manage seemingly paradoxical values such as flexible workforces and employee loyalty, globally driven change imperatives and local empowerment, and a willingness to enter new markets and highly disciplined risk management.

High-performance businesses understand that, depending on the circumstances, they must have the ability to be both tortoises and hares. And they harness their technology investments with a focus on long-term success, not just short-term profit maximization. In fact, the real-time business has a "today" focus on cost-effective, secure delivery of IT, as well as a "tomorrow" focus on using technology innovation to enable future success.

> " High-performance businesses understand that, depending on the circumstances, they must have the ability to be both tortoises and hares. "

GETTING VALUE FROM IT SOLUTIONS

But what's the real catalyst for the future of the real-time enterprise? We believe the answer lies in getting value from IT solutions, yet that is not a given. Buyers today are seeking outcomes tied to business results that help to drive real economic value. IT partners are on the hook for outcomes.

Without question, the information technology industry is at a critical stage in its evolution. Thirty years ago it was largely craft- and skill-driven. Everything was customized for each client. Today it has reached a level of maturity that is ushering in an era of both standardization and commoditization. These forces have led to a huge increase in the use of global resources, common tools, and replicable methodologies that have lowered costs significantly.

The good news is that academic and business researchers have found strong positive relationships between IT investments and operating efficiency, business performance, competitive advantage, and shareholder value growth.

But IT value is not created equally. There are clear winners and losers because companies vary greatly in their ability to derive business value from IT investments. In an age where IT matters more than ever, knowing how to capture the most value can separate the winners from the losers.

In fact, the "I" in IT remains a challenge. Using information to run a business is still an evolving management science. Executives in both the private and public sectors often admit to not having the right information to make the right decisions at the right time. They run their organizations from gut feel and are frustrated by the lack of timely information — especially as more and more processes directly link companies with suppliers and customers outside the enterprise's walls. These executives are seeking the same efficient and "frictionless" decision-making capability that many manufacturers achieved with just-in-time manufacturing.

Although many companies have installed a core set of enterprise applications, they have not yet implemented the necessary change management or done the required business optimization to capture the value inherent in their enterprise solutions.

Most know they are at the stage where their core investment can be leveraged to drive significant value both inside and outside their enterprise. They *integrate* their enterprise solutions through the entire organization to provide a common platform for maximum efficiency. They *optimize* their business processes so they flow and fit with their enterprise systems and ensure that information is provided to critical workforces. And they *extend* the functionality of their core systems to take advantage of further enterprise solutions capabilities that provide more functionality.

The real value comes from integrating business processes and information across functional areas to enable real-time decision making, realizing the vision of the real-time enterprise.

THE TECHNOLOGY TRANSFORMATION AHEAD

The notion of the real-time enterprise holds tremendous power. With technology infrastructure more robust than ever, we are headed toward another significant wave of technology change and innovation. Web services, RFID (radio frequency identification), mobility, and insight technologies are converging to create the real-time enterprise supported by real-time decision making.

> " We call this vision of the future Reality Online; it is defined by technologies that are *always on, always aware,* **and** *always active.* "

In this next era, technology will be defined more broadly, going beyond transaction processing to embed technology in everything we do and transform modern life. This includes adding information and maintenance services to your car, adding status services into your supply chain, or adding intelligent communications to heart implant devices so that your doctor can monitor your heart as you go about your daily life.

We call this vision of the future Reality Online; it is defined by technologies that are *always on, always aware,* and *always active.*

- An **"always on"** business is connected to every customer and every product or service all the time. It knows where its products are, how they are performing, how they are being used, and how they are being maintained. It adds a new dimension to products and services that massively increases customer intimacy and creates significant top-line growth opportunities. For example, think about a low-cost, low-risk wireless solution that empowers field agents with real-time information that helps them provide higher and more consistent levels of customer service and improves staff utilization.

- An **"always aware"** business truly harnesses the massive information it is collecting to drive business intelligence and insight faster than the competition. But the need for real-time data brings challenges, including efficiently managing what can often be an overwhelming stream of information, and getting data quickly enough to make the right decisions. In response, we have created a business intelligence prototype that allows users to aggregate, view, and manipulate real-time data from multiple sources — including enterprise systems and trusted third parties — via the Internet.

- An **"always active"** business knows what is happening and acts on that information to correct errors, improve performance, and satisfy customers. Always active companies exploit their superior business insight ahead of demand — when it's possible to get the best price from a supplier or to deliver a unique innovation to the customer. Think about an application that enables product marketers to issue instant surveys via a mobile device to grocery shoppers in return for a discount at the checkout. Or consider a utility company that sets up an intelligent agent that contacts homeowners while they are away to determine whether they wish to turn down the heat to save energy.

In summary, in the world of Reality Online, every product provides a platform through which services may be delivered. This new world has its roots in the visions of Hasso Plattner and all of SAP's founders. They laid the foundation for a new generation of business applications, and their early innovations have evolved to the real-time enterprise of today. The future holds great promise as we prepare for the next step, what SAP calls the enterprise nervous system.

In closing, I want to personally congratulate Hasso Plattner on the successful company he has built with SAP and on his contribution to the technology industry. I also send my very best wishes for his 60th birthday. Speaking on behalf of Accenture, we look forward to continuing our long-standing relationship with SAP, further enhancing the value we can jointly deliver to our clients.

A real-time global marketplace will emerge with clear winners and losers. The winners will embrace technologies that will help them increase revenue; stay connected to every customer, product, and service; and harness the right information at the right time, enabling them to make more accurate business decisions. Competitive advantage will be largely driven by technology innovation. Those who make appropriate investments with a focus on long-term success will outperform their competitors and become the real-time enterprises of the future.

9

Seamless Computing

Bill Gates is chairman and chief software architect of Microsoft, the software giant he co-founded with Paul Allen in 1975. Gates stepped aside as CEO in 2000 to work more directly with product groups and focus on the company's long-term technical strategy.

Bill Gates

How have things evolved in real-time business since the publication of *Business @ the Speed of Thought*? What lessons have been learned?

In the past 3 years, we've seen major advances in software and hardware that have enabled many companies to start building what I called a "digital nervous system." Breakthroughs such as the Tablet PC, advanced productivity software like Office 2003, and industry-wide support around XML and web services have made it possible for companies of all sizes to connect the people, processes, information, and relationships that create real business value. But we still haven't realized computing's full potential. Our industry must work to seamlessly connect all these technologies and make them flexible and intuitive enough to match the way the real world works.

What effect will the real-time enterprise have on corporate structure, strategy, and operations? Who will win and who will lose as the real-time enterprise emerges?

Software will be more important than ever. In some ways, every company will become a "software company," since powerful software is the key to unlocking the value of technology, gaining a strategic advantage, and sustaining growth. Companies that use advanced software to enhance and extend their unique business processes, forge deeper connections with customers, and innovate to meet their customers' changing needs will have a much greater chance of success in the coming years.

What is the role of trustworthy computing in the real-time enterprise?

As computers move to the center of the way we all do business, expectations around security are much higher. At Microsoft, this means a fundamental transformation in how we write software. The visibility of our products and their impact on people's daily lives demand that we make trustworthy computing our number-one priority. We are addressing the issue of security at every level, from the way we write and test our code, to our efforts to help customers become more secure, to a next-generation architectural approach to computer security.

Microsoft has voiced a strong commitment to web services. Are services-based architectures where personal productivity and enterprise applications meet? How will they impact the way business applications are conceived and deployed?

XML and web services have been a focus for Microsoft for many years, and building XML support into all our products is enabling us to create a new generation of connected software. This will fundamentally transform business computing, through software networks that span multiple applications, devices, services, and organizations in a dynamic and distributed way — enabling developers to easily and quickly create software that integrates real-world business processes at every level and seamlessly connects with partner and customer networks.

How should customers improve their productivity and efficiency to get ready for the real-time enterprise?

There are many things that businesses can do today to unlock the value of the technologies they already have, streamline business processes, and achieve productivity breakthroughs. Web services can connect existing systems and islands of information both within a company and with its partners and customers. Advanced productivity software offers information workers the ability to find, visualize, and act on a growing sea of digital information. Powerful creation and collaboration tools can clear the path from insight to action and drive tremendous productivity increases. Companies that make information technology the center of their business today will be in a far better position to benefit from tomorrow's innovations.

10

The Process Revolution and ERP

It would have been impossible to address the real-time enterprise without involving Michael Hammer, who has spent his life studying how processes can enable corporations to reach new levels of success. One of the most sought-after business speakers and President of Hammer and Company, Hammer has been named by Business Week as one of the four preeminent management thinkers of the 1990s, and Time magazine included him in its first list of America's 25 most influential individuals. He is the author of many highly regarded books including Reengineering the Corporation, Beyond Reengineering, and The Agenda: What Every Business Must Do to Dominate the Decade. Since he began his research, information technology has advanced to levels previously unimaginable, the world economy has gone from multinational to global — and Hammer's thinking has evolved into a comprehensive vision of the real-time enterprise at work.

Michael Hammer

THE CUSTOMER ECONOMY

Since the philosopher and economist Adam Smith penned *The Wealth of Nations* in 1776, the industrial revolution has been built on two principles: the specialization of labor and hierarchical controls. We take a process and break it down into atomistic activities, as simple, narrow, and self-contained as possible. We then assign these tasks to people who perform them over and over — and we install levels of supervision to ensure that these people are performing their tasks efficiently. This was the structure of industry and business in the mid-eighteenth century, and it was still the structure in the late twentieth century. As Henry Ford himself once said, "Nothing is particularly hard if you divide it into small jobs."

Ford may have been right when he said it, but in today's world he's wrong. The historical practice of creating isolated pieces of work in functional departments and organizations is now obsolete. It does not meet the needs of modern enterprises.

The trouble with the division of labor is that it creates enormous amounts of *non-value-adding work*. Non-value-adding work is work that

> " The historical practice of creating isolated pieces of work in functional departments and organizations is now obsolete. It does not meet the needs of modern enterprises. "

an enterprise performs but that is of no direct value to the customer. When work moves from one person to another, someone has to check it, review it, assign it, prioritize it, schedule it, and see that it gets done. All of this is non-value-adding work since the customer is not interested in paying for any of it. And all of this adds time and cost and offers opportunity for error, while creating complexity and inhibiting flexibility. Non-value-adding work is the bane of contemporary organizations.

Very few people, including economists, have any sense of this problem, even though it is the single most important issue facing corporations today. Why is it so important? Because the defining characteristic of the modern age is the power of the customer.

Today the developed world faces a situation where supply consistently exceeds demand — overcapacity in virtually every global industry — an unprecedented phenomenon. This overcapacity is a consequence of globalization, dramatic increases in productivity, and shortened product lifecycles. Technology has crushed barriers to entry in new businesses, and Wall Street has increased its demand for unrelenting growth. The commoditization of products and services and the widespread availability of product information have enabled customer choice to explode in all directions. Now the power in business relationships has shifted from the seller to the buyer. What the customer demands is speed, low cost, and flexibility — yet the classic business structure delivers none of these because of non-value-adding work.

It might seem natural that organizations operating in a customer-driven economy would orient themselves around customers' needs, yet it's rarely so. Most corporations are focused internally, not on customers. They are organized to make life easier for themselves, not for their customers. Different departments perform piecemeal activities, different units sell disparate products and services, and none work in concert to achieve common customer-focused goals. In fact, many large companies have evolved into a collection of independent divisions that are, at best, ignorant of the goals and achievements of others around them and, at worst, actively in conflict.

Modern corporations bulge with checkers, expediters, and supervisors — all making the organizations sluggish and clumsy, while doing nothing of importance for the customer. They suffer from rigid hierarchies, internal conflicts, and pointless bureaucracy. Delays, misunderstandings, and rework are the hallmarks of the traditional corporation.

Perhaps the hoariest cliché in business is the story of the drill manufacturer who addresses his employees and announces that none of their customers want to buy drills. In fact, they never have. "They don't want drills," he says. "They want holes."

Buying the drill is part of the cost of getting the hole. Studying drill specs, talking to a sales rep; placing an order; receiving, checking, and inventorying goods; receiving an invoice; and cutting a check are all part of the cost of getting the hole as well.

In a typical company, each manager drives his or her department to strive toward goals not directly related to the customer's desires — the sales manager strives to generate new orders, the warehouse manager wants to minimize inventory, and the shipping manager attempts to minimize costs. Each employee focuses solely on a very small piece of organizational value — pricing the product, taking the order, checking the customer's credit, allocating inventory, picking and packing the goods, planning the shipment, or making the delivery.

Customers, however, care about none of this. Customers care only about holes. And in most companies, making sure customers get what they want is the responsibility of nobody.

THE POWER OF PROCESS

Some companies have learned to thrive in a customer-driven environment by creating new ways of working. They have created new business models that offer the customer higher quality, lower costs, and more options. They are quick, flexible, and agile — not only capable of doing things fast, responding to special requests and circumstances, but also capable of changing quickly, of recognizing and seizing new opportunities. They are process-focused and real-time organizations.

Instead of putting their employees in functional silos with little understanding of the customer or the context in which they work, process organizations focus on end-to-end processes — performing work that is of value to their customers, work that takes into account the larger context, work that is directed toward achieving results rather than performed as an end in itself. A *process* can be defined as an organized group of related activities that together create value to customers — a coherent structure that defines which tasks are to be performed, in what order, in what location, when, and by whom.

> " Instead of putting their employees in functional silos with little understanding of the customer or the context in which they work, process organizations focus on end-to-end processes . . . "

A process, such as filling an order, consists of many activities — taking the order, checking the customer's credit, allocating inventory, picking and packing the goods, planning the shipment, and making the delivery. One of the recurring themes of processes in a process organization is that a whole series of activities previously distributed across many people and departments is now performed by a single person. For example, a major oil company recently redesigned how it fills orders for lubricants. Before, an order for lubricants would hopscotch back and forth among seven different departments. Now, one person handles it from beginning to end.

By performing work in a manner that follows a disciplined and repeatable design, process organizations are able to align everyone in the organization around common goals, eliminate unproductive activities, build teamwork, flatten hierarchies, and, in general, reduce non-value-adding work to a minimum. Customers, processes, and results are bound together in an iron triangle. You can't be serious about one without focusing on the other two.

Also, a direct connection exists between processes and real time. A process organization eliminates the hand-offs and non-value-adding activities that prevent it from responding in real time to customer needs and changing circumstances.

Not every organization is able to rise to this challenge and opportunity. Organizing around processes means changing everything about the organization, from jobs and roles to relationships and metrics. Yet vast amounts of inertia weigh down large organizations, and many find making these changes beyond their capacity. Already we are seeing a winnowing of organizations that are too slow or unwilling to make this shift.

However, those that do make the shift feast on the markets of those that don't.

PROCESS WORK

A process-oriented, customer-focused organization that operates in real time is not nirvana. It has fantastic benefits in terms of reducing overhead, improving customer satisfaction, and increasing speed. For employees, it leads to more fulfilling work lives and higher morale — but at a price.

Focusing on process shifts power from managers to those on the front line. Many contemporary organizations are accustomed to treating employees as organic machines, the hands and fingers of the managers. Operating in a process mode requires that the duties of traditional management — decision-making, assigning, and scheduling — be integrated into the jobs of front-line workers. And that means that every person in the organization needs to perform a broad range of tasks. You must make use of your employees' brains. They have to understand what customers want, and they have to understand the larger process. Most important, they have to know enough about the business to make choices.

Because focusing on process means that vital decisions could be made by employees without high-school educations, becoming a real-time enterprise involves a huge increase in the amount of training and education required. Employees have to be trained and provided with the tools and data necessary to perform their jobs at a high level. They also need to be educated so they have the insight, understanding, and values to make decisions on their own.

Process work is by its nature team work. Since it is not always possible to compress an entire process into a single job, many processes will be performed by groups of people. These groups must work as teams. Everyone performing a part of a process needs to see how his or her work fits with, and impacts, the work of everyone else. Working within a larger context and toward the achievement of common goals is an effective definition of what it means to work in a team. Team members may possess different skills, but all share an understanding of each other's roles and all work together toward a common objective.

Working in a process enterprise entails a lot of responsibility and accountability. Expectations are high, and the work is not nine to five. All the positions in a process-oriented organization are rewarding but demanding. The reality is that not all employees are ready for this kind of job.

PROCESS-BASED MANAGEMENT

Just as front-line jobs are redefined in a process environment, so are the jobs of managers. Managers no longer need supervise workers. Process workers have the knowledge and authority to get work done without managers looking over their shoulders and without needing results-oriented measures to focus them on achieving outcomes. Conventional managerial roles must be replaced by ones that support rather than control the front lines. Process owners have the job of designing, measuring, and improving processes on an end-to-end basis. This is a vital role in an organization that recognizes that competitive success comes by creating extraordinary customer value and that customer value is created by world-class business processes. However, it is a role unfamiliar to most managers, revolving as it does around innovative work design, meticulous measurement, performance analysis, and focused interventions.

The other primary managerial role is that of a coach. Process workers operating in teams don't need heavy-handed supervisors, but they do need someone to go to for development, mentoring, and assistance. That is the role of the coach. As one coach put it to me, "In the old days, I spent all my time telling my people what to do. Now the process teams allocate and monitor their own work, which frees me up to get my people the tools and training that they need." *Coach* is a widely used, but also widely misused, term. A process environment forces conventional managers into real coaching roles.

Not only is learning these new roles a drastic change for most managers, but so is adopting the style that is demanded of whoever fills these roles. No longer can managers look after their narrow areas of responsibility and wash their hands of everything else. Customers are not content if one part of the enterprise performs while others do not; they demand that the entire enterprise operate as a seamless whole. To that end, managers must learn the unnatural behaviors of cooperation and collaboration. Process

> " *In a traditional organization, managers are the stars, and managers have the power. In a process environment, employees are center stage, and managers are in the wings.* "

owners and coaches, and even divisional heads, must work together — as a team — for the common good.

Above all, managers in a process enterprise must adjust to a new self-image and a reduced sense of their own importance. In a traditional organization, managers are the stars, and managers have the power. In a process environment, employees are center stage, and managers are in the wings. They must lose their egos, moving from babysitter and overseer to facilitator and coach. Where are the coaches on a sports team? They are on the sidelines, not in the middle of the field.

THE ROLE OF LEADERSHIP

The transition to a process orientation may be the most important and the most difficult change that organizations have ever undertaken. This degree of change is scary, and if it weren't for the transformation of the global economy, no one would want to attempt it. However, the economy has been transformed and radical changes *are* necessary. This is a new epoch, like the industrial revolution of 250 years ago.

Even companies that recognize that change is necessary sometimes fail in their attempts to do so. Some companies stumble by moving too slowly. Others fail by not dealing forcefully with inertia and resistance. Still others fail by not demanding early results.

The technical problems are easy. The hardest problems are organizational — the cultural and the human problems — and the most vital agent for change is a dynamic leader. A leader must have passion, intensity, and a vision that inspires others to leave the past behind and embrace the future. Real leaders help people overcome their fear.

Persistence, commitment, and a willingness to go wherever the changes take the organization are prime characteristics that a leader needs to encourage participation inside and outside the company. A leader must also deal with Wall Street and investors who are focused on the company's short-term financial picture rather than its long-term strategy. The cult of quarterly earnings and short-term results can cripple a company's ability to engage in the kind of strategic change needed to become a real-time enterprise.

Leading a process enterprise is made even more demanding because many processes extend beyond the walls of the organization, and a real-time leader must follow them — down the supply chain to the raw materials suppliers and up the distribution chain to the customer.

> **"The cult of quarterly earnings and short-term results can cripple a company's ability to engage in the kind of strategic change needed to become a real-time enterprise."**

For example, a process might begin in a retail outlet, go back to a distributor, then to the manufacturer, then to the raw materials supplier. The consumer buying a product triggers the raw materials supplier to ship to the manufacturer, who then adds the information to its production cycle, which causes the distributor to adjust the transportation schedule from the manufacturer to the retail outlet. The leader of a real-time enterprise must embody the organization to those outside the corporation across the process.

Leading an organization engaged in a cross-enterprise process entails shifting corporate culture from an "us against them" mentality to one that says, "We win together." Does this mean you will be sharing information with the customers and suppliers? Absolutely. Does this reduce your bargaining power with them? Absolutely. But if you don't try to win at the expense of your customers and suppliers, if you try to work together with them and they try to work with you, the potential for success is great.

Buying and installing software is easy. Organizing around process is difficult.

REAL-TIME TECHNOLOGY

SAP software was one of the major forces behind the growth of the process phenomenon. Initially, though, the company itself wasn't particularly aware of it.

Most technologies are poorly understood in their early days. When a new technology comes along, we tend to see it only as a tool to solve old problems. Only later do we discover broader uses. History gives us many examples: the phonograph, the radio, the telephone, and the Internet are all inventions that vastly exceeded their inventor's initial intent. Edison thought the phonograph would be useful for recording the deathbed wishes of dying gentlemen. Marconi was trying to replace the telegraph, not create radio as a broadcast medium. When Hasso Plattner and his colleagues developed SAP software, it is not certain that they fully grasped its transformative effect.

In a traditional organization with traditional information systems, people doing functionally focused jobs have access only to the limited transactional information that comes from their departments' narrow information system. Older software reinforced the traditional functional business model — accounting, marketing, and production scheduling. Integrated Enterprise Resource Planning (ERP) software was something different. It performed the same functions, true, but it was actually process software. Employees using integrated systems like SAP have access to information from all departments across the entire process. Suddenly, processes become visible. Front-line employees realize how their work affects the work of others, and they become aware of everyone else working on their process. They also have the wherewithal to do bigger jobs, *and* they have access to the kind of information that even managers didn't have previously. This is hugely empowering.

Besides information transparency, process-oriented business software also created a revolution in metrics. Traditional organizations use metrics that are generally financial and backward-looking. The new ERP software allowed organizations to trace the connection between overall results and what was required of employees. Metrics could be used to examine, analyze, and predict, not just to perform autopsies. Using real performance metrics in a disciplined management process meant that instead of getting alarmed at financial metrics and making random, desperate attempts to improve results, companies were (and are) able to quickly spot and address performance-inhibiting problems.

In the late 1990s, dissatisfaction with ERP software didn't really have anything to do with the software itself. Our research showed that, by and large, it was easy to differentiate those happy with ERP from those who were dissatisfied. Organizations that attempted to implement ERP applications as if they were typical software had either meager or disappointing results. Successfully implementing an integrated ERP system requires building a business model that identifies which performance aspects of your processes contribute to enterprise success, redesigning your processes to improve these aspects, and then using the software to support the new processes. Organizations that didn't manage ERP in process terms had little to show for their efforts, while companies that implemented ERP as part of an effort to transform and improve their business processes enjoyed huge successes.

KNOW THY PROCESS

Michael Hammer points out that his research shows that the key element to successful Enterprise Resource Planning (ERP) implementation is a process-centric approach. That's what Martin Klitten of Chevron says implementing SAP forced him to do: to understand his processes in greater detail than ever before (Chapter 3). Colgate focused on process to reduce order fulfillment times from 2 weeks to 5 days (Chapter 18). Vinod Khosla stresses in Chapter 13 that the key criteria for design should be the ability to evolve a system. Thinking and designing produces a better result than just throwing software at a problem. On the other hand, Hammer notes that the way in which processes are embedded in SAP software provides a powerful agent of change. When these processes are understood, the software becomes a powerful method to transmit them to a wide audience. In Chapter 4, August-Wilhelm Scheer notes that SAP did more to transmit German concepts of business administration to the world through its software than the combined total of that nation's considerable academic research. Geoffrey Moore recommends in Chapter 16 that for stable processes that fall into the category he describes as *context,* companies should adopt the best practices for these processes embedded in software like SAP's.

The importance of SAP was that for the first time companies had software systems that could support a complete end-to-end business process. What people believed was merely a software system was actually something fundamentally different, a powerfully subversive tool for highlighting and transforming business processes. For some companies, it was the most important tool in their efforts to transform and improve their business. Companies that use SAP have visibility across the

> " *The importance of SAP was that for the first time companies had software systems that could support a complete end-to-end business process.* "

whole process. The process, and the software that supports it, is an enormous force for information democracy in an organization. People who were aware of only their own tasks now share data and communicate with people across the entire process. And people are no longer limited by the information to which they have access, but by their ability to use it. Empowering employees to own processes and in so doing to satisfy and nurture customers is the heart of the modern enterprise.

11

From Vision to Reality: The Emergence of the On Demand Era

As IBM's Senior Vice President for Strategy, Bruce Harreld is responsible for the formulation and execution of the company's overall strategy and for its emerging growth initiatives. Prior to joining IBM in 1995, Harreld was an adjunct professor at Northwestern University's Kellogg Graduate School of Business Administration. Harreld holds an MBA from Harvard University and a bachelor of science in Industrial Engineering and Operations Research from Purdue University. He has held executive positions at Boston Chicken, Kraft General Foods, Inc., and The Boston Consulting Group.

Bruce Harreld

Every day more and more businesses are confirming what visionaries like Hasso Plattner knew years ago — the very nature of business is being flipped on its side, as entirely new business designs are enabled through the flexible delivery and management of open, non-proprietary computing products and services. In other words, SAP's "real-time enterprise" — and what IBM calls "on demand business" — is transforming the business landscape.

On demand businesses are rethinking their business designs. In many industries, business leaders are thinking about their businesses as a group of components that need to be optimized, integrated, and sometimes outsourced to create an operating model that yields improved financials and competitive advantage. Leading information technology companies like SAP and IBM are making this easier for organizations, allowing them to look at themselves as a series of logical components, and to prioritize a set of actions based on the level of difficulty and potential payoff.

New options are available that allow organizations to leverage the scale and capability of strategic external partners while focusing valuable internal resources on their core competencies. Consumer products giant Proctor & Gamble decided to outsource its worldwide human resources operations — including payroll, benefits administration, and travel management — enabling the company to focus more intensively on its core business.

> **" The Internet and a host of new technologies built upon open industry standards enable the more flexible business models of the on demand era . . . "**

The Internet and a host of new technologies built upon open industry standards enable the more flexible business models of the on demand era, letting enterprises quickly and cost-effectively integrate a wide variety of applications and business processes end-to-end. Seeing open technologies like Linux as a boon for competitiveness and economic development, hundreds of country, state, and local governments are working to drive its adoption.

More flexible financial and delivery models for IT products and services give enterprises of all shapes and sizes new options for acquiring computing capability. Nearly half the Fortune 500 now use flexible hosting of applications, which provides access to built-in extra server capacity that can be turned on at will. On demand access to the most advanced supercomputing technology is enabling fledgling Hollywood animators to reduce production time for features to 18 months, allowing them to compete aggressively with major studios.

THE COEVOLUTION OF BUSINESS AND TECHNOLOGY

A variety of factors is responsible for this evolutionary shift. A number of economic drivers force companies to develop and adopt new business models, including:

- Volatility unseen since the depression of the 1930s
- The "boom and bust" of IT precipitated by the bursting of the dot-com bubble, which has forced a new sense of reality into IT organizations
- A recovery in which, so far, job creation has been limited by increased productivity enabled by IT investment and sellers have been unable to raise prices because the Internet has dramatically reduced the seller's traditional information advantage
- The increasing rate of commoditization of IT and the increasing difficulty of attaining enduring competitive advantage through IT innovation

At the same time, key technology enablers are creating new opportunities. Today's IT infrastructure enables interenterprise communication with the speed and intimacy previously confined to intraenterprise communication. The effect of this cannot be overestimated. The ease and ubiquity of interenterprise communication dramatically lowers transaction costs between firms. As transaction costs decline, the drive to outsource business processes will increase. This industry deconstruction and reconstruction will likely be *the* major disruptive change in business designs over the next several years.

> **❝ What will separate the winners from the losers will not be the vision so much as the ability to broadly execute against that vision. ❞**

There is a renewed recognition that this is not possible without a tight linkage between business strategy, business processes, and IT. The current focus on business process modeling, business process monitoring, and related areas is evidence of this change.

It is this confluence of economic drivers and enabling technology that leads many to believe that we are at an inflection point in the coevolution of business and IT. However we choose to refer to this future

state, all industry players largely share a vision of the next major stage of
evolution in IT. What will separate the winners from the losers will not
be the vision so much as the ability to broadly execute against that
vision.

THE ON DEMAND VISION

What is the on demand vision? It can be summarized as follows:

- End-to-end truly is end-to-end. Historically, we sought to integrate and to
  optimize *within the scope of a firm*. Going forward, end-to-end refers to the
  entire supply chain and demand chain.
- It involves constant rebalancing of fixed and variable costs. One of the
  ways businesses are doing this is by mapping fixed costs to components of
  their business and by outsourcing those components that do not achieve
  enough leverage on the fixed cost basis. They then pay for the component's capabilities on a more variable basis. Historically, the transaction
  costs of outsourcing consumed most or all of these savings, but this is less
  and less the case.
- Firms are making decisions about what components of their business truly
  differentiate them and in turn are deciding how to prioritize their trans-
  formational efforts, their technology investments, and their outsourcing
  decisions. As firms consider these new process outsourcing arrangements, it
  is becoming clear that this is very much a continuum, allowing a firm to
  decide how much to insource or outsource. While we sometimes think of
  outsourcing as something new, it is as old as the notion of division of
  labor. Today's interest in outsourcing is not something fundamentally new,
  but rather a natural evolution of the nature of the firm accelerated by
  rapidly declining interenterprise transaction costs.
- As a result of business process outsourcing enabled by a robust communications and computing infrastructure, we will see the industry deconstruction and reconstruction described earlier.
- Business strategy will be much more tightly linked to IT. Again, this will
  be a natural part of the evolution and maturation of IT, dating back to
  when the "MIS executive" became a "C level executive."

It is the confluence of these evolutionary forces that, in our view,
defines the new era in the co-evolution of business and IT.

THE EVOLUTION OF THE IT INDUSTRY IN SUPPORT OF ON DEMAND

So far, we have focused on the evolution of the enterprise toward on demand. Let's now turn our attention to the role of IT. To manage complexity, the IT industry focuses on architecture — the specification of interfaces. This often manifests itself in a "stack" — a collection of functions that build on each other. For the better part of two decades, IT has focused on the build-out of a communications stack based on the Open Systems Interconnection (OSI) model. This seven-layer stack starts with the physical layer and progresses up through data link, network, transport, session, presentation, and application layers.

Today, the IT industry is redefining this traditional seven-layer stack into a more business-oriented four-layer stack. These layers, starting from the bottom, are IT infrastructure, application infrastructure (including the application), business process execution, and business design. The traditional seven-layer model is subsumed in the first two layers of this new on demand model, clearly acknowledging the stronger linkage of business strategy with IT.

Business design addresses the fundamental strategic decisions faced by a firm. Once a strategy is set, firms seek scale and predictability of outcomes by defining and managing business processes. Each of these processes depends to some extent on IT applications. These applications are enabled and supported by applications infrastructure (for example, database systems, web application servers, and collaboration tools) and underlying IT infrastructure (for example, servers and storage networks).

The relationship of a business process to the underlying applications is critically important. From an IT perspective, a transaction is typically viewed at a fairly microscopic level — posting a payment, updating an address record, and so on. From a business perspective, however, a transaction often occurs over a very long period of time and involves many IT transactions. Business processes in most large enterprises have evolved over a long period of time in response to many demands, and they are complex and often fragile and inflexible. A new generation of business modeling tools has recently been introduced by a number of suppliers, including IBM, to precisely model these processes and monitor their execution. An on demand enterprise will be very focused on analyzing business processes across the value chain and implementing interenterprise IT systems to optimize them. Indeed, it is at the business process level where business strategy and IT intersect, and firms that best understand this will lead the next wave of evolution.

This four-layer model is also a very useful way to think about what a firm can outsource. In many cases, a firm will choose to insource the business design, business process execution, application infrastructure, and IT infrastructure. However, for a particular business component, the firm can choose to outsource just the IT infrastructure, the IT and application infrastructure via application hosting, the IT and application infrastructure plus the business process execution via a business process outsourcing (BPO) relationship, or the entire stack through a business transformation outsourcing (BTO) relationship. In the case of BPO, the outsourcer commits to execute the process as it is already defined. In the case of BTO, the outsourcer commits to transform the business process by optimizing the business design. Whatever the level of insourcing or outsourcing, the IT function is likely to be intimately involved in the decision making and the subsequent supplier management.

> " Indeed, it is at the business process level where business strategy and IT intersect, and firms that best understand this will lead the next wave of evolution. "

SUMMARY

Ultimately, as Hasso pointed out many years ago, what firms care about is innovating and maximizing organizational productivity. As firms have attempted to optimize against these goals, they first optimized at the business process level. Then they integrated across these resulting "stovepipes" to achieve some form of enterprise-level optimization. Now the challenge is to look beyond the firm and optimize across the entire value chain and value net. To accomplish this, firms must have a far more dynamic posture in virtually everything they do — just in time applied to everything. This is the essence of the on demand era.

12

Real-Time Case Study: The Future of Marketplaces in a Business-to-Business Environment

Claus Dieter Hoffman is chairman of the supervisory board of SupplyOn AG. SupplyOn is an Internet marketplace tailored to meet the needs of the automotive supplier industry. Prior to this, Hoffman held a variety of executive-level positions during his tenure of nearly 30 years at Bosch. In his latest position, he was a Member of the Board of Management with responsibilities for Corporate Finance and Controlling as well as Corporate Purchasing (CFO). Since his retirement in 2002, Hoffmann became Managing Partner of H + H Senior Advisors GmbH. He is the author of publications on the management aspects of multinational corporations and the prospects of Asian economies and serves as member of the Supervisory Board for the ING Group, EnBW, and several other companies.

Claus Dieter Hoffman

I s there really a future for online marketplaces in business-to-business commerce? In the year 2000, many users and software and Internet reporters answered this question with a resounding *yes*. A wealth of initiatives and, consequently, companies emerged whose founders contributed vastly different experiences and competencies. As a result, a correspondingly wide range of marketplaces and business models exist today.

From a user's perspective, two categories of marketplaces exist:

- A horizontal approach, which is a solution approach offering a specific category of applications across all industries
- A vertical approach, which focuses on functions and application clusters within the value chain of one industry

The initial euphoria about the increased value potential of e-marketplaces was followed by a period of considerable disillusionment. The anticipated quick successes failed to appear and a shakeout started that continues to this day. At SupplyOn, we observed that, although vertical marketplaces experienced a significant shakeout, the effect on horizontal business-to-business marketplaces was more severe.

DISILLUSIONMENT WITH E-MARKETPLACES

All companies, both those that survived and the failed e-marketplace initiatives, had considerably underestimated the difficulties of the ramp-up phase.

The first mistake was in the assessment of system infrastructure requirements. High levels of simultaneous and interdependent user access to the platform require systems to be powerful in a way that had not previously been recognized. The first systems had evident problems with these increased demands, which were reflected in poor stability and only moderate response times. Then, as now, the quantitative expansion of the infrastructure alone was not sufficient; it had to also be enhanced by improved qualitative solutions.

These progressively increasing demands for more powerful systems naturally led to unplanned overspending of development and investment budgets. Real-time interaction between companies does not come free of charge.

The next painful step in the learning curve was the realization that the traditional, sequential organization of quality assurance processes for application development, in which the final debugging is performed alongside pilot customers, does not work for online marketplaces. When an application is integrated into the marketplace, it must be absolutely free from errors from the beginning, or it can paralyze the marketplace.

> **" Real-time interaction between companies does not come free of charge. "**

Furthermore, for several reasons, the potential for growth was generally overestimated, both in terms of the number of participants and in terms of transaction volume.

One of the reasons that marketplaces failed to take off was the lack of ease of use for the marketplace user. The more difficult applications are to use, the greater the inhibition threshold of the user.

Another aspect for supply chain applications is the connection to vendors. This is a significant factor for the growth and success of the implementation. However, the further down the value chain you get, that is, in the direction of second- or third-tier vendors, the more frequently you are dealing with small- to medium-sized businesses. In these companies, the extent of IT product penetration is generally less, and thus there is hesitancy to use e-marketplace applications for business processes.

At the end of the day, many of the original business models proved to be unsustainable, particularly in cases where pricing was calculated on per-transaction basis.

Do all these realizations now cast doubt on the future of electronic marketplaces? We are of quite the opposite opinion. The integration of e-platforms in transactions between business partners, particularly in business-to-business relationships, will ultimately prove to be a very efficient and effective instrument.

E-MARKETPLACE SUCCESS FACTORS

An increase in the popularity of e-platforms is still subject to some important prerequisites, which we explain in the following discussion of e-marketplace success factors.

These success factors have been gleaned from practical experience with SupplyOn, the dominant marketplace for European automotive suppliers.

SELECTION OF APPLICATION CLUSTERS

When creating applications for the SupplyOn marketplace, we focused on automating the following processes:

- The purchasing process with quotation request, the availability of all documentation associated with the request, provision of a quotation by the supplier, and the evaluation and acceptance of a quote
- Supplementary processes that occur in the general purchasing environment:
  - Support of communication in product development
  - Exchange of quality data
- Logistics processes with contact with suppliers, particularly the transfer of delivery schedules, the transfer of delivery and transport information, and the visualization of inventories and demand

These applications all have the following features in common:

- They are typical processes in a business-to-business environment.
- They are processes that frequently use transactions and handle large volumes of data.
- Until now, these transactions have been developed using conventional communication media such as faxes and letters, supplemented by the use of the telephone. IT penetration in this area has been limited. Individual EDI connections existed only in a few exceptional cases and were limited to a handful of large suppliers, because the installation of conventional one-to-one business connections is not economically feasible.
- We chose applications for which, by definition, many-to-many business relationships exist in the industry, making a marketplace is the most suitable medium.

FOCUS ON REDUCING PROCESS COSTS

The applications used in the marketplace were specifically selected for their cost-saving potential.

- Repetitive applications of a process-based procedure that can be standardized have the greatest rationalization effect. While many marketplaces have concentrated on indirect material in purchasing and supply chain management, which typically only represents 10 to 20 percent of the purchasing requirements of a production company, we have concentrated from the beginning on direct material, which accounts for 80 to 90 percent of requirements.
- The savings potential is greatest in processes that have previously only been processed using conventional procedures instead of IT.
- The additional value of an e-marketplace really begins to make an impact if the selected processes require parallel communication with a large number of participants.

Cost savings are not the only advantage; using a platform of this sort to process purchasing functions also leads to increased market transparency, enabling more successful purchasing, which can far outweigh even the cost-related advantages.

We consider this to be an inherent side effect of the system, which greatly depends on how intensively the marketplace user already analyzed the purchasing market.

Added Value

When designing marketplace applications, it is important to streamline the basic processes of purchasing and logistics in the marketplace, but it is also important to offer additional functions and information that has not previously been available. We achieved this by including an industry-specific business directory.

All potential suppliers register in this business directory and are listed according to their specific expertise. Each company's specialization is described in terms of procedure/process technology, and the facilities required are listed.

This provides sustainable support for the purchasing process, as purchasers receive a proposed list of competent suppliers corresponding to their specific needs and can immediately incorporate these suppliers in the request for quotes.

The suppliers can then present themselves in a qualified situation with a detailed description of their spectrum of expertise in the marketplace. This information is available to all potential customers.

INDUSTRY FOCUS

Having clearly focused applications and thus clearly defined participants in a marketplace proved to be a very productive strategy.

Because the depth of industry-specific, application-specific solutions was more important for us than the breadth of the application spectrum, we decided on the vertical approach described earlier. Major suppliers in the automotive industry helped initiate the marketplace. The applications were focused on the supply chain, that is, the relationship between these tier 1 companies and their second- and third-tier suppliers.

We were therefore able to call upon the industry and IT expertise of these companies when defining the functional specifications. The accumulated knowledge of the experts has therefore been incorporated in the design of the marketplace functionality. This enabled us to create tailor-made solutions for the automotive industry (and similar high-volume production industries) while avoiding the necessity to develop individual company-specific solutions.

The development process produced some modules that are highly relevant to this industry but that have since found increasing acceptance in other industries as well.

By consolidating the strengths of leading companies in the supplier industry in this e-procurement system, we have combined more than half of the purchasing volume for tier-1 suppliers in Europe. For these industries, this has resulted in *de facto* standards for Internet business processes.

The vendors in the relevant material fields can simultaneously conduct sales and supply transactions with several customers within one e-business environment. This considerably simplifies business processing in most medium-sized businesses because only one user interface is required, which displays information on different customers, and system access requires only one registration and password.

The partnership between these leading companies and the rollout of the e-business functions has caused a significant increase in marketplace usage figures. The more the marketplace is used by these companies and the more suppliers are connected, the greater the attraction for more tier 1 companies to join.

TECHNOLOGY PARTNERSHIP

Selection of the correct technology partner is the long-term decisive factor for the success of a marketplace.

Marketplace applications will be accepted only if the technology partner is able to implement the specifications for the applications compatibly and in accordance with the demands of the marketplace. Furthermore, the marketplace infrastructure and its capability of supporting a large number of simultaneous transactions securely are of equal importance. Finally, the partnership must be based on a long-term outlook and allow for further development and expansion of the application modules. We have found this partner in SAP.

One further important aspect for the choice of the technology partner is competence in the connection of back-end systems. Back-end integration is one of the

> " *Selection of the correct technology partner is the long-term decisive factor for the success of a marketplace.* "

most important factors for success in both ease of use and cost-cutting potential. Users will fully accept the e-business functions in the marketplace only if they can execute a process from beginning to end within one interconnected environment, without system interruption.

This back-end integration has been established for all applications in the SupplyOn marketplace, enabling transfer of data in both directions between the user's systems and the marketplace. Standardized "connect solutions" enable implementation of these back-end connections in the companies within a short space of time and with a minimum of effort.

It should also be possible to switch between application modules of the marketplace. In our case this was realized by appropriate configuration of the central marketplace.

THE BUSINESS MODEL

It has become apparent that purely transaction-based calculation of rates is not an acceptable business model. Aside from the complexity of the accounting workload in a transaction-based price system, the concept of a proportional or variable increase in costs in relation to increased use also holds little attraction for the user.

In the IT environment, the "natural" expectation is a fixed-cost regression, where increased use corresponds with a relative decrease in cost.

Concepts that calculate the connection and service costs at a flat rate are thus considerably more likely to be successful. License fees can be calculated based on company size.

SUPPORT SERVICES

Our experience has shown that offering additional services contributes considerably towards the acceptance of an offer to join the marketplace.

End-user training is an obvious service, but it is also important to provide a competent call center to help users with problems and questions. Implementation support for the rollout in larger companies and at the vendor sites is also particularly important.

SUMMARY

So, are business-to-business marketplaces a temporary phenomenon? On the contrary, if the success factors here are taken into account, the marketplace is an exceedingly effective tool for fulfilling the requirements of communication applications in the supply chain.

Proprietary portal solutions are only a partial competitor. For reasons of cost, these solutions can be considered only by larger users. They cannot fulfill the multilateral transaction and communication functions necessary for purchasing and logistics. The use of marketplaces is also the only realistic method for establishing the *de facto* industry standards needed for the real-time enterprise.

13

The Real-Time Enterprise

Vinod Khosla is a recognized leader in the venture capital community. Since 1986, Vinod Khosla has been a General Partner of Kleiner Perkins Caufield & Byers. He cofounded Daisy Systems and was founding CEO of Sun Microsystems, where he pioneered open systems and commercial RISC processors. Vinod Khosla coined the phrase "real-time enterprise" in a 2002 white paper coauthored with Asera VP Murugan Pal.

Vinod Khosla

Current market trends, global competition, and technological innovations are driving enterprises to adopt the practices of the "real-time enterprise." To a degree not seen before, real-time enterprises rely on the automation of processes spanning disparate systems, different media, and even different enterprise boundaries. Such organizations provide real-time information to employees, customers, suppliers, and partners and implement processes to ensure that all information is current and consistent across all systems, minimizing batch and manual processes related to information.

Any business process within the enterprise, including relevant processes in use by its trading partners, must be reflected instantaneously in all enterprise systems. In other words, within a real-time enterprise, all information is real time. All manual or batch processes related to information in an enterprise are inefficiencies in the delivery of products and services — that is, unless the manual or batch processes are integral to the nature of the business.

What all this makes possible, I would argue, is such tremendous efficiencies and significant, ongoing reductions in selling, general, and administrative (SG&A) costs that the emergence of the real-time enterprise arguably represents an important watershed. It's a do-or-die challenge for corporate America in general and for the IT industry in particular. Corporations that don't strive to be real time in their use of information technology risk being forced out of business by more efficient rivals. One has only to look at retailing, where Kmart has fared so poorly against Wal-Mart, largely because of the latter's superior use of technology. While Kmart's SG&A expenses are about 21 percent of revenues, Wal-Mart's comparable figure is just 17 percent, which is enough of a difference to have helped to force Kmart into bankruptcy.

INCREASE IT BUDGETS

Equally important, I believe that the whole future of the IT business depends on reaching the real-time enterprise goal. Today, we live in an age when every CEO says to his CIO, "Let's reduce the cost of IT." I actually think that is the dumbest thing one can ask for. What the IT industry should do is have CEOs ask, "Where can we increase spending on IT and gain productivity elsewhere?" If a company spends an extra 1 percent of sales on technology, it should get back 1.5 percent to 2 percent in reduced SG&A.

> ❝ The move to the real-time enterprise will not come immediately or without facing some difficult technical and cultural challenges. ❞

If, in fact, we can do that, IT budgets will go up, because the corporation is getting an economic return on its IT spending. Clearly, we want to make IT as efficient as possible and reduce costs there, but that shouldn't be the CIO's main goal. If we as an industry can make that vision of recurring SG&A savings happen, IT budgets will go up faster than they are today.

The move to the real-time enterprise will not come immediately or without facing some difficult technical and cultural challenges. As it is, all of us in the IT business think in terms of building applications as opposed to running the applications. Ask any CIO and he'll tell you that 70 percent of his budget is spent on maintenance and operations. All of us in IT are worrying about the other 30 percent of his budget, the money he spends on hardware, on software, and on new applications and gadgets. The big payoff is in that 70 percent portion of the budget that CIOs spend on running SAP, servers, and datacenters. If we can apply technology to the operations problem and design applications that are simpler to run, modify, and decommission and replace with the next generation, the IT shop's productivity will go up, and IT spending will go up, too.

I believe that this is the key to continued growth in the IT business. Currently, corporate America spends an average of about 5 percent of corporate sales on IT. That's a sizeable sum, but I don't see why it can't increase to 10 percent if that extra spending results in a recurring 10 percent reduction in SG&A. Already, companies such as Cisco Systems, Dell, and Wal-Mart have proven that every dollar spent on IT produces such a payback that more money for IT means less in labor costs. That is where IT will grow.

Today's business practices and models demand an operational environment acting as a virtual enterprise, with insight into the status of customers, partners, and suppliers on a real-time basis. Some examples illustrate the nature and power of the real-time enterprise:

- All systems would immediately recognize the entry of a new product in a catalog system. Billing and customer service could be done from the moment the product becomes available.
- A real-time wireless carrier could activate a cell phone as soon as a credit card payment is processed, with no time lost and no need for manual intervention.
- A real-time credit card company could improve customer loyalty by automating dispute notifications, from the customer on back to the credit card company, the merchant's bank, and the merchant itself.

Yet, automation of an end-to-end value chain has not been widely adopted or fully achieved. Even though technologically this has been possible for some time, only lately has it become realistic with the advent of Internet-driven standardization. This has led to orders-of-magnitude cost reductions, plus the elimination of debate regarding the technical infrastructure to be used. With the advent of Internet technologies such as HTTP and HTML, and with standardization initiatives around XML, web services, UDDI, and SOAP, it is now possible.

CHANGE AS PROCESS

But something else is needed, something as important as standards but probably much more difficult to achieve. The key to realizing the real-time enterprise is to make systems adaptable to change and to accept change as an ongoing process. Change itself must be a core competency of the entire organization, especially within IT. This requires a transformation of IT, a move forward from the stark reality of relying on legacy applications to the promise of systems that are more malleable, more pliable, and more easily adapted to ever-changing business processes. The goal should not be a radical transformation of software or hardware but rather a continuous migration of systems, thereby transforming the organization into an adaptive enterprise.

The inflexible structure of conventional systems has long been the subject of loud complaints by top management. Enterprise IT problems are tied to the "islands of information" caused by many legacy architectures distributed across geographies, business units, and subsidiaries. The technology evolution has forced many enterprises to buy new software and hardware. This has resulted in "best in class," sometimes "most in class," and many times "try, buy, throw" environments. The challenge is to leverage existing operational systems, evaluate "most in class" systems, and reuse the most meaningful of them. Many times the real problems are legacy processes rather than legacy systems. In such cases, integration is a wrong approach to achieve the necessary plasticity and adaptability.

> " The key to realizing the real-time enterprise is to make systems adaptable to change and to accept change as an ongoing process. "

THE CHANGE GAME

Agility is a central theme in this book. Khosla argues for a fundamental rethinking of IT architectures, starting with a major focus on enabling continuous changes to systems over time. Legacy systems should be encapsulated, he writes, and the customizations of each software product a customer uses should be captured in declarative, not procedural form. The result would be a new level of malleability in systems, better returns on investment in IT, and a chance for the IT industry as a whole to start growing at a healthier rate than usual. For another view of how enterprises can and must avail themselves of ongoing change in IT and business process, see HP CEO Carly Fiorina's thoughts on what she calls the *Adaptive Enterprise* in Chapter 7.

According to Gartner Group, 70 percent of all infrastructure efforts fail or substantially miss their objectives. Large integration projects like Boeing's I–Man portal fail to achieve the desired results 60 percent of the time, according to Giga Information Group. That firm reckons that companies put too much faith in technology's ability to cut costs and fail to adapt old processes to make use of new technology.

What's really needed, I believe, is some kind of Excel-like tool for business processes, an authoring environment that would do for business processes what the electronic spreadsheet has done for financial numbers. Spreadsheets are wonderful tools for modeling financial scenarios, and the tool I envision would help business people and technologists to model business processes with the same ease and accuracy. Such an authoring tool might look like Microsoft Visio, being quite graphical, but its models would be immediately actionable, not just static diagrams. Using this tool, individual users would be able to iterate on a process very rapidly, adapting portions of it to their peculiar needs.

What's most important, though, is not that this tool uses the Visio process but that it works across multiple applications, enabling companies to combine selected pieces into composite applications. These composite apps would bring together information and process from many different apps and present it all on a single screen or single set of screens. And built into these composite apps would be the people part of a workflow — the tasks that people engage in when helping to execute a particular business process.

MALLEABLE SOFTWARE

The idea is to take pieces of existing transaction systems, preserve their complexity in the background, make them more usable, and have them follow a business process that is external to the business application. An example might be order entry, a fairly complex process and a classic example of a system in need of a simpler front end. Once, at a certain large telecommunications manufacturer, I saw that in order to enter an order, their customer service reps had to access four different systems. Moreover, they had to go through 77 different screens across those four systems. Embedding a composite screen that shows data from three or four applications relevant to the task is what those service reps needed. In some sense, we've built the Ferrari but we're still relying on the double-clutching gear change when we drive it.

The real-time enterprise requires a fundamental shift in our thinking. In the past, we've tended to think of applications as software with business processes existing somewhere else. How we do order entry is a business process, but people have not matched that up exactly with the systems involved. We must understand that if a business process is highly inefficient, it may need restructuring. Just putting new software in place may not do the job. Software today is not malleable enough. If you want to change or customize it, IT has to get involved in a fairly big way. It would be much better if IT didn't have to get involved and the end user or business analysts could do that work themselves. An Excel-like front end, therefore, would be a big help.

> **" The real-time enterprise requires a fundamental shift in our thinking. "**

Yet, such a front end will be of no use if the underlying software is not made more malleable and open to modification and reconfiguration. Ideally, when a system is installed, the user should install with it the mechanism needed to decommission that system — to uninstall it, so to speak, without disturbing the business processes that rely on it. As it is, most of corporate America is living with systems built in COBOL as much as 30 years ago, primarily because they have no way to eliminate them. These systems are woven too tightly into the business processes companies rely on day to day. If the function of these legacy systems were encapsulated, however, this could change. Imagine if all the specifications of the customizations I wanted in SAP, for example, were declarative, not procedural. That is, they were stated in a way external to the software rather than described in terms of actual software logic. When it came time to install the next release of SAP, I could take all of these declarative statements and apply them to the new release. I wouldn't have to customize the new software. These declarative statements would "say" *what* you want to do, not *how* you want to do it. And this would make it easy to decommission old systems: You'd have captured what you're trying to do separately from how you're doing it.

This notion of declarative as opposed to procedural statements is very important. Today, the problem is that the *what* is captured in some code, in some variables deep inside a piece of software. It may define, for example, how an insurance company should measure the life of a bond. It now becomes very hard to separate the assumption from the code, and you can't just throw away the code.

Now, some people will say, "Don't customize software, use standard programs." The fact is, though, that you run into another problem. Standard software doesn't necessarily adapt to the business process that a company wants to use. So, the company ends up split between two ways of executing that process, namely the way the organization wants to do it and the way the software is programmed to do it. And to bridge this difference, some kind of translation is required, and by definition, that is *not* a real-time enterprise. Costs and complexity increase, and information is lost in this translation. If the software were more malleable, however, you could adapt its actions to the way people want to do things. This adaptability is precisely where we need to get to, as opposed to always looking backward and trying to adapt the organization to the software.

GET THE ARCHITECTURE RIGHT

As a result, the most important thing a CIO can do as a first step to getting his or her enterprise into the real-time circle is to get the company's IT architecture right. Enterprise architecture is clearly the single most important thing. Years of experience show that the optimization of this architecture and its systems can be achieved along four dimensions: flexibility, cost, performance, and reliability. The real-time enterprise demands that flexibility be given top priority, ahead of cost, reliability, and performance. The transformation to the right architecture will not be accomplished with a single decisive stroke, however. It will take place through a thousand small cuts and changes. We can't do a massive overhaul of whole companies. The good CIO will get the architecture right and then implement lots of short-term projects — 90- or 100-day projects — and hack away at the cost structure bit by bit.

The changes needed to realize the real time-enabling architecture range across all aspects of IT. Disparate information resources will need to be virtualized, so as to create an information base, or iBase. This calls for extracting documents from various legacy systems and converting them to XML as queries are invoked. Another key step is the encapsulation of legacy systems in a way that preserves their function yet hides their complexities and idiosyncrasies, such as unforgiving user interfaces.

> " *The real-time enterprise demands that flexibility be given top priority, ahead of cost, reliability, and performance.* "

The use of web services creates an environment in which end users as well as technicians can assemble and reuse these applications and their components to generate new composite apps. Applications would be loosely federated, not tightly integrated, thus supplying much needed malleability. This environment would operate within the constraints of corporate business processes, often coded into the end user programming environments by business analysts (often as those declarative rules or objects, not as computer programs) and to a limited extent by programmers to create components and services in languages like Java and C#. The front end of this environment would be the Excel-like authoring tool described earlier. The aim is to create a "mass customization" environment for business processes, workflow, and collaboration, with support tools provided for administration, personalization, versioning, upgrading, and more.

Hardware and software makers will help, no doubt, but again, without any radical change to their products. I don't believe in the notion of radical change, in which somebody comes out with an all-new design and it takes over the world. I think processors, for instance, are already changing in ways that will help the real-time enterprise. I wouldn't be surprised if Intel and AMD start producing processors that have hardware support for the kind of virtualization of processing power that will be required in the future. But they'll do that without making it incompatible with today's standard Windows or Linux or Solaris platforms. In short, we'll see 100 small changes that will add up to a fundamental change in server architecture. And I believe software will have to change the same way. This is why I speak of a "continuous migration approach" to the real-time enterprise.

KNOWING YOU'RE IN REAL TIME

If the change is so gradual, how might we know when we've reached our goal? I believe the following is a good, public litmus test: Today, every corporation in America reports quarterly financial results. There's a conference call with Wall Street analysts, and so forth. What if these companies could close their books every single day because, in fact, all of their information is in real time? If you could produce financial statements every single day, because all of your systems carry all the information, and every business process is automated and captured in real time, working intricately with transaction systems, then all the systems would be up to date. A financial analyst could ask, "What's the P&L, bookings, or revenues today?" A customer support rep could ask, "What's the status of this order, has it shipped?" Those two questions should reflect exactly the same information. If an order has shipped, it should be indicated in terms of revenue, too — contingent, of course, on the shipment meeting a set of criteria defined by contractual information that's part of the appropriate business process.

So, if you can accurately produce two such financial statements every day, then in fact you are a real-time enterprise. If you cannot do this, it's because certain processes are either manual or batch-oriented, and all the information in the enterprise is not concurrent in all systems. And any process that's done in batch or manually will require extra staff and extra cost, and this will mean less efficiency. Indeed, building the real-time enterprise is a process of eliminating manual and batch processes; that's where the cost efficiency comes from.

Quite related, of course, is making sure everything that happens in one system happens within the context of every other system and that it's reflected instantly in all those systems. There can be no such thing as manual entry of an order, as is often done today at the end of a financial quarter to make sales look better. There's no such thing as a status check that isn't always there. And there's no more customer support rep calling manufacturing and manufacturing calling a contract supplier to ask if an order has shipped or not. All information is concurrent.

> " Indeed, building the real-time enterprise is a process of eliminating manual and batch processes; that's where the cost efficiency comes from. "

Consider the benefits of having all information current in all systems such that books can be nominally closed within hours of the close of a quarter (or day!). Cisco Systems is able to do this today, and after adjustments including managerial and auditor input, it can announce financial results within 3 days of the end of a quarter. Think of the cost savings in finance alone! Cisco's much-vaunted electronic order-entry system has decreased the rate of errors for the company from 20 percent to 0.2 percent. If a majority of the orders come in untouched by humans, think of the sales force efficiency and yield improvements. If most employee information (such as vacation days and 401Ks) is "self-service" on the intranet, think of the savings in HR. If order status, product configuration, and "available to promise" dates are self-service for customers on the web, think of the improvements in customer service that are possible, while reducing costs. These improvements are not just about a web site but a structural change to web-enabled IT.

SELF-SERVICE SAVINGS

The benefit of "self-service" is enormous because data will be cleaner when the owner enters it and the process will be efficient because it is outsourced to the end customers themselves. This is how the Internet is being used for information transport rather than simply as a browsing medium. It represents a change in the way finance, operations, HR, logistics, and the whole corporation work. According to Reinhard Geissbauer, head of the North American Industrial Equipment practice at Roland Berger & Partners, manufacturers already using the Internet see annual cost savings of 6 percent across the value chain. From procurement to web-based supply chain management and after-sales service, it may be possible to cut costs by as much as 8 percent to 10 percent. The savings are potentially larger. On the other hand, Cisco a few years ago failed to automate its supply chain deep enough into its partners, resulting in hundreds of millions of dollars worth of excess inventory — beyond what a normal demand forecasting error would have caused in a full real-time, full-visibility environment.

The reality is that the vast promise of IT, by and large, has been a mirage for most corporations. But does this have to be true? Does the promise work only for some organizations? Are missed opportunities or productivity gains just that, or can they be realized? Are budget overruns, process delays, and "additional costs" to recover the investments already made an unavoidable fact of life? We have gone from MIS departments with large in-house software development efforts to inexpensive desktop enablement, to large packaged software applications, to productive application development tools, client/server applications, portable environments such as Java, and system integration tools. We have gone through IT consultants, outsourcing vendors, ASPs, and the Big 5 and their system integration expertise, but the problems of IT remain largely the same.

Even more tantalizing are the stories of "benefits" of good IT strategies:

- Cisco has substantially higher revenues per employee than its direct competitors, Nortel and Lucent. The cost of doing business is lower at Cisco, and their responsiveness and customer service levels are higher.
- Geissbauer stresses that many of the top challenges for manufacturers relate to competitive pressure and manufacturers need to respond faster to customers in order to achieve their top-line sales goals.
- Dell can offer "mass customization" and still maintain much higher inventory turns than its competitors, generating greater profitability in its PC business.
- Wal-Mart and Amazon have used IT technology as strategic weapons to increase their competitiveness.

- FedEx could not economically provide the level of customer service that it does without IT. The cost to FedEx of a "package pick-up call" or a "where is my package" inquiry has declined substantially because of the use of appropriate technology.

We estimate that each 1 percent (of sales) of increased IT spending or spending redirected from rigid and outmoded forms of systems integration in a corporation should reduce SG&A spending by 1.5 percent to 2 percent (of sales) beyond the improvements in IT productivity. It is important to note that the bigger role of IT is not managing IT functions and expenses, but rather managing expenses and service levels for the rest of the corporation.

IT can be a strategic weapon and help reduce SG&A costs relative to competitors while improving customer experience. The rate of savings depends on industry sector; those sectors with high SG&A can realize the most significant benefits. This applies especially to business processes, collaboration environments, and personalized applications where the bulk of enterprise activity can be automated. It is clear that every business process, every manual or batch process, and every human touch point that is properly automated and eliminated will result in an economic saving as well as an improvement in quality by reducing the risk of human error and improving the availability of information. That is the great promise and potential of the real-time enterprise.

14

Real-Time Case Study: Fire Safety at Frankfurt Airport

The real-time enterprise doesn't always have to make corporations safe to do business on the other side of the globe. Sometimes it keeps us safe on the way there. This case study from Frankfurt Airport demonstrates how the combination of a few simple ideas and software that knits them together can improve safety and efficiency at the same time. Ulrich Kipper, an IT executive at the airport, led the implementation of RFID tags and customized PDAs that ensured the airport's fire shutters — a vital but invisible safeguard for visitors — were inspected and working properly. Kipper holds a doctorate in physics and has been working in IT since 1990.

Ulrich Kipper

While it would likely never occur to passengers that our airport's air conditioning system could turn deadly in the event of a fire, we worry about the possibility every day. Whether a fire broke out in a terminal or in an area used only by staff, the ventilation ducts that normally carry cool air could suddenly fill with toxic smoke, endangering everyone in the building. That's exactly what happened during a tragic fire in Dusseldorf Airport on April 11, 1996.

To protect against this, our airport's system is equipped with fire shutters that can seal vents in seconds, trapping the heat and smoke locally. German law requires we inspect each shutter annually to ensure it is working properly — and more often if it has a history of trouble — which is a formidable task when you have 22,000 shutters to examine. Some are only a few centimeters wide; others are as large as 2 meters across. Each usually requires completion of a three-page form as proof of inspection.

We didn't need the cost or the trouble of so much paperwork. The rest of our maintenance operations run over the web atop SAP® R/3®; we wanted inspection data to work in real time as well. If we could make shutters remember when they had last been inspected and store that data digitally, we could verify results with our government in real time, streamline our maintenance requests, and save money by shifting the process to an R/3 implementation we already had in place. Some-day, we hoped, an inspection that found a malfunctioning shutter would cause the software to automatically generate a work order to fix it. But that will have to come later.

We thought about this for a long time. We needed a way to store data next to the shutters, some of which are in inhospitable environ-ments. We needed portable devices to read that data, because many of the shutters are at the top of ladders 7 meters above the ground. And we would have to implement most of it ourselves.

We asked SAP for advice, and the company came back to us with a simple solution that harnessed some cutting-edge technology. SAP sug-gested that we install radio frequency ID (RFID) tags on the shutters to store inspection data, which our maintenance staff would read with cus-tomized PDAs that would be synced to our SAP system at the end of each day. We presented them a list of our exact requirements and launched a pilot program with SAP in February 2003. Testing started just 5 months later — but it might have taken an extra year to get started if we had worked with another SAP customer instead of SAP itself.

The RFID tags were ordered — we purchased 30,000, which are being installed one by one as each shutter comes up for inspection. Each tag contains four pieces of information: a barcode, which is visible on the front; an ID number; another ID used by SAP's system; and the date when that shutter was last inspected.

By the end of 2003, 70 technicians were using the PDAs to examine shutters daily. They begin each day by downloading their slate of maintenance requests to the device from their desktop machine. The requests cannot be altered by input from the technician. Only later, when they scan a tag during their rounds, does the request queued to that tag open, which causes the PDA to read the date stored on that tag and then save it, after which it writes the date of new inspection back onto the tag.

If the shutter is fine, the technician's work is done. If it's broken, the technician has to log that information and file it back at his or her desk later. So far, this is the only area requiring manual data entry. Installing a wireless network to send inspection results to our server instantly is cost-prohibitive, because most of our maintenance staff works in out-of-the-way corners of the airport.

Implementing this solution and weaving it into our IT infrastructure actually led us to upgrade our entire SAP system — we added a mobile device engine that connects any PDA to our R/3 data using a web application server. We've just begun to scratch the surface of what we can do. The paperwork is gone for good, freeing our technicians for more pressing tasks. And now that we've linked inspection data to our SAP Business Information Warehouse, other departments are analyzing the data, looking for patterns in part defects, average lifespans, and failure rates.

> " RFID sensors and PDAs have helped us create a corporate nervous system for our fire shutters, allowing us to work in real time and leave paper forms behind. "

Ultimately, we want this system to generate its own maintenance requests, reacting in real time to shutters that fail and sending a technician to fix it in minutes rather than days. We'll continue to save time and money, and it could very well save lives.

Now that we have the mobile engine in place, we've launched an internal pilot program to apply a PDA approach to our logistics needs. We're experimenting with different devices that can log incoming shipments of parts and supplies. We're aiming to build up an entire family of devices that can handle a wide range of requests and possibly use wireless networks to keep data flowing faster than arriving packages. RFID sensors and PDAs have helped us create a corporate nervous system for our fire shutters, allowing us to work in real time and leave paper forms behind. Integration of technologies like these with our corporate software continues to inspire similar projects, helping us fully realize our vision of becoming a real-time enterprise.

15

IT and the Future of Outsourcing

Anil Kumar is a Director with McKinsey & Company Inc. located in Silicon Valley. He is responsible for McKinsey's global business process outsourcing and offshoring practice as well as its electronic business practice. Kumar is the founder and chairman of a 24/7 research and information McKinsey Knowledge Center in India and co-founded the Indian School of Business (ISB) as a joint venture with Kellogg, Wharton, and the London Business School (www.isb.edu). He has published in the Sloan Management Review, McKinsey Quarterly, and Harvard Business Review, and co-authored Customer Value Optimization, a book on capturing Customer Relationship Management's (CRM's) benefits.

Anil Kumar

IT defines the contours of business processes. Improvements in IT have invariably reshaped processes, including those across enterprises. IT has in fact enabled an increasingly multi–locational, multi-enterprise world, including the outsourcing of products and services. Hasso Plattner has a special appreciation for the new global enterprise. He epitomizes the global citizen — personally living a multi–locational life in Germany, South Africa, and the United States. He also has interests across enterprises — from SAP to sailing, tennis, and golf. In integrating his life across these locations and interests, he has pushed the expectations from IT.

> " Today, systems supporting the real-time enterprise are poised to have a transformative impact on business by increasing visibility and predictability, driving standardization and consistency, and improving the speed of decision-making. "

Today, systems supporting the real-time enterprise are poised to have a transformative impact on business by increasing visibility and predictability, driving standardization and consistency, and improving the speed of decision-making. This next frontier of automation will lead to new, more extensive, and more varied types of outsourcing — enabling major managerial innovations that will be crucial for executives to harness.

LESSONS FROM THE PAST

IT advances have typically fostered outsourcing. For the earliest corporate entities, business decisions had three critical properties: they were local, customized, and end-to-end. These traits fixed the limits and nature of firms (Figure 15-1).

Historical constraints on business decisions	Nature of decisions enabled by real-time IT
• Limited to a single location within a specific geographic region	• Multi-locational and global in scope
• Customized according to local conditions and traditional practice	• Standardized and drawing on global best practice
• Decisions require end-to-end management of production through delivery	• Focus on specific narrow skills or parts of the value chain

Figure 15-1. Constraints Removed by Real-Time IT

For centuries, business decisions had been local because information traveled slowly and expensively. A manager 100 miles away from a plant simply knew too little about it, and his decisions took too long to arrive. Managerial processes were therefore closely tied to the physical site. However, beginning with the telegraph, fast and cost-effective communications let managers make decisions at a distance and thus divorced them from physical location. In a sense, one of the earliest forms of outsourcing was the provision of third-party communication to firms.

Companies had always customized decisions because diverse managers — working with varied resources, tools, and training — developed and drove their processes. Here, technology enabled standardization of tasks (for example, document production) so that personnel could perform them identically within other entities. The advent of Enterprise Resource Planning (ERP) software broadened this standardization to business processes across various industries and enabled outsourcers to offer such processes as a service. The providers were able to differentiate themselves by building core competencies on these standardized processes and leveraging IT economies of scale by aggregating services to multiple customers.

End-to-end decision-making meant that managers within a single company had to make the full set of decisions from production through delivery because these business processes were inseparable. However, as data, process, and automation standards have improved, the unbundling of business systems has become increasingly possible. The semiconductor industry — with its outsourced manufacturing and design — provides a clear example of the possibilities that arise from deploying standard IT solutions.

In each case, new IT capabilities removed managerial constraints — widening geographic reach and increasing uniformity and modularity — and thus increased the opportunity for reliable outsourcing. Real-time IT lifts further constraints and creates additional opportunities.

THE PROMISE OF REAL TIME

Real-time IT opens up new outsourcing possibilities, such as remote management of many operational activities, collaboration with outsourced services groups, and greater outsourcing of complete, extended supply chains. In aggregate, these changes will drive a new wave of multi-locational, cross-enterprise activities — as well as new business configurations taking advantage of new outsourcing options.

Remote management becomes possible once office workers have real-time access to immediate operational data from anywhere in the world. For example, many companies are now implementing "digital-dashboard" performance management systems that give managers instant access to production data that in the past wasn't easily available outside of the factory floor. Now, whether walking around the factory connected to a wireless LAN or in an office halfway around the earth, managers can get real-time production data and act immediately. This further separates decision-making from the physical location — and in principle allows new types of outsourcing.

Real-time collaboration can enable true global, multi-party design — across the full scope of mechanical, industrial, electrical, and software design (Figure 15-2). It will permit the outsourcing of design tasks without impairing the collaboration essential to execute them successfully. For example, GM's engineering-collaboration system has grown from 100 users a few years ago to more than 16,000 today. This system electronically connects most of GM's global design groups and lets them easily share engineering drawings. Groups from different regions can work together on a project in real time, balancing workloads. For instance, GM design groups in Russelsheim, Germany, and Sao Paolo, Brazil, can work simultaneously on a car for the Brazilian market. Such collaboration has cut the design cycle from 36 months a few years ago to 18 months today. Other real-time IT systems such as Product Data Management have enabled concurrent operations, so design, manufacturing, and marketing can work together sharing product design ideas, production schedules, marketing requirements, and other information. Increasingly, real-time supply chain software and web-based services enable the outsourcing of these critical operations, without compromising collaboration.

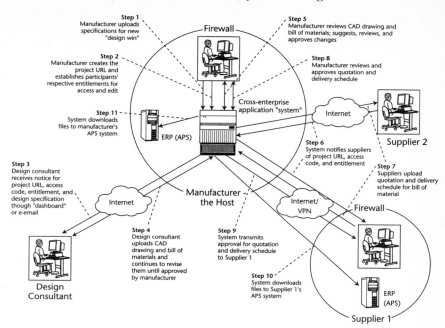

Figure 15-2. Collaborative Product Design

Real-time IT systems will also compel the standardization of information and process architectures and will slowly phase out the proliferation of standards that exist throughout today's enterprise IT systems. As a result, partners in supply-chain and customer-facing activities will be able to work together much more closely. Leading telecom equipment companies such as Alcatel have implemented collaborative planning software with standard interfaces and protocols that allow real-time monitoring of inventory, supply commitments, and forecast changes. These types of systems allow these companies to manage outsourced manufacturers as if they were internal departments.

> " *Real-time IT systems will also compel the standardization of information and process architectures and will slowly phase out the proliferation of standards that exist throughout today's enterprise IT systems.* "

Standardization based on web protocols has allowed other companies to deploy real-time services to effectively extend their corporate footprint. Here are a few examples.

- Dell uses Internet-based software to act as order-taker and customer interface for many third-party products it never touches.
- Amazon uses a web services platform to integrate several third-party sellers onto its storefront.
- Yahoo! aggregates a wide variety of content based on standard protocols and offers it as a single information portal.

Increased standardization invariably leads to new outsourcing opportunities. Just as the standardizing of manufacturing automation (MRP and other systems) led to outsourced manufacturing and supply chain services, so will the standardizing of service workflows lead to service outsourcing opportunities. For example, as additional processes in the insurance industry become standardized and supported by real-time systems, we would expect to see more functional specialists offering outsourcing of risk management, claims processing, and other services. The promise of real-time standardized service processes is opening up new sectors of the economy to functional reconfiguration — this will be the next frontier of outsourcing

ECONOMIC IMPACT OF REAL TIME

As with other major shifts in IT capability, the transition to real time will have important economic consequences. Today, enterprises keep many functions integrated in-house because of a perceived coordination advantage. Historically, enterprises have been reluctant to outsource because of the hidden costs associated with external coordination. For example, outsourcing manufacturing and separating it from design could hinder collaboration, resulting in cost, quality and time-to-market problems. Real-time IT can overcome physical barriers, ensure effective collaboration, and eliminate these concerns. With outsourcing representing some $300 billion in value in 2001, even a small increase in the types of activities that can be outsourced has enormous economic implications. Our analysis suggests that by the year 2008, outsourcing will reach more than $800 billion (Figure 15-3).

Overall growth of value of business outsourcing
$Billions

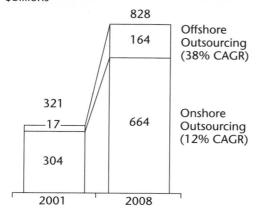

CAGR = Compound Annual Growth Rate

Figure 15-3. Growth of Outsourcing

Consider the automotive industry, which has leveraged real-time systems for collaborative design, sourcing, and manufacturing. Most car companies outsource parts manufacturing and increasingly assembly, focusing on product design and marketing. Volkswagen AG, for example, manufactures less than 15 percent of its parts. It can outsource so much because of a strong IT infrastructure and a push towards more real-time systems to ensure close collaboration. Real-time systems also accelerate remote outsourcing and offshoring. Ford, for example, operates a facility in Chennai, India, with more than 700 employees engaged in application design, engineering, development, and maintenance. The breadth and depth of the global pool of talent now available because of the deployment of real-time systems is staggering and will continue to drive shifts of this nature for many years to come (Figure 15-4).

> ## THE BIG HANDOFF
>
> Anil Kumar sees real-time information technology as greatly reducing
> the risks of outsourcing critical tasks and even entire processes. Increased
> standardization in IT, he argues, finally makes it possible for corporations
> to separate, for example, the manufacturing of a product from its design.
> In Chapter 11, Bruce Harreld, IBM's Senior Vice President for Strategy,
> looks at what IBM calls on demand computing, which applies the real-
> time outsourcing model to computing resources such as processing
> cycles and mass data storage.

Real-time IT systems will also lead to more standard interfaces and
software packages across industries, substantially lowering the cost of
switching outsourcing providers. Enterprises have viewed outsourced
relationships as locked in, primarily due to high switching costs. The IT
systems typically took long periods to integrate, causing significant
operational inefficiencies. Standard interfaces should make switching
seamless from a systems integration standpoint and will encourage outsourcing. For example, with the advent of web services and related standards around content description (XML) and access (SOAP),
applications can begin to seamlessly share information with other vendor's applications as well as with legacy systems, eliminating integration
pain points from switching outsourcing providers. Although the rate of
adoption of web services remains a subject of some debate, in the long
run these standards will dramatically lower switching costs. The economic potential of the growth in outsourcing created by these trends
will be tremendous (Figure 15-5).

Real time also has the potential to open up "internal" capabilities —
that is, capacities based on specific intellectual property and/or differen-
tiated talent — to broader external markets. It can do so by establishing
standard interfaces for real-time processes. Finally, real-time IT can optimize business value by matching best practice design with best practice
production with best practice sales, marketing, and channel management. The potential revenue upside here could be as large as, if not
larger than, the cost savings from the initial shift to back office outsourcing and shared services models.

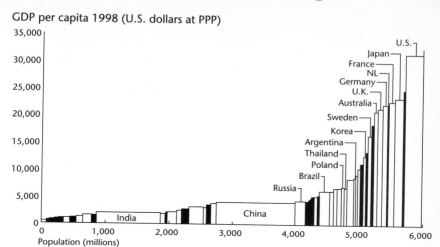

Figure 15-4. Global Talent Pool

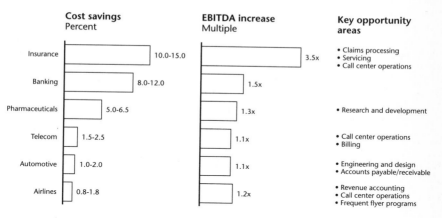

EBITDA = Earnings Before Interest, Taxes, Depreciation, and Amortization

Figure 15-5. Economic Potential of Outsourcing

TAKING ADVANTAGE OF REAL TIME

As businesses migrate to real-time platforms, they should take advantage of the increased flexibility and new economic models that these platforms offer. The first step is to map an ordered progression towards real-time system architectures to front-load benefits from:

- Optimizing existing outsourced relationships and/or interfaces between multiple internal business units
- Leveraging opportunities to use additional external best-in-class providers to perform internal functions (design, sales, marketing, and production)

It is of course vital to grasp which internal capabilities could yield value if leveraged in an external, global market. The company must identify the core competencies in which it can be world class and on which management should focus.

The firm should also thoroughly investigate other functions for the potential to outsource them, using at least three criteria:

1. The importance of strategic control of that function and comparison of internal capability versus best-in-class third-party provider
2. The optimal geographic site, based on importance of physical proximity, talent base, infrastructure requirements, intellectual property risks, and risks related to the country
3. Cost advantage

Businesses should ensure a staged, pilot-based approach to additional outsourcing opportunities, leveraging experiences from past moves to shared services and/or back-office outsourcing. They should use the pilot to demonstrate early benefits, resolve possible system and organizational issues, and drive a standardized approach into the rest of the company. Pilots should be undertaken with a commitment and game plan for whole-hearted movement to optimized outsourcing.

A VIEW OF THE FUTURE

How different will an enterprise that has fully taken advantage of real-time systems become? Where will it differ, in structure, organization, or scope from a typical company today? We believe that as the benefits and increased flexibility of real time become part of the DNA of every company, the nature of the typical enterprise will change. The sharpness of focus on specific processes and sources of advantage will increase, the boundaries of the overall corporate entity will blur, and the importance of real-time innovation will require development of new managerial skills. Specifically, in this view of the future, real time will change enterprises in the following ways:

- **Competition focused on defining skills, not markets** — In the past, a company could be successful simply by identifying a new market to pursue and bringing together under one roof the skills necessary to succeed in that market. In the future, the broad use of real-time systems will result in many companies being able to bring the best skills to bear at the same time on any opportunity — effectively competing away any initial market advantage. Instead, companies will have to focus on specific skills that lead either to the creation of intellectual property or the management of production or distribution networks. Dell, for example, outsources most of its manufacturing but retains both key product configuration and sales skills. NVIDIA outsources its semiconductor fabrication and most actual product design to focus on high-performance engineering.
- **Company boundaries blur and reshape constantly** — While in the past companies could succeed or fail based entirely on their own actions, in the future it will not be enough to manage one's own operations. Increasingly, managing the aspirations and evolution of one or more webs of partners surrounding the core enterprise will be necessary for any company to succeed. The definition of where the corporate boundary begins and ends will become much less clear — instead, managers must cope with a constantly evolving corporate organism consisting of the core enterprise, partners, outsourcers, and other service providers.
- **Responsiveness becomes the primary executive priority** — In the past, with managerial response dictated by the often-lengthy time required to receive operational reports, much of the job of management was to focus on incremental improvement of results obtained from prior events. This led to slow decision-making cycles and weak response to changing market conditions. With real-time systems, however, companies can emphasize rapid response and active innovation — influencing events as they occur to improve the corporate outcome. Whether the event is a customer interaction, a production cycle, a design review, or a risk assessment, real-time systems will bring to light new opportunities — and a new approach to management.

CONCLUSION

Like IT advances of the past, real time will bring substantial changes to business processes and outsourcing. It will give access to production data all over the world, ensure transparent collaboration from afar, and compel a new Esperanto among information and process architectures. It will thus enhance "plug and play" with outsourcing providers and reduce risk for businesses seeking outsourcing relationships. The ultimate implications of real time will be no less than a change in the way enterprises focus on specific advantages, identify their boundaries, and respond to events. Hasso's vision of a global SAP is one that draws on the best resources, talent, and innovations in developing and delivering software from any enterprise, anywhere in the world. This will be possible once IT delivers on the promise of real-time outsourcing.

> " The ultimate implications of real time will be no less than a change in the way enterprises focus on specific advantages, identify their boundaries, and respond to events. "

16

Context versus Core in the Real-Time Enterprise

When Geoffrey Moore published Crossing the Chasm, he changed the way the high-tech industry thought about itself. Moore's analysis rang profoundly true not only with senior executives and CTOs, but also with field sales staff who encountered roadblocks they didn't fully understand. Moore pointed out that the way that technology was presented and sold to innovators and early adopters, who were obsessed with functionality and willing to tolerate substantial risk, absolutely horrified the early majority, who were risk-averse and looking for proven solutions. The chasm is the distance between these two groups that every high-tech company has to learn to navigate on its way to success. Moore is now focusing on how large organizations can overcome the inertia that holds them back. As it turns out, Moore's analytical tools, the concepts of core versus context activities, are directly applicable to the real-time enterprise.

Geoffrey Moore

The real-time enterprise is a goal that we continually move closer to without ever achieving. In every generation, new technology comes forward and spawns innovative ways of doing business. New technology expands the domain of automation and increases outsourcing. As companies become more efficient and focused on creating value, the gap between what we can imagine our businesses can do and what they can actually do becomes smaller.

Of course, our imaginations are more powerful than our ability to execute. We will always have a gap. The full-blown real-time enterprise will stay just out of our reach. But it is important to note that today, because of the massive proliferation of technology, the nature of the gap between the possible and the actual has changed.

> " *Now, the barrier to the real-time enterprise is understanding how to put all of this power to use to the fullest.* "

In the past, cost and latency constrained the real-time goal. We could not afford a real-time enterprise nor could we move fast enough to achieve it. We did not have ready-made technology available to solve the next set of problems in our way. When companies did solve the problems, they did so by building the needed technology.

Today, technological constraints are less of a problem. We are awash in computing power in every corner of the corporation. Technologies such as wireless and broadband connect a mature suite of tools and enterprise applications. We have huge computing platforms and massive storage capabilities.

It is more technology than we can really absorb. Now, the barrier to the real-time enterprise is understanding how to put all of this power to use to the fullest. We need to make each of the modules more articulate and more vertical, that is, more tailored to problems in a particular industry. The architecture works end-to-end, but how much of that architecture is actually assisting our processes throughout? Can we get the right architecture out of our imaginations and into reality?

So the real-time enterprise is about getting real — taking thoughts and visions, and making them real. It is about realizing the capabilities we already possess in current technology. In theory, the real-time enterprise already exists, but in practice we are not there yet. Getting closer to the vision — closing the gap — is the challenge going forward.

CORE VERSUS CONTEXT

In my earlier work, I outlined a path for the successful growth of high-tech companies in which the key to success was learning to "cross the chasm" between different types of customers. My fundamental point was that each segment of customers along the technology adoption curve has different interests and motivations. To successfully move a product from the new thing to the low-risk choice, companies had to speak differently and take their products to market in a whole new way, but they didn't realize it. The warm welcome that early adopters offered to explanations of advanced functionality provoked hostile reactions from the early majority who wanted to reduce risk and solve common problems.

Now my research and consulting is focused on helping companies overcome the inertia that afflicts large organizations. My latest book, *Living on the Fault Line* (HarperBusiness 2002), uses the concept of core versus context activities to attack this problem. The book examines a variety of questions:

- Why is change so difficult?
- How can stock price be used as a barometer of success?
- What natural forces increase inertia and how can they be combated?

In a nutshell, core activities increase a company's sustainable competitive advantage. Core activities create value for customers in a way that is hard for competitors to replicate and by doing so increase the market power of the company. Investors notice and reward the company with a higher stock price.

In today's market, core doesn't stay core for very long as competitors copy successful companies. At one point a web site to distribute marketing information was a core activity. Now it is a context activity, a basic requirement that does not differentiate a company.

Political factors also drive context to encroach on core. Everyone wants to feel important, meaning to feel like core, even though his or her activities might more reasonably be considered context. In most organizations, context activities compete with core activities for resources, and when context activities win, the company loses.

My recommendation is that companies never lose sight of the distinction between core and context. Invest as much as possible in core activities. Seek to reduce costs and outsource context activities. If you have to cut spending in a downturn, don't do it across the board, cutting core and context by equal measures. Instead, seek to actually increase your investment in core while making even more drastic cuts in context to achieve the total cost-reduction goal.

In my book, I describe in detail the nature of competitive advantage and its impact on technology adoption, management practices, and corporate culture. In this article, I want to focus on how core versus context applies in the struggle to create the real-time enterprise.

INNOVATION THROUGH INTEGRATION

The challenge today is overcoming the historical notion that competitive advantage rests in creating new technology. That used to be the case. To make dramatic advances and create new core activities, new technology was required. But as companies become more successful, as their earlier generations of products become standard infrastructure, the challenge shifts to one of orchestration and integration. The key question now becomes how we can achieve the real-time enterprise by taking advantage of current technology rather than by inventing new technology.

This concept is new for Silicon Valley. Unlike past generations of technology, today IT in and of itself is no longer a differentiator — what differentiates a business is its application of IT.

By nature, innovation darts around. In the 1980s and 1990s, categorical, technological innovation was the focus, massively symbolized by the PC, relational database, client/server, dot-com, and Internet booms. In this decade, however, that form of innovation is temporarily on the shelf while we exhaust the possibilities at hand. Today, the action is in application innovation and process innovation working hand in hand. As the application becomes more articulate, the process can become more articulate — it's a coevolution.

> " " *IT in and of itself is no longer a differentiator — what differentiates a business is its application of IT.* " "

- For example, Dell takes the same technology everybody else has and dramatically creates competitive advantage on top of it. Dell does not have a secret software module hidden in a mountain; it simply has a much more articulate, refined version of every module. In addition, Dell has a business process and a business discipline that is extremely well aligned with its technical systems. Dell's advantage lies in the way it rethinks its business processes.

- Wal-Mart is another example of a business successfully focusing on core. As a retailer, it is not necessarily very imaginative, but when it comes to the myriads of details, the little things, the company is so precise and thoughtful. Wal-Mart has used IT to impose a discipline. As a result, it has more than 30 percent of the retail market.

It will be exciting to watch industries, from government services to document-driven services, experience this approach. Real estate is about to get reengineered. Medical recordkeeping is about to get reengineered. Of course, these are huge, decade-long challenges, but they won't require better networks or better computers.

HOW CAN THE REST OF US GET THERE?

The important question here is "What about the rest of us?" Focusing on large, successful companies is like being in a class with Albert Einstein and watching your grading curve. Albert's grade, along with Dell's and Wal-Mart's, is 27 sigmas off to the right. And then there's you.

We are not all Albert Einsteins. We are not all gifted seers. However, a lot of us are pretty good at being fast followers. Help is available from software companies, service providers, and outsourcing companies that help manage change and take context off our hands.

The agenda for improvement is pretty well understood at most companies. The challenge is in overcoming the cultural changes and the ensuing business process changes. Generally, the to-do list is so long that it can't all be done. Realistically, only a few changes of any significance can be accomplished. Here the core versus context distinction becomes phenomenally important. Any company can change some number of processes, but the budget is tight. It's a horrible mistake to spend the budget changing a process that isn't core. It will send a company to the back of the line.

SAP was the first company to convince the world that if an area is not core, it should be automated by the best vendor solution available. For context, change your process, not the program. Don't modify the code. Don't invest in expensive customizations in context areas. Just swallow the application as delivered. For core, you want to change the program.

Enterprise applications make managing context a commodity. They level the playing field. If a company buys SAP, they are at parity with the marketplace for everything except core. That's a phenomenal gift. It sweeps context off the table and provides the room to let companies be inventive about defining core. The key is merging the capabilities of the software with new business processes and the zeal to do better.

Of course, it's easy to lurch too far in the direction of core. When a company becomes successful because of core activities, competitors seek to imitate the core practices, eventually turning core into context. As a company grows, it invents more and more core over the years. The ability to invent more core and stay ahead of competitors is the fundamental engine of growth.

Somewhere along the line, as a company becomes bigger and more successful, the problem is overwhelmingly one of inventing new ways of managing context, not core. Large mature companies experience this problem. How can they squeeze resources from context and repurpose them for core? The largest companies will require a decade to address this problem.

> " *Perhaps the best way to define the real-time enterprise is one in which the investment of resources is balanced properly between core and context in a program of continuous innovation in core areas and methodical outsourcing of context areas.* "

Core versus context helps clear up these problems and establish priorities for companies of all sizes. Too much time on context means that your competitive advantage disappears. Too much time on core means that context will grow out of control because of natural forces. Perhaps the best way to define the real-time enterprise is one in which the investment of resources is balanced properly between core and context in a program of continuous innovation in core areas and methodical outsourcing of context areas.

STRATEGY AND CULTURE

Most large organizations can come up with a strategy to focus on core activities but lack the ability to execute. Context gets in the way. Even when the CEO and the executive board are totally committed, massive legacy inertia is still almost impossible to overcome.

When we at TCG Advisors work on developing new strategies, we engage the senior executives, and we all get very crisp about the new direction. We look at what parts of a business process enable the core and how to extract resources from processes that are no longer core. What we find is that businesses are happy to assign people to the new core but are reluctant to take money away from the old processes. This is a losing proposition: if the inertia in context is not reduced, the change management problem cannot be solved.

Reengineering is key to reducing context. When this idea was introduced in the early 1990s, it got off to a very bad start. It was introduced in a way that was extremely offensive to corporations. One of the key barriers to managing context is the enormous cultural anxieties around this problem. People associate security with not changing, but the paradox is that the only true security actually lies in change, specifically in changing ahead of the curve. That's a hard concept for individuals, and especially groups, to absorb.

THE PEOPLE FACTOR

Moore points out that changes in IT systems and business processes are inextricably linked to changes in corporate culture. This thought is echoed by Michael Hammer in Chapter 10 and by Esther Dyson in Chapter 27. Moore sees corporate cultures as typically wedded to the status quo and essentially opposed to the kinds of changes that technology often makes possible. Hammer's take is that both front-line jobs and those of managers are inevitably redefined by the needs of what he calls the "process environment." For Dyson, a renewed sense of corporate culture can, with help from technology that supports core competencies, provide a sustainable competitive advantage. Technology, she writes, will come to life only with the right social and cultural underpinnings.

In the old traditional organizational structure, particularly in the bureaucratic command and control structure, an enormous number of resources are needed just to make the processes work inside of the corporation. Ideally, in mature markets you'd like to have more and more of resources at the surface of the corporation where they can interact with the marketplace and with customers, partners, competitors, and suppliers. You'd like to have a Southwest Airlines type of organization, where the company has enabled a high percentage of employees to actually touch the customer. In effect, such organizations have more nerve cells at the nerve endings. By contrast, their competitors tie up a lot of these same resources just making connections within their own organizations.

> " People associate security with not changing, but the paradox is that the only true security actually lies in change . . . "

Technologies have also enabled little organizations, like TCG Advisors, to be much more powerful. A handful of people have an enormous effect because technology takes care of so much context, allowing time to be spent on core. In a bigger enterprise, it's a bigger challenge, but in a smaller enterprise it's unbelievable how much more powerful a company can be than when I started in 1978.

TECHNOLOGY ADOPTION AND THE DOT-COM HANGOVER

One of the most significant barriers to the real-time enterprise is the memory of the irrational expectations of the dot-com area. Remember how the Internet was going to revolutionize the supply chain? We heard promises of a world in which enormous non-value–adding costs were removed, latency would disappear, and visibility would extend from end to end. The just-in-time process would start with the customer order and flow through every crevice of the supply chain. Similar visions were put forth in many other areas.

In fact, nothing was wrong with any of those ideas except the time-frame. To make those visions a reality requires hundreds of companies to make thousands of process changes. The companies can't do it on their own. Companies like SAP will add the required functionality to enterprise applications, which will be implemented, which will enable the required process changes. This takes years and years of just plain old hard work.

There are of course huge rewards for getting there first. Maybe a dozen companies are at the state of the art for the real-time enterprise today. Perhaps 100 companies are making good progress, and 1,000 more are piloting some aspect. But that leaves ten of thousands of companies at the starting line. There is so much to gain by just getting those companies onto at least the first stair of this staircase. Smart CEOs won't let the memory of hype get in the way of progress.

Smart CIOs will make sure that they are preparing for the changes ahead at an architectural level. Web services have opened the door to service-oriented architectures, but, again, laying the groundwork and building the skills is going to take years of work.

What service-oriented architectures do in the short term is allow more business process flexibility, and that's particularly important for core. It is a way to add capabilities that will differentiate and add to core on top of the powerful enterprise applications that more or less take care of the context, and that's exciting.

In the long term, service-oriented architectures will provide the basic plumbing that will enable dramatic transformations in the supply chain and elsewhere.

HOW WILL WE KNOW WHEN WE GET THERE?

While the real-time enterprise will always be out of reach, and will be defined afresh by each generation of IT professionals, we can look at a few metrics for our progress. Real-time companies will be able to:

- Dramatically reduce the time from idea to product to half or less of what it takes today
- Respond intelligently to requests from customers for services that combine many different services from a company

- Remember customers as they are transferred from one part of the company to another
- Respond to the customer with pertinent information in real time

> " We will never finish the job of creating the real-time enterprise. We know that. But right now, we should start the job and not wait around. "

These capabilities show only the most visible aspects of the real-time enterprise. We will never finish the job of creating the real-time enterprise. We know that. But right now, we should start the job and not wait around. There is more to be gained by just turning the cranks in front of us than by waiting to install a new set of wheels.

17

The Networked Enterprise

Hubert Österle is the director of the Institute of Information Management at the University of St. Gallen, where he has taught since 1980. A frequent speaker and author on information management, business engineering, and process and system development, he is also founder and president of The Information Management Group (IMG).

Hubert Österle

N etworking is the lifeblood of the real-time enterprise. This chapter describes where the networked enterprise is going and the roadblocks to getting there. Before we examine the dynamics of today's networked economy, it's worthwhile to trace the evolution of the real-time enterprise to get a deeper understanding of the underlying mechanisms.

BEFORE THE NETWORKED ENTERPRISE

In 1967, Peter Mertens published a book on intercompany collaboration and integration. In 1969, I was part of a group of students at the newly founded University of Linz in Austria. We were mesmerized by Mertens' vision of integrated data processing (Mertens 1966). At the time, the concept was based on file exchange and batch processing.

In 1974, as an employee of IBM Germany, I was asked whether a particular financial accounting software package might have a chance on the open market. The vision was that each employee and program in a company would have real-time access to data entered by any employee. The solution ran on a database, but due to performance issues would probably not be used for business. This solution was an application developed by Hasso Plattner and the other founders of SAP.

In 1984, August-Wilhelm Scheer published a groundbreaking book (Scheer 1984). He described a data model for an integrated manufacturing company, a model that influenced database integration research not only at universities but also development in many corporations.

In 1986, Getzner Textil AG, a leading European textile manufacturer with 800 employees, evaluated a new software solution for business processes. The goal was to enter data once and allow every employee and program to access real-time, consistent data. Getzner chose SAP® R/2®, although the related hosting and software costs were at the limit of the possible for that midsize enterprise. Years later, Getzner calls that decision a key to its business success as a textile mill in a high-wage country.

In 1989, Professor Beat Schmid at the Institute for Business Information Systems at the University of St. Gallen in Switzerland founded the Electronic Market Competency Center. Research focused on intercompany collaboration across the rising Internet. In 1995, as part of a research visit to SAP's research lab in Silicon Valley, I had the opportunity to discuss intercompany processes with Hasso Plattner. Encouraged by similar visions, we created a business networking research area at the Institute, and, at The Information Management Group, we started implementing these ideas through seamless processes in and among companies.

In 1997, at SAP's 25th anniversary celebration, Plattner declared that the company had been following the vision of real time ever since its founding and that it would continue to do so.

The Internet hype of the late 1990s highlighted the enormous potential for connecting companies. The bursting of the dot-com bubble showed that the wired economy couldn't develop in a big bang, but rather incrementally, using sound business and economic decisions, which Plattner emphasized all along during the dot-com era.

The networked company is a fascinating vision for technologists, but is it also a prudent business goal? What is networking and what can it bring to a company?

AUTOMATION

The first goal of computerization was automation, with computers replacing human labor for highly repetitive tasks. Using programs for billing, payroll, and warehouse management lowered personnel costs.

The programs could read huge amounts of data and produced huge amounts of data. Data exchange was via punch cards and magnetic tapes. The user interface consisted of forms and printouts. Computers provided processing capacity, replacing manual labor.

Visionaries such as Mertens saw the potential of electronic data exchange between programs and dreamed of a network of programs, but turning that vision into reality was difficult with the limited tools at the time.

DATABASE INTEGRATION

Magnetic drives brought about a breakthrough, enabling real-time data exchange between programs via databases. At the same time, CRT terminals resulted in a quantum leap in usability. The prerequisites were in place to ensure that every program and every workstation had immediate access to all company data entered in the system, and that the data was consistent, providing, of course, that the programs used the same data model. Database integration was coming, but it took almost 20 years from the time of the first trials at the end of the 1960s to widespread use in the mid-1980s.

Integrated applications reduced or eliminated duplicate entries. Using the system for receiving goods, for example, a company could not only enter the quantity stored, but also automatically update financial accounting information with the value of the quantity stored, based on the prices in the supplier contract.

Such integrated applications also accelerated processes. Accounting could immediately report on the value basis of the quantity stored and more quickly assemble a balance sheet. Product cost planning could access the current average delivered price in real time. Getzner Textil AG was able to realize its vision of real-time order confirmation. When a customer requests a price and delivery date for an order of 5000 meters of fabric, the employee can answer the question while the customer is still on the phone. SAP® R/3® provides access to the availability of raw materials and starting materials, delivery times for starting materials, capacities of weaving machines, current cost data, and finally the conditions for that specific customer. Getzner can lower costs and, more importantly, provide faster service for customers, which is essential in the fast-paced textile world. This is a competitive advantage as long as the competition cannot match this service level. Once they can, this level of service becomes a requirement for all competitors to meet customer expectations.

Integrated processes and the underlying applications require formalization and standardization. By formalization, I mean that procedures and workflows, such as customer-specific rebates, must be described in such a way that they take all possibilities into account. Formalizing therefore means modeling business reality in data and program functions. Prerequisite for interaction of programs is not only having a formal description of the world. In addition, all involved systems must speak the same language, that is, use the same model of the real world.

In the 1970s and 1980s, many companies invested in company-wide data models designed to create company-specific formalization and standardization. Unfortunately, the resources required to construct a prototype, particularly for realization of a company-wide application system, on the one hand and political barriers on the other impeded the realization of this vision.

STANDARDS TIME

Information technology's essential goal is to model, or describe, the world or some piece of it: a document, the sound of a pop song, a complete business process. But only by adhering to standard elements — standard data formats, standard communications protocols, and standard interfaces — can these models be shared effectively and without loss of meaning. Indeed, in a world where such notions as collaboration, partnering, and integration are increasingly important, so are all forms of IT standards. Österle sees standard data and message formats helping companies to integrate their applications and processes across the Web. In Chapter 4, August-Wilhelm Scheer argues that standardized data models are crucial to helping decentralized enterprises make sense of their disparate databases. Along similar lines, Anil Kumar writes in Chapter 15 that the push for real-time IT will inevitably drive standardization within companies and across the IT landscape. Further discussion of the importance of standards shows up in Kumar's look at the growing use of outsourcing.

It took independent software houses, such as SAP, Baan, and J.D. Edwards, to help companies implement company-specific, seamless processes. Their software mapped more and more functional areas of a company using a generic model.

Integrated applications triggered the wave of business process redesign in the 1990s. When employees and programs can access real-time data anytime anywhere, many former restrictions on processes cease to apply. For example, when processing an automobile insurance claim, every employee at any location can access the customer's policy, the accident report, and the cost estimate from the garage. The largest benefits of integration lie in new processes, reduction of required tasks, improved use of capacity (for example, of call centers), accelerated claims processing, and new services for the customer. The goal is to create a seamless process where data processing causes no delays in business and where data is never manually reentered.

Executives at companies that have implemented processes based on integrated applications often emphasize that the value of software such as SAP R/3 lies in standardization and execution of processes in the company, particularly for companies with a global presence.

INTERNET-BASED COLLABORATION

Internet-based collaboration is the next level beyond database integration. For interenterprise communications, Internet-based collaboration is about loose coupling rather than complete integration. The attraction for Internet-based collaboration is obvious. The Internet is a cost-effective, global network, and the browser allows interaction with innumerable programs through one device (for example, a laptop, cell phone, or PDA), as long as the program uses HTML or XML.

As we discussed, seamless integration within a company has yet to be fully realized. The need for integration is only increasing due to mergers and acquisitions and process integration. However, the most immediate improvements have been realized in many areas. If you compare continued incremental intracompany improvements with the potential for intercompany processes, intercompany processes offer far greater untapped potential. Except for a few areas, such as electronic payment, we are, in spite of 20 years of Electronic Data Interchange (EDI) and 10 years of business Internet usage, still very much at the beginning.

Internet collaboration takes several forms, including portals, messaging systems such as EDI and XML, eServices, and Internet marketplaces or exchanges. I discuss each of these in more detail in the following sections.

PORTALS

The most common form of collaboration between companies, or between companies and consumers, is through a portal, a human-to-machine interface. The fact that a company has a web site describing the company and its products goes without saying. In addition to a simple marketing presence, many companies offer numerous services through their portals (IWI St. Gallen/Tuck School Dartmouth 2003; IMG *Web-based Customer* 2003; IMG *SAP Portals* 2003). Consider these examples:

- Dow Corning, the world's leading silicon manufacturer, provides self-service ordering of commodity products through its Xiameter.com portal, saving process costs, which Dow then passes onto the customer in the form of a 15 percent discount.
- RAG Coal International uses a portal to coordinate its transport chain from the coal mines to the ports to cargo ships on the canals, and from the train to the coal power plant. The simple portal replaces time-consuming, problem-prone communication via fax or telephone for the numerous transportation companies involved.
- Through a portal, international light manufacturer Zumtobel Staff offers its agents — distributors located in various countries without their own sales organizations — their own specific price list, product catalog, reference projects, and the ability to order products. Zumtobel Staff makes sales easier for these distributors and more closely connects them to the processes at headquarters.
- ABB Turbo Systems supports over 70 service stations around the world in maintaining marine diesels. A database with 180,000 ship-specific configured turbochargers helps service stations schedule required maintenance, find replacement parts, access technical drawings and installation guides, and search for the closest warehouse with the required parts. Its portal also identifies opportunities for selling replacement parts and additional business. The portal did not require much additional functionality. Instead, it extended in-house IT functionality to the service stations. Previously, only employees at headquarters had access to these capabilities.

Portals enable many other forms of intercompany processes (for examples, see Green 2003), including collaborative product development at Mattel, coordination of construction workers at Bovis Lend

Lease, package tracking at UPS, freight exchange at Landstar, configuration of automobiles at BMW, and supply chain management at Whirlpool. In the consumer world, we have long used Internet search engines, electronic banking, travel booking, and purchase of standardized articles, such as books or CDs. Over 100 million people have access to the Internet through a portal, which makes portals an established technology, but intercompany applications offer huge untapped potential (IWI St. Gallen/IMG 2003).

More so than telephones and faxes, Internet portals have dissolved the boundaries between companies. Business partners no longer need to communicate through expensive employees. Instead, portals provide 24/7 access to a very well-informed and reliable computer. Thus, business partners are included in processes just like internal employees. The benefit of a portal lies in the instantaneous transport of data and documents (such as product catalogs or CAD drawings) at a very low cost, transfer of process steps (such as the creation of an order by the business partner rather than an employee), consistent information for all involved in the collaboration process, and, last but not least, convenience for the customer.

> " *Over 100 million people have access to the Internet through a portal, which makes portals an established technology, but intercompany applications offer huge untapped potential.* "

Pure-play consumer-oriented portals, such as eBay and Expedia, have largely disappeared (except, of course, for the two just mentioned) or been acquired by companies such as banks, travel agencies, publishing houses, and the like.

On the surface, portals can be seen as a new type of user interface that unifies access to various programs at a low cost. Their more substantial potential includes business-to-business integration, exchanging information between applications, and offering additional functions, such as authorization and security.

EDI AND XML

Electronic Data Interchange (EDI) based on standard EDIFACT messages is machine-to-machine communication focusing on the processing of transactions between companies, such as offers, orders, invoices, and so on. High investment and operating costs in the pre-Internet era precluded wide use of EDI and limited its use to large corporations and their suppliers. Easier, cheaper network access through the Internet, XML's flexible exchange format, and the availability of standard software with XML interfaces are accelerating data exchange between applications across company boundaries (IWI St. Gallen/Tuck School Dartmouth 2003).

- L'Oreal is driving vendor-managed inventory for its corporate customer, German drugstore chain DM-Drogerie Market. L'Oreal handles the inventory of its products at DM, providing sales figures and sales forecasts using web-based EDI. Using this service, DM-Drogerie Market reduced its inventory by 30 percent, and L'Oreal improved the customer relationship.
- SIG Combibloc, a leading manufacturer of packaging for the beverage industry, implemented a Collaborative Planning Forecasting and Replenishment (CPFR) solution with Coca-Cola. Here, XML messages are exchanged between the Enterprise Resource Planning (ERP) systems at Coca-Cola, SIG Combibloc, and their supplier. Data exchanged includes sales forecasts, current inventory, and orders. This system allowed SIG Combibloc to reduce inventory, improve its service level, and reduce process costs in production planning.
- Brose, a global automobile supplier for power windows and seat adjusters, reorganized the request process between its procurement, product development, and production departments and its suppliers. This reduces workflow time and helps avoid unnecessary process loops. In contrast to the previous examples, Brose primarily exchanges documents, such as requests and supplier contracts, rather than transaction data. These documents are then integrated in Brose's ERP system, SAP R/3.

Besides some specialized areas such as electronic payment between banks, message-based collaboration between applications, particularly between applications at different companies, is still in its infancy. In the ideal situation, messaging will eventually replace database access and the network of database management systems, as described by SAP in its Enterprise Services Architecture, discussed in more detail in Chapter 25. However, we are not there yet. Currently unsolvable problems in assuring data consistency as well as the substandard performance of today's networks cannot yet match the reply times within ERP systems.

At the SAP Analyst Summit 2003, SAP Executive Board member Peter Zencke illustrated SAP's vision of the networked company using the example of an extended order fulfillment process. In this example, a company can receive an order through various channels, from portal to EDIFACT; split it into separate items; decide on shipment from the warehouse, production, or a supplier; and create all invoices for each part. In the extreme case, order fulfillment is replaced by a set of independent item fulfillments and the business object "Order" is relevant only for tasks such as a credit check or order-specific rebates. More importantly, order processing is handled only by the relevant ERP systems seamlessly without human intervention.

Such cross-company processes are a long-term goal that can be realized only in small steps. More serious than the performance barrier is the lack of standardized direct communication between applications.

Consider a seemingly simple integration problem at a Swiss engineering company that delivers machines to Malaysia. The customer in Malaysia maintains the equipment and needs replacement parts. The company can order parts from the Swiss manufacturer or from a number of cheaper Chinese manufacturers. Before the Malaysian company can decide based on all aspects, such as guarantees, it needs a cost comparison. It first uses the Swiss manufacturer's maintenance por-

> " More serious than the performance barrier is the lack of standardized direct communication between applications. "

tal to identify the parts needed. The Swiss company doesn't necessarily manufacture the part but may instead procure it from a supplier, which offers multiple variants of the part. For the correct price, the sales system at the Swiss manufacturer accesses, in real time, the product database at the supplier and offers the customer in Malaysia all the variants with pricing. Because transportation costs between Switzerland and Malaysia often cost more than the part itself, the customer needs a detailed offer including transportation costs. The sales system determines the costs for various transportation methods using an eService (described later in this chapter) and completes the replacement part offer for the customer.

From a technical point of view, it is not difficult to convert customer requests to XML messages and to receive XML messages with prices from suppliers. Even response times are fairly good. What is difficult is the semantics behind the messages. For example, the manufacturer's

ERP system may store shipping costs as "costs including insurance and customs processing" while the transportation company's system may store shipping costs as "costs without insurance and customs processing." Related but unstructured information such as restrictions on the use of alternative replacement parts is difficult to exchange; it would require a large amount of programming. XML and EDIFACT clarify only data formats and simple broad content questions; the programs, the processes, and the legal and contractual requirements determine the semantics. Figure 17-1 illustrates the integration that can be achieved when a common semantic model is in place.

It is easier but still challenging when both sides of the communication exchange use the same software. For example, a company with multiple production and sales locations uses SAP software exclusively. We already see numerous companies with end-to-end logistical or financial processes, across several organizational units. Prerequisite here is that the applications involved use the same master data and very similar customizations. This is why many companies are running projects to harmonize processes, software infrastructure, and data models.

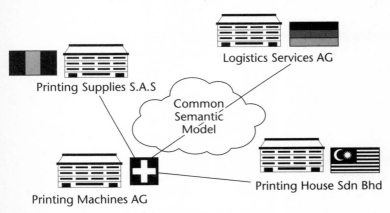

Figure 17-1. Integration with a Common Semantic Model

Two applications can "talk" only if they are based on the same semantic model. They must not only display data in the same way but interpret it in the same way. The replacement part example shows that network-based application communication still has a long way to go. A study of collaborative processes by the Institute of Information Management at the University of St. Gallen (Senger 2004) indicates that currently, in America as well as in Europe, only simple forms of message-based machine-to-machine communication are being implemented.

Compared to pure machine-to-machine message exchange, portals are much more successful because a human, who understands both ends of the communication, is the interface.

ESERVICES

An eService is a widely automated service that can be used by any application or process. Some use this term to mean reusable program components (web services, modules, and software components). Others use this term to refer to whole corporations that provide their service almost exclusively electronically. Others dream of a LEGO-style economy in which companies can create processes using off-the-shelf eServices. Slowly but surely, new forms of the division of labor are beginning to establish themselves in business. Here are a few examples.

- With its eService eScore, InFoScore offers a payment solution that can process all current payment methods for online shops, such as schlecker.com or myToys.de. eScore supports dealers by performing customer credit checks, handling the payment processing, and, if necessary, collection. PayPal is a similar service with 8.5 million private accounts and 2.1 million business accounts. PayPal processes 70,000 transactions per day; it was acquired by eBay at the end of 2002.
- Based in Wolfurt, Austria, inet-logistics handles tasks such as selecting the cheapest shipping method and transportation company, processing the transport order with the transportation company, customs, and monitoring delivery right through paying for transportation. In effect, inet-logistics handles all the details of order processing, which is something medium-sized businesses in particular need help with due to lower volumes (Reichmayr 2003).

- Using North American mailing addresses, MapPoint.net calculates geographic information, searches for local addresses, calculates distances, and also provides other services. ptv.de offers similar services for transportation, mobility, and logistics in Germany. In both cases, this is a new type of service, made possible by Global Positioning Systems (GPS), geographic digitization, and the global network.
- SINFOS is a master data service for retailers and their suppliers. About 1,100 suppliers and 100 retailers as well as market analysts and logisticians use this service to publish data for all their products. Market stakeholders can view and search for 280,000 items by European Article Number (EAN). The manufacturers involved therefore no longer need to send changes in product data to all customers in different forms. Retailers can access all data in one format using one process.

eServices (see Figure 17-2) outsource single tasks from business processes. Companies that provide eServices have deep, specialized knowledge and an economy of scale. Network tasks like message transfer or directory service have a central role. Many of these services communicate machine-to-machine and will be an integral part of the application world and the customer's processes, which is why this is also called "silent commerce." eServices — in particular network services — allow many-to-many relationships from the user's point of view.

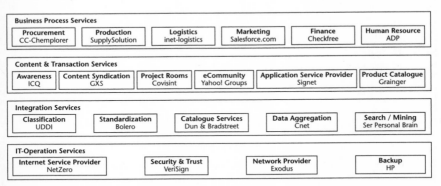

Figure 17-2. Business Collaboration Infrastructure

The technical implementation of eServices is less critical for success than one would think. Few today use standards such as UDDI, .NET, RosettaNet, ebXML, and SOAP. More important than the technical implementation is the relative adoption of the service by the market. From a technical standpoint, the customer is mainly concerned with minimizing any future conversion costs when selecting a solution and therefore attempts to choose the market leader to avoid such costs.

eServices produce network effects and tend toward monopolies, similar to telephone networks. That is why the companies that offer large networks are fighting for dominance. Services such as PayPal from eBay, PayDirect from Yahoo!, and MSN Bill Pay are fighting to be the standard for payment. In the race for largest authentication service, Microsoft .NET Passport, the Liberty Alliance (consortium of over 100 companies), and ScreenName from AOL are fighting for first place in the portals of the Internet.

eServices help businesses with a particular but important task, and the eService provides it faster and cheaper than they can themselves. Further, such solutions are often better than any individual solution, particularly because they have critical mass in the marketplace and simplify the lives of end users. In the case of authentication services, for example, individual solutions cannot possibly handle the task. We can expect to see an explosion in growth in a new service industry,

> " eServices help businesses with a particular but important task, and the eService provides it faster and cheaper than they can themselves. "

which over the next few years will grow faster than the software industry and will eventually have a higher market value.

In spite of this euphoric estimation, we must be cautious about illusions. Besides the fact that a long, drawn-out battle around the monopoly position will massively hinder development, the problem of semantic integration, as described above, remains. eServices are successful as long as they are seen by users as network services that cannot be done without, or services that cover small tasks with simple semantics and accepted standards (such as the classic payment form, credit card payment, directory assistance, and so on). Over the long term (more than 20 years), eServices will not replace large areas of business process software, ERP components. The LEGO economy will remain an illusion due to the unsolved problem of generally accepted and valid semantics, even though it has been brought up and disappeared since the beginning of business computing again and again at regular intervals and under different names. Examples are modularization and the abstraction of data types in the 1970s, object orientation and artificial intelligence in the 1980s, the middleware and service architectures of the 1990s, and now the web services of the current decade.

EXCHANGES

Electronic marketplaces are the highest form of network services, at least in terms of their potential. They allow collaboration between an unlimited number of companies, perfect the market economy by creating total transparence of all products and services, offer dynamic sourcing with dynamic prices, and process transactions as efficiently as within a company. This ideal form, in the year 2000, saw 6,000 marketplaces designed for all kinds of industries and uses. In 2003, only a few remain, and their original vision has been reduced considerably.

As an auction house for new and used consumer goods, eBay is the ideal type of electronic marketplace. Electronic stock exchanges, Transplace as a freight exchange, GNX as an industrial procurement marketplace from the 1980s, and WorldWide Retail Exchange (WWRE) as a retailer marketplace are other examples of marketplaces that like eBay balance supply and demand.

Most marketplaces have changed from an emporium to an exchange that supports business operations between businesses:

- Chemical specialist Degussa uses the industry marketplace Elemica to improve its relationships with customer, such as those in the tire industry. Elemica does not offer auction functions or buying aggregation. Instead it sees itself primarily as a neutral infrastructure for transferring, validating, and transforming business messages. Elemica supports data and process standards for supply chain functions and offers transport optimization and order monitoring services through integration with logistics partners. For Degussa, the partner integration on a central platform provides enormous cost savings compared to previous point-to-point ERP connections.

- In 2001 DaimlerChrysler, Ford, General Motors, Nissan, Renault, Commerce One, and Oracle founded Covisint as a platform for collaborative product development, procurement, and supply chain management. The automobile manufacturers in this marketplace benefit less from new suppliers or lower prices; they gain primarily from more efficient processes between the involved parties. But, as some players in this value chain see their cooperative processes as a competitive instrument, the future of Covisint is unknown, despite participation from large automobile manufacturers.
- click2procure, Siemens' procurement marketplace, is a "private marketplace," which Siemens has opened to third parties for buying and selling products.
- Bolero.net is an exchange for secure electronic transmission of international trade documents. Bolero.net is both a standardization body and a trusted third party. It is both an infrastructure and a service provider for those involved in the trade process, including importers, exporters, transportation companies, banks, insurance companies, and government bodies. Bolero.net's Business Collaboration Infrastructure (BCI) allows many-to-many relationships between parties across the entire global trade chain. Otto (GmbH & Co KG), the world's largest mail-order company, was the first important customer to begin using Bolero.net in September 2001.
- TollCollect is primarily an infrastructure for processing highway tolls but can also be understood as the beginning of an IT infrastructure for mobility in Europe. This infrastructure could aggregate numerous disparate services, such as GPS via Galileo (the European navigation satellite system), geographic information services, and traffic control systems.

Marketplaces with auctions in the sense of exchanges are limited to commodities in a few areas. Exchanges in the sense of a business collaboration infrastructure for limited value chains build an infrastructure consisting of legal and organizational regulations (such as the Rulebook from Bolero), data standards (such as ebXML or boleroXML), and process standards (such as SURF for secure payments with Bolero) as well as eServices (such as secure data exchange, the Title Registry from Bolero for maritime freight bills of lading with rights and responsibilities, supply chain visibility, or credit checks). Such marketplaces will become the business bus for specific value chains, define or implement standards, handle tasks (such as transport, routing of messages, and currency conversions), and provide additional services, such as partner directories and product catalogs.

Exchanges turn one-to-one and one-to-many relationships into many-to-many relationships. Numerous companies are already feeling pressure from powerful customers. A small or midsize automobile supplier is forced to adhere to the procurement process of every automobile manufacturer, which means they must understand and handle numerous supply and delivery processes. This results in high costs, complexity, and dependence. For these companies, exchanges become an important tool.

While eServices tend toward monopolies, marketplaces do this even more so. The movement of power structures to the value chain causes enormous resistance to the potential losers who develop counterstrategies. This slows the realization of marketplaces and exchanges. Big players in the value chains therefore attempt mergers and acquisitions and other forms of power consolidation to build market share, which they can use to push their standards and their solutions. You can get an idea of the possible development by looking at the history of stock exchanges and the shakeout of the securities business, the airline industry, travel reservations, and so on.

In certain areas, such as flight booking systems and stock exchanges, we already have functional, economical marketplaces, often consortiums of the most important players in the market. In other areas, we may need to wait as long as three decades when we compare the development of intracompany networking integration in the 1970s and 1980s. And intracompany integration is actually politically easier, because companies often have a central power with the ability to push through and drive internal company standards. We must take into account that exchanges change the market and the structures are just growing today.

THE REAL-WORLD CONNECTION

The forms of intercompany networks described thus far simplify processes by making real-time data available on all electronic media to all relevant parties; this data then supports seamless processes. One interface does remain: that between reality and the mapping of the real world in the information system. A human is at work here entering data, observing and classifying reality, and entering it in the computer. Sensors and actuators, mainly in mobile form (transponders, radio frequency identification or RFID tags, and intelligent devices such as GPS receivers), are taking over for humans for primary data entry (Fleisch

2001). They reduce process costs, accelerate processes to real time, and work more reliably. What applies to sensors for data entry also applies to actuators when accessing the real world (such as heating regulators and traffic light controls).

- An international semiconductor manufacturer uses a RFID system to track boxes for internal logistics and achieves complete transparency of stock and transport activities. It uses real-time asset and transport information for production control as well for identification of potential shortages.
- Volkswagen is using RFID tags to identify and pinpoint new cars in delivery parking lots.
- Frankfurt Airport is equipping 22,000 fire shutters with RFID chips that are monitored and maintained via PDAs (see Chapter 14 for details). The installation enables Frankfurt Airport not only to comply with new legislative requirements but also to run more efficient processes that reduce costs by as much as €100,000 annually (Spindler 2003).
- A chip manufacturer in Dresden procures temperature-sensitive photochemicals from a supplier in Amsterdam. Digital temperature logs in the transport containers continuously record the temperature range, which is read via infrared at the factory (Thede et al. 2001).
- Miele is working on equipping future washing machines to report technical problems to the user and service technician proactively.

Transponders and related technologies have been around for years and are being used, but up until up now were limited to specific uses because of their cost. RFID developments are making these devices and tags available to the mass market at a reasonable cost.

In spite of this, use of new technologies for connection to the real world are locally limited and in pilot projects. Lack of a common infrastructure hinders cross-company collaboration using such devices. IT components, protocols, and processes are not standardized. With RFIDs, for example, some hindrances are technical, such as interference from water or metal or insecure communication channels. High costs for widespread use and user privacy concerns also slow their adoption (Strassner and Schoch 2002).

Companies such as Wal-Mart are driving automatic real-world connections. The U.S. retailer, with 17 percent of the worldwide trade volume, is requiring its top 100 suppliers to use RFID tags on all cartons and pallets by 2005. If the pioneers see the potential for improvement, other companies will follow — indeed they must.

A VISION OF THE NETWORKED CORPORATION

Integration and networking are not implemented in self-interest. Nor are they a toy of technically minded academics or a gigantic cash cow. This latter fallacy became all too apparent to dot-bombs as well as to banks, insurance companies, media companies, and others. It became most apparent to investors during the ebusiness hype. In reality, business and companies are changing too quickly, and each company must prepare itself for this increasing change.

Companies that succeed will tailor their products and services to the people who use them and their individual requirements. Customers want their problems solved quickly, easily, and comprehensively, independent of where they are, how late it is, and how they need to contact the company (see Figure 17-3). Hilti, a construction tool vendor, has analyzed the processes of its customers — the construction industry — and now provides not only screwdrivers and rotary hammers but also complete management of these tools, since building and construction companies usually don't manage administration and maintenance processes for their tools very efficiently.

BUSINESS NETWORK

Networked companies start at the customer process, that is, from the workflow needed to help the customer solve a problem. This process determines which products and services are needed by the customer and which should or must be offered by the supplier. The company creates a network with its suppliers and business partners to buy services that others can perform better and more quickly.

SERVICES

More and more services, such as delivery time requests or troubleshooting, will be available electronically. A process portal, such as SAP® Enterprise Portal, provides real-time, secure access to several internal applications such as pricing, explosion diagrams, and product catalogues as well as to external eServices, such as credit checks, logistics selection, and payment. The portal brings all this together to create a seamless process.

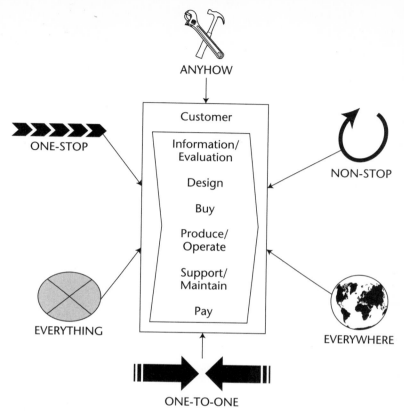

Figure 17-3. Customer–Focused Process

COLLABORATION PROCESSES

The customer relationship in the information age means more than just creating electronic versions of existing forms and following existing processes. Services, such as a supplier managing stock for the customer (vendor-managed inventory) or the control of the supply chain, require process adjustments on both sides. The coordinated activities of the customer and the supplier build a collaborative process (or workflow). Slowly but surely, collaborative processes will begin to replace classic internal processes and make a value chain as manageable as an integrated organization.

PROCESS COMPONENTS

The transformation of ERP processes to collaborative processes is the big challenge for the business engineer over the next few years. Modularization, the move from monolithic software to a services-oriented architecture, is a Herculean task for software engineers at companies like SAP. On the one hand, rethinking customer processes requires a complete ripping apart of functions into modules that can be easily combined. On the other hand, the integration problem still has the restrictions we described earlier in the chapter. Companies such as SAP, Oracle, and Microsoft are often accused

> **" The customer relationship in the information age means more than just creating electronic versions of existing forms and following existing processes. "**

of constructing a monolithic software world that squeezes out competitors. Perhaps more correctly, they are reaching the limits of software development. Integration requires that the modules and services use the same semantics, that is, the same model of the real world. So far, finding the congruence of models from different developers is possible only by testing the collaborative ability of modules.

The image of the LEGO economy (see for example Hagel and Brown 2001), in which companies are made of components that can be quickly assembled and where needed taken apart and reassembled, is an easily sold marketing message, but it remains more an illusion than a vision as long as we do not have a widely accepted model of at least the core processes.

ESERVICES

Service architects, mainly the suppliers of eServices that we described previously in the chapter as a fast growing area, are fighting the restrictions of integration. Each company can ask itself whether it has specialized functions, such as a credit check database for a certain market segment, which could be offered to other companies as an eService with high customer value at negligible cost. Many successful eServices come from brick and mortar corporations.

In addition, outsourcing opportunities can be exploited to purchase additional functions instead of running them yourself. Many portals already use eServices, such as credit checks, document exchanges, payment processing, logistics, and other subtasks.

eServices influence the connectedness of a company. But it is not about choosing the cheapest, most technically advanced, and easily implemented web service. Instead, companies must go beyond choosing individual services and choose a more comprehensive business collaboration infrastructure that incorporates web services.

EXCHANGES

A one-to-one network can generate much benefit, but this is only a temporary solution. A company cannot maintain 100 different collaborative processes with different interfaces to 100 different customers or suppliers. This results in a cost explosion and blocks any further development. Exchange infrastructures (business-to-business) must handle this for certain value chains. Such infrastructures can standardize the rules for collaboration along the lines of the trade agreements (such as the fact that exchanged electronic messages are legally binding). It can also define the components of collaborative processes, such as the updating of commonly used article data, eServices, message formats, foundational technology (such as security), and others, to make collaboration across the Internet possible, so that it seems as if all employees in a company are working in one software world and in one database.

This standardization is often *de facto*, led by the most powerful market leaders rather than set by standards bodies. Each company must decide for itself in which value chains it wants to participate and which standards and exchanges it will enforce and promote.

CONCLUSION

After 30 years of intracompany integration, we will see at least 30 if not 40 years of intercompany collaboration. Humans and companies are not LEGO blocks but social systems that learn collaboration slowly and create collaboration solutions. Ultimately, every customer, every workstation, and every program will access all the data in the value chain and the economy in real time, as if the data were in one intracompany database, as long as all involved agree this is what they want. Customers will require their suppliers to support their processes in such a way that they no longer see the companies, but rather collaborate with a virtual process assistant. Never before in the history of information and communication technology were there so many new developments, from RFID to eServices, close to maturity. Innovation and transformation will more than ever before become the most important virtues of business.

BIBLIOGRAPHY

Fleisch, E.: Business Perspectives on Ubiquitous Computing. M-Lab working paper No. 4. University of St. Gallen, 2001.

Green, H.: The Web Smart. *Business Week European Edition*. Nov. 24, 2003: 56–69.

Hagel, J.; Brown, J.: Your Next IT Strategy. *Harvard Business Review* 79. October 2001: 105–113.

The Information Management Group (IMG): *Web-based Customer Service ABB Turbo Systems — the Right Information in the Right Place at the Right Time — Success Story*. IMG 2003. http://www.img.com/PDF/SuccessStories/45009e.pdf

The Information Management Group (IMG): *SAP Portals at Zumtobel Staff — Architecture for the Future, or: Ready for "e" — Success Story*. IMG 2003. http://www.img.com/PDF/SuccessStories/45012e.pdf

IWI-HSG, IMG: *Marktstudie von The Information Management Group (IMG) und dem Institut für Wirtschaftsinformatik (IWI-HSG): Einsatz und Nutzen von Portallösungen in der Schweiz Zielgruppe: Unternehmen, die SAP Systeme im Einsatz haben (SAP-Kunden)*. IMG AG, St. Gallen 2003. http://www.img.ch/portalstudie

IWI-HSG, Tuck School of Business: *The Electronic Collaboration Case Study*. Glassmeyer/McNamee Center for Digital Strategies, Tuck School of Business, Dartmouth College, and Institute for Information Management. University of St. Gallen, Hanover (NH) and St. Gallen 2003, http://cases.iwi.unisg.ch

Mertens, P.: *Die zwischenbetriebliche Kooperation und Integration bei der automatisierten Datenverarbeitung*. Verlag Anton Hain. Meisenheim am Glan 1966.

Reichmayr, C.: *Collaboration und WebServices: Architekturen, Portale, Techniken und Beispiele*. Springer, Berlin, 2003.

Scheer, A.: *EDV-orientierte Betriebswirtschaftslehre*. Springer, Berlin, 1984.

Senger, E.: *Potenziale und Erfolgsfaktoren von Kooperationsprozessen.* Dissertation in Arbeit, St. Gallen, 2004.

Spindler, M.: *How Fraport AG Utilizes mySAP Mobile Business to Ensure Legal Compliance.* Presentation at SAP NetWeaver Conference. Basel, October 2003.

Strassner, M.; Schoch, T.: *Wie smarte Dinge Prozesse unterstützen.* Universität St. Gallen und ETH Zürich, 2002.

Thede, A.; Schmidt, A.; Merz, C.: *Integration of Goods Delivery into Ecommerce Supply Chain.* In: Fiege, L.; Muehl, G.; Wilhelm U. G.: Electronic Commerce, Second International Workshop, WELCOM 2001 Proceedings, Heidelberg, November 16-17, 2001, S. 206–218.

Zencke, P.: *An Enterprise Services Architecture Blueprint for the Extended Order to Cash Process.* Presentation at SAP Analyst Summit 2003. Boston, November 2003.

18

Real-Time Case Study: Shortening Cycles at Colgate-Palmolive

Colgate-Palmolive is a $9.3 billion consumer products company that oper-ates in over 200 countries and employs 37,700 people worldwide. Globally recognized brands include Colgate, Palmolive, Softsoap, Mennen, Irish Spring, Ajax, Axion, Fab, and Hill's Science Diet. Ed Toben joined Colgate in 1990 as Vice President of Information Technology and was promoted to CIO in 1999. In 2000, he was named one of Computerworld's Top 100 IT Leaders.

Ed Toben

Colgate operates globally, doing business in over 200 countries with 70 percent of sales from international operations. It is incredibly complex, a huge IT challenge, but if you look at the company as a very simple model, we have one line of business: consumer products. And the very core of growing that business is improving our margin structure. By improving our margins, we are able to invest in new products, research, marketing, and advertising. Fundamentally, for the past 10 years Colgate has been working with SAP in support of that program. And, although we rarely use the term, Colgate has become a real-time enterprise.

End-to-end integration now seems like an obvious solution, but if you go back 10 years, it was breakthrough thinking. Ten years ago, our entire industry was going through a transformation, and we needed to improve our margin structure so that we could invest in new products. Back then, a purchase order from a major retailer would take us, on average, 2 weeks to delivery. We had a long list of steps: taking an order was a step, figuring out distribution was a step, and every step needed information from the previous step. It took too much time to complete the order fulfillment cycle, and generally speaking, this meant we had gaps in the process. And gaps in the process mean excess inventory sitting in the warehouse.

STREAMLINED PROCESSES

We concluded that we needed to streamline the process and reduce the cycle from 2 weeks to 2 days. Now, one way of doing this would be to spend a zillion dollars keeping inventory in many locations, but clearly this wasn't the right solution. Instead, we began analyzing our business, taking a purchase order through our whole process until it becomes cash in the bank. We went through order management, inventory management, manufacturing, distribution, finance, dealing with our suppliers, and everything else. At this time we had separate systems for order

> " *Integration is the key. It is a huge advantage that you can extend further and further.* "

management, inventory management, manufacturing, and distribution. We discovered that one of the places where we lost time was that our information systems had trouble talking to each other. That's how we found our way to SAP and the breakthrough: integrated systems.

CIOs and their business counterparts typically go through agonizing reviews of software: Is this a better order management system than that one? Is this a better accounts receivable system? However, at Colgate, we've learned that this isn't the point. Integration is the key. It is a huge advantage that you can extend further and further. Connecting different products and different vendors, even individual best-of-breed products, doesn't deliver the same advantage. Integration delivers the biggest immediate payoff, and, with innovation and research and development, SAP will make its components best of breed over time.

INTEGRATION IMPACT

It took a long time to understand the impact of integrated, real-time systems. For example, traditionally a financial system has its own information base, and all the financial processes take place within the confines of this system. SAP R/3® software allowed us to take the discrete functions in dealing with our customers — accounting, customer service, order procurement, distribution, transportation — and combine them functionally. All the data is in one place, and whenever any information touches the process, it moves with the process. It is a very different way of thinking. You can see the process in motion: for someone in the financial group, a shipment arriving at the receiving dock becomes more than just a ledger entry.

Many times we were SAP's pilot customers. For example, we've been working with the Advanced Planner & Optimizer module (SAP® APO) since before it was called APO. With R/3 as the base and APO, we optimized our supply chain and extended the whole real-time principle. We started with our U.S. and North American business, which is an approximately $2 billion company within the company. This business is extremely important to us, not only because we are an American company, but also because we typically use the United States as a test market before we launch new products internationally. The SAP integrated database allowed us to take snapshots of our process as we handled our cycle from order to delivery. We were able to think of the process as a whole and take a lot of time out of the cycle. It's rather a cliché, but time is money. Today, we've installed the new system in 95 percent of our business and collapsed 17 inventory databases into 1. Now we average 5 days per cycle. We could reduce it further, but one insight that the system provided was that we needed to be not only fast but also accurate. Our biggest retailers now tell us they want their delivery on Thursday morning and we deliver Thursday morning, not Wednesday night or Thursday night.

Conceptually, an end-to-end, real-time, integrated system is very easy to understand. From one perspective, it really doesn't matter how you do it. Each generation — from mainframe to client/server to web — is a faster, slicker way of doing things, but the technical challenges haven't fundamentally changed: Your infrastructure has to be in place. Your systems have to perform flawlessly, quickly, and with no downtime. However, the devil is in the details. You can't just plug in the new system and have money pour out the other end. First, you need to be clear on your objectives and then use SAP to align your processes. If we hadn't standardized on SAP, we'd be a couple of years behind where we are. We'd have spent a lot of our time putting pieces together — a lot of integration and a lot of interfaces — and that's a lot of hard work.

If you don't have your business vision lined up, you're not going to get much out of the system. One of our biggest lessons was that you have to approach building an integrated system in an integrated way, with an integrated project team. When we first started, our team was literally all over the planet. We don't have a central location where everybody is, so we had our people each working in their normal locations. It took us a while to realize that you can't possibly do it this way. You have to get people looking at the process from multiple perspectives, and you can't do it by giving a PowerPoint presentation. The only way it works is by putting everyone in one place, really executing and understanding the whole system. Later, they can go back to their own locations, but they have to become experts first. Something really interesting happens then. The people who do the planning and execution move from being reactive to proactive, streamlining and smoothing the process. They start running ahead of the system, coming up with ideas, wanting to try new things, trying to figure out if they can do this or try that.

> " You have to get people looking at the process from multiple perspectives, and you can't do it by giving a PowerPoint presentation. "

It never gets easy, but now we have the template for how to do it. We understand process, we understand integration, and we understand what has to happen and how to get the benefits. Now it is about continuous improvement — and that is a process as well.

PART IV

REAL-TIME INTERFACES

B efore we can give birth to the real-time enterprise, we have to invent a way to see it. The very words *real time* imply the ability to see a business as it is happening — to see manufacturing, sales, and delivery as they occur. This power isn't going to be granted by new infrastructure, faster networks, or reengineering. Seeing inside real time will begin and end with the interface, which is poised to (finally) escape the desktop and leave windows behind.

A real-time interface will be one that provides a metaphor enabling us to see inside a process, rather than see inside the machine, as all computer interfaces have done before. The blinking command line was a metaphor for the calculations being crunched by low-level code in mainframes. The GUI invented by Alan Kay at Xerox PARC in the '70s and perfected by Steve Jobs at Apple in the '80s created windows that peered into the file structures of PCs. And the browser's frame resolved the complexity of the web's infinite branches into a simple page. All three tamed complexity by reproducing functionality in a familiar metaphor. The challenge of designing the real-time interface is to keep complexity at bay while allowing the user to see entire landscapes of data at a glance. The dream of their designers was to make the interaction between the interface and the user as natural as possible. This impulse drives all the contributors to this section.

While the authors of the preceding chapters focused on the infrastructure and underlying code of the real-time enterprise, this part of the book dwells on the key role the human-computer interface plays in bringing the real-time enterprise to fruition.

But when does the real-time enterprise begin? Any interface that would presume to see inside the enterprise must take a conceptual leap that none has before and address head-on the idea of time itself. Each interface that has come before, whether it be a blinking prompt, a floating cursor, or a button waiting for a stylus' tap, has stood outside of time, prepared to wait an eternity if need be for the user to set it into motion.

To faithfully depict real time, the interface will now have to switch from passive and reflective to active and projecting. The inner life of the enterprise will appear on the screen, with or without input from the user.

With the exception of the brief "push" media fad in the mid 1990s, the screen has always waited for the user to "pull" information from it in response to outside stimuli. Whether it was an email from a colleague asking for a scrap of information, a note to self to check a particular column on a spreadsheet, or any of the countless other ways we remember to perform tasks, we always needed to know exactly what to ask our interface to do.

But the interface to the real-time enterprise will answer us with what needs to be done, finding, displaying, and continuously updating information we might never have thought to ask for. It will not wait for us.

The interface we need will also be uncoupled from the operating system on which it is running. Beginning with Steve Jobs and the Macintosh, the GUI became wrapped so tightly around the OS as to be considered inseparable. Microsoft followed suit over a decade later, finally rewriting Windows so that it was no longer a wrapper for the DOS command line, but the OS itself.

Real-time interfaces will ride atop the OS and be dedicated solely to the enterprise itself. The one-size-fits-all approaches of Windows, the Mac OS, and the browser have intrinsic limits and will never be equal to the challenge. "That user interface is the overlapping windows and icons interface that we originally designed for children," says Alan Kay. Now, the problem is, if you look at the versions of that today, "it looks like the panel on a submarine."

The implication of the real-time enterprise is one that doesn't unnecessary tasks in between you and what you need to get done right now, according to Alan Cooper. This means getting the human user closer to their goals and eliminating intermediate tasks. That's just extraneous stuff that's there for the software's sake, but not for the human's sake.

But proliferating interfaces will create new problems, as well as tradeoffs — at what point does standardization become desirable for maintenance and compatibility reasons instead of simply a hindrance? And who should be allowed to make this decision — programmers or users? The former are most keenly aware of what's possible and practical, but the limitations produced in a fast-and-dirty solution that sticks — the web browser being the obvious example — can have crippling effects on functionality should they catch on. Real-time interfaces must be designed with the users' goals and process in mind. Anything less is counterproductive.

And what happens when we leave the desktop? The small screens and keyboards of wireless devices introduce an entirely new set of challenges at both a metaphorical and physical level. Every variety of phone, PDA, game machine, or all-in-one device is a different puzzle to solve for interface designers. As Nokia president Pekka Ala-Pietilä notes, no matter how small our technology might have the potential to become, we are confronted with the limits of the human thumb. At the same time, it's hard to accept that wireless devices, which currently lag behind PCs in terms of total functionality, will be able to make the leap to a real-time interface when the time is ripe. But until the applications beneath the interface are written and the desktop fixed, their designers will have plenty of time to catch up.

CONTRIBUTORS TO PART IV

- Nokia president **Pekka Ala-Pietilä** is responsible for the strategic direction of the company, identifying growth opportunities, and, as head of Nokia Ventures Organization, developing and investing in new businesses. He was president of Nokia's mobile phones division during its groundbreaking years in the mid 1990s. He is also a member of the SAP Supervisory Board.
- Adobe CEO **Bruce Chizen** has led his software company's push behind the Portable Document Format — the ubiquitous PDF — since ascending to the job in 2002. The PDF has done more to realize the paperless office than any technology yet.
- **Alan Cooper** is considered the father of the Visual Basic programming environment and is chairman of Cooper, an interactive design consultancy that specializes in improving usability and interface design.
- **Friedrich Fröschl** joined Siemens in 1995 as president of the business services division. Currently he is Corporate Vice President of Corporate Information and Operations (CIO).
- **Alan Kay** was present at the creation of object-oriented programming, the graphical user interface, Ethernet, the laser printer, and the client/server model, all while working at Xerox's Palo Alto Research Center through the 70s. He is a founder of Viewpoint Research Labs, and since 2002, has been a senior fellow at Hewlett-Packard's HP Labs.
- **SAP Global Research & Innovation**

19

Real-Time Interfaces for Real-Time Enterprises

Virtually everyone using a computer today greatly benefits from Alan Kay's fundamental contributions to the science and technology of computing. No matter whether you use a Mac or a Windows PC, the GUI windows and icons are derived from the groundbreaking research Kay led 30 years ago at Xerox Corp.'s famed Palo Alto Research Center (PARC). Likewise, the quite indispensable technique of object-oriented programming (OOP), popularized in computer languages such as Java and C++, descends from Kay's development at PARC of a revolutionary programming environment called SmallTalk.

Alan Kay

Historically, most of our interactions with our tools and associates have been in real time and as instantaneous as possible. Writing was also done in real time but introduced delay. This was less than desirable when it was trying to simply imitate oral communication, but world changing when the delay could be long enough to transport the written ideas and their copies over many miles and centuries. Musical instruments were interesting examples of artistic tools used to amplify and extend extremely real-time expressions of ideas about feelings. Assistants were examples of agents who could be interacted with in real time but then could add process and their own powers of thought to carry out desired communications and goals.

It's pretty clear that the term *real time* with regard to computing was coined because early in the digital computer's history, most interactions were not. But between the "calculating engines" of Charles Babbage and the stored program computer of John von Neuman, many of the interactions with analog computers were done in real time, especially for control of vehicles (Norden bomb sight), weapons (predictive antiaircraft artillery), and sense extensions (radar and sonar). Vannevar Bush, an early inventor of analog computers and President Roosevelt's science advisor, proposed in 1945 an interactive information desk that he called "memex" that could not only hold the equivalent of a small town library but could form cross-indexed (we would say hyperlinked) "information trails." He realized that the crosslinkings would be more valuable than the base information and that there would be a profession in the future to make worthwhile crosslinkings that would then be sold as products.

> " *It's pretty clear that the term real time with regard to computing was coined because early in the digital computer's history, most interactions were not.* "

EARLY REAL-TIME USER INTERFACES

Interest in real-time information about and control of airspaces heightened with the cold war of the 1950s and 1960s, and digital computers started to get big and fast enough to interact in real time. Many ideas appeared that we would consider "modern" a half century later. Among others, John McCarthy, a pioneer in artificial intelligence, proposed that everyone should have a computer terminal with access to shared computer resources worldwide. In 1959, McCarthy wrote a very influential paper describing an intelligent computer agent he called the Advice Taker that would deal with human users in commonsense terms and reasoning. Part of the motivation for the Advice Taker was his realization that a worldwide network with millions of users plus the universality of computing would lead to an explosion of millions of useful tools and pieces of information that would quickly be overwhelmed by complexity unless new ways were invented to interact with and control computing.

PERSONA TO PERSONA

As Alan Kay in this chapter and Alan Cooper in the next make clear, designing effective user interfaces involves much more than situating graphical buttons on a screen or choosing colors. The best user interfaces invite and facilitate psychologically rewarding interactions between computers and human beings. The best user interfaces are comparable to a language, Kay insists: familiar enough to useful without much training yet powerful enough to express unanticipated ideas. Kay himself draws inspiration from musicians and their instruments, the educational theories of Piaget, and even Elizabethan theater. Cooper, meanwhile, has developed the notion of personas, which attempt to capture the mental models of the people for whom a particular piece of software is being built. A further exploration of the user interface problem, specifically as it's encountered in the mobile realm, is central to Chapter 22 by Pekka Ala-Pietilä.

J.C.R. Licklider, Director of the Information Processing Techniques Office (IPTO), a division of the Pentagon's Advanced Research Projects Agency (ARPA), wrote an influential paper in 1960 called "Man-Machine Symbiosis" that proposed and predicted a near future in which interactive computers would be complementary intellectual partners with the result that "[humans] will think as no humans have thought before."

The founder of the field of computer graphics, Ivan Sutherland, created Sketchpad, the first real interactive graphics system, which included the ideas of objects, icons, clipping and scaling windows, and problem-solving agencies, among others.

Cliff Shaw at the RAND Corporation designed and built JOSS, the first interactive system whose designer really thought of most users as noncomputer scientists and truly cared about them. The level of care and scaffolding in JOSS has rarely been approached and never surpassed. It was an environment that had to be experienced rather than explained, one of the few ever in which the knowledge that one was going to be able to use it later in the day set up a pleasant tingling of anticipated pleasure, a most unusual feeling for most users of computers today.

Douglas Engelbart, inventor of the mouse, noting that most important things are done by groups of people trying to work together, decided that a worthy goal would be to boost the combined intelligence of groups using real-time interactive computing. Those interested in the real-time enterprise would do well to study his work.

Wes Clark, seeking to get real-time computing to real users in biomedical research, invented the LINC in 1962, arguably the world's first real personal computer. Thousands of these were built and used in the 1960s.

In 1962, Licklider was given a large amount of funding by the Advanced Research Projects Agency and started up many projects in both universities and businesses to invent great designs for what appeared to be the manifest destiny for computers (to be personal complementary tools) and communications (connected by an "intergalactic network"). He funded the ideas mentioned earlier in this section, and many others as well, and quite a few of the best ideas in our computing world today (and quite a bit of the wealth as a new business sector twice as large as the automobile industry) were the result.

In 1964, Engelbart and Bill English invented the mouse as an attempt to make an inexpensive and handier pointing device than the light pen, and, concurrently, Tom Ellis and others at RAND created the first really good stylus and tablet that would allow pencil-like interactions and started work on a graphical successor to JOSS.

Graphical user interfaces abounded in the 1960s. The most pervasive were made by people who thought that interfaces are mainly for access and control of function. This was extremely naive, but represented the older and dominant thought of several generations of engineers from an era in which the technology made it extremely difficult to contemplate really assisting the user. For example, the interfaces for large ships, airplanes, hydroelectric power generation stations, nuclear reactors, and air defense systems, and so on were very extensive, complicated, and assumed highly trained personnel who would essentially be part of the total machinery. This "diminished humanity" perspective ("humanity as the control system machinery for the machine") had been noted by many critics of the industrial revolution but was generally accepted by most people.

In early computer systems, this style showed up in airlines' reservations systems and later in the mind-numbing non-designs associated with much of IBM's products and American business in general (for example, the deadly embrace between business, databases, and 3270 terminals was especially infelicitous with regard to the end users). A more interesting perspective, held by many in the ARPA community, was the "supertool" view — somewhat analogous to the way musicians feel about their instruments — that training is okay if the tool is terrific because the result is both great efficiency and range of expression. For example, the interface of Engelbart's oNLine System (NLS) required a dozen or so hours of learning, but fluency was greatly rewarded by being able to have multiple interactions per second with subsecond response. It's hard to adequately explain this to today's computer users and especially to computer programmers. Engelbart's computer in 1968 was a time-sharing system with about 20 users. It had a clock speed in today's terms of about 1 MHz and a total memory of 192K! But the programmers were outstanding, and they had enormous will to have subsecond response. They were able to achieve this — because they *really wanted it.* In contrast, many people today have their own personal computers with clock speeds and memory capacities more than 1,000 times as fast and large, but rarely are delivered subsecond response in important areas of their work.

Another interesting "supertool" from these early days was the GRAIL system at RAND that grew out of JOSS and the stylus and tablet. It had the first really great character recognition system (done by Gabe Groner) and required a few hours of learning. But once learned, one experienced for the first time an intimate relationship with a computing system, a kind of magical and instant transformation of one's ideas sketched with the tablet into dynamic computer simulation models. (Sketchpad had much of this earlier but was done on a much older and slower machine so some of the romance of what it was about was lost.)

Spacewar, the first video game, was created at MIT by Steve Russell, as a serendipitous offshoot of the several ARPA projects there. This was real-time interaction in the extreme and inspired much more than the subsequent video game industry. As with the other supertools, its forte was great payoff for doing a fair amount of learning. One should guess right away that because children like to play games, are willing to get good at them, and eventually become adults, the real second stage user interfaces of the near future, even in business, will start to look more and more like games, in no small part because much of the learning that businesspeople don't like to do, regardless of the payoff, will have already been done by the children much earlier. The simplest way to have a revolution in interfaces is to do better games with much better interface designs and then 10 years later introduce real-time enterprise systems using many of the same ideas.

An enormous amount of work went into the "other face" of user interfaces, which is the use of computers as agents analogous to human assistants. One of the difficulties in user interface design in general is that the UI is there to facilitate something other than itself, so there is a very important sense in which it has to be invisible and essentially foolproof. We don't like our tools to have any hitches at all — musical instruments work essentially perfectly for most of their modes of use. Most musicians are not aware that their instruments are machines — they think of them as amplifiers of their musical ideas. On the other hand, we are more tolerant of human and animal agents, but only in narrow learned ways (and often not as tolerant as we should be). For example, we can deal with simple misunderstandings relatively well, but any hint of real stupidity where an agent is not supposed to be stupid is not tolerated. This puts a tremendous burden on most attempts at using artificial intelligence as an interface agency — particularly if it is in areas in which the user thinks of the interactions as being tool-like. For example, hand-drawn character recognizers are essentially "AI-like," even the simple ones. But they are used in a context that is only slightly removed from the perfect tool use of writing on paper. An error is really jarring and so different from pencil use that it subtracts mental chunks from the central tasks at hand.

In the early 1970s, two more interface styles showed up whose ways of dealing with users were interesting enough to be considered new. The first (we will consider the second in detail in later in this chapter) related to virtual reality, stemming from Ivan Sutherland's first virtual reality helmet in the late 1960s and further developed by Nicholas Negroponte and his ArchMac group at MIT. This interface simulates the real world when things the user already knows and can do can be directly adapted to fruitful interactions. The work of the ArchMac group was decades ahead of its time, and many of the excellent and usable ideas are both in use today and have yet to show up in the commercial world of computing. Of course, we really want something more magically pliable than the real world as a payoff for using computers, so some of the best designs in this area have been an artful mixture of "slightly magical yet pretty intuitive" objects. The amount of magic that can be tolerated is pretty constant for most people, but what is considered magical and what is considered mundane changes generationally. "Technology is all that stuff that wasn't around when you were born," so children of each generation grow up in a mundane world that would be considered magic to previous generations.

XEROX PARC: INTERFACE AS LEARNING ENVIRONMENT

The second interesting style of interaction developed in the 1970s came out of Xerox PARC, which was in many ways the research successor of ARPA. The context for much of this work was the desire to create a children's environment in which they could learn the most powerful ideas of our civilization by creating them in their minds with the aid of the personal computer as "supermedia."

The primary aim in this style of interaction is "the interface as learning environment." We made this central partly because we were dealing with children, but, importantly, because it is the nature of both the computer and knowledge to be open ended and expansive over time. Thus, the real difficulties in interface design are somewhat similar to the difficulties of language itself: it has to be somewhat conventional and conservative to provide continuity with the past but still capable of representing new ideas and ways to represent things. Ordinary language is much better at the former than the latter and worked much better in the past when there was

> " *Thus, the real difficulties in interface design are somewhat similar to the difficulties of language itself: it has to be somewhat conventional and conservative to provide continuity with the past but still capable of representing new ideas and ways to represent things.* "

very little change of ideas from generation to generation. It's pretty clear that this is a serious difficulty with UI design as well.

Along with many previously good notions, especially from the ARPA community, a number of fundamental ideas were used to create the supermedium, including:

- Psychologist Jerome Bruner's perspectives about multiple mentalities and different modalities of representation
- Dynamic objects as universal representors

- Universal authoring, including of processes
- The theater as a "magic mirror"
- A simple but profound perspective on communication
- An even simpler idea about context
- A notion about actual creative processes for play and work

We will discuss each of these in a bit more detail now.

USE DEVELOPMENTAL PSYCHOLOGY

Bruner argued convincingly that we have multiple ways of "thinking and knowing," three of which are as follows:

- **Kinesthetic: enactive** — Muscular and proprioceptive learning and doing
- **Iconic: figurative** — Visual, sonic and olfactory "spatial" configurations
- **Symbolic: linguistic** — Reasoning using symbolic representations and logic

Developmental psychologist Jean Piaget saw these as serial stages of development in childhood, but Bruner was able to show that they operate in parallel but are quite modal in dominance (for example, young children can think symbolically, but are often dominated by what they see before them).

The interesting survey of creativity in math and science by French mathematician Jacques-Salomon Hadamard indicates that much of the creative process is not done using ordinary symbolic languages, but instead is conducted in the more mysterious realms of figurative, and even muscular, thinking (as Einstein, among others, reported). This argues for inventing ways to deal with ideas on the computer through muscular, visual, and other figurative means, and with various kinds of symbologies. One phrase at PARC, "*Doing* with *Images* makes *Symbols*," was used as a kind of slogan to inspire designs that used all three of Bruner's main ways of knowing and to have the flow of interactive process invoke them in the general order in which most ideas are best learned: by doing with ones hands, by putting in configurations that allow comparing and contrasting simultaneously, and by the vast powers of abstraction and logic that allow ideas too large and different from common sense to be dealt with.

Use Objects, Universal Building Blocks

One of the most interesting properties of computers is their ability to simulate other computers including themselves. This means that "computers" made from software could be a universal building block for all things that can be made with and from computers from the smallest bit to the largest worldwide network. An earlier version of this had been termed *object-oriented programming,* and this descriptive phrase was applied to the more streamlined, universal, and powerful conception of objects that was developed at PARC.

Create a Changeable Interface

A universal material invites universal authoring including and most importantly by the end users. JOSS and GRAIL at RAND and LOGO at BBN and MIT had shown that end users could be tremendously productive with carefully designed "programming systems." The idea at PARC was to make a new kind of powerful object-oriented programming system that was "JOSSified" and "LOGOified" so that it would be usable and fun for children and also to make this system capable of implementing all of its other tools, including its user interface and even its own operating system. The result was quite successful and, among many interesting things that were done in this system, the first overlapping user interface with icons, etc., was indeed programmed in the very same language that the children learned (and in fact, they could even make interesting changes in it).

Beam Intelligence Back

The theater is often called the "magic mirror" by theater people because they realize that the theatrical process is not to successfully "communicate" very complicated ideas in a few hours to a random audience of hundreds of people, but is instead about evoking from the audience ideas that they know or almost know, but have forgotten. Coleridge, who was a theatrical critic as well as a poet, once wrote, "People go to bad theater hoping to forget; they go to good theater tingling to remember." So the "mirror" metaphor is that the theater when it is working well seems to beam back the audience's own abilities to think about the human condition with a little selective filtration representing the author's special interests. This is a very interesting way to think about how a computer interface that doesn't have any AI behind it can nonetheless seem better and smarter than it is: use the fact that the user is intelligent and beam that intelligence back at them (hint: you don't have to have anthropomorphic characters to do this). Having the universal building material be objects simulating all other processes is an analogy in the large to players on the stage assuming all roles (including the scenery, as often was done in Elizabethan theater).

Tell What the Computer Is Thinking

The "absurdly simple" idea about communication is related to the theatrical metaphor with another metaphor: that language and communications in general are extensions of the gesture. If we picture two people trying to communicate and show what is in their thought clouds, we quickly get the simple notion that they are essentially pointing (mostly with words but sometimes with actual gestures) to their thought clouds. The amount of communication likely to happen has a lot to do with the overlap of their thought clouds on the subject at hand. In other words, as in the theater, not a lot of direct new information in communication is learned instantly; instead the process is dominated by cues and agreements and disagreements. Ricky Wurman, who has written about 80 books, likes to say somewhat sarcastically, "Most writers, if they tell the truth, they think they've done their job." What he means by this is that "telling the truth" simply doesn't work if the receiving thought clouds are not already almost aligned. The art of essay writing is mostly about how to build the shared thought clouds that are necessary for the central idea of the essay to be understood (and to do this building in a way that keeps the reader interested until the main points are reached).

Why is it so difficult to communicate with computers? The absurdly simple answer is that most users (even experts) don't often know what is in the computer's "thought cloud." How can we know this most easily? Perhaps by just putting the computer's thought cloud on a graphics display and allowing the user to literally point to the ideas in common for the communication at hand! Of course, another way to know what is in the computer's thought cloud is to learn many things that are not on the display, and this is the most common path, even today. But since we were dealing with children, we thought it would be a good idea to try to show "what the computer was thinking" even if done crudely with windows, icons, and menus.

SHOW MULTIPLE POINTS OF VIEW

"Point of view is worth 80 IQ points." That is, our limited ability to think and the great power of the (usually invisible) context to influence our intuitions and conclusions argues for including powerful abilities for multiple perspectives for visualizing (including noniconic ways) ideas we are trying to think about. The earliest uses of multiple windows were for providing different views of the same objects or worlds, and the general lack of this (or poorly done versions of this) can be quite debilitating to the end users without their even being aware of what they aren't thinking about.

PROJECTS, NOT APPLICATIONS

We need to have a larger and richer sense of the user as a person who has many processes and projects at play in her life. Some projects are ephemeral, but most extend over time and may involve a hefty subset of all the capabilities of the computer. So a project-based interface would not have "applications" at its center but would instead be much more organized about allowing the user to create many different parallel play and work environments with full access to all of the abilities of his or her personal computer system and network. An interesting side effect of such an interface is that one doesn't need a separate weaker presentation system (such as PowerPoint) because the environments themselves can be sorted, arranged, sequenced and

> " *[A] project-based interface would not have "applications" at its center but would instead be much more organized about allowing the user to create many different parallel play and work environments with full access to all of the abilities of his or her personal computer system and network.* "

shown to do all the things necessary for a presentation but with far greater power and almost no new interface to handle it.

IDEAS ON THE OPEN MARKET

Now, if we look at the commercialization of some of these ideas from the 1960s and 1970s — from both the ARPA community and its off-shoot, PARC — in the 1980s and 1990s, an immense low pass filter seems to have been inflicted to the point where we are lucky to even get a "dial tone" in the systems we have to buy today! It is not worth-while in this short chapter to dwell in any detail about how and why this happened. But one point is quite relevant and telling: from the introduction of the Univac 1 onward, businesses especially, and many other organizational entities, have never been very creative, innovative, or prescient about computing. Marketing being what it too often is, there has been a deadly embrace between unsophisticated organizations and almost as unsophisticated vendors only too willing to "sell them what they want (or what we can try to make them want)" rather than to invent what they really need. These stultifying processes predate per-sonal computing by many decades, but the immense gravitational clutchings between mainframe users and vendors from the 1960s and 1970s became colossal black holes in the 1980s and 1990s.

As media critic Marshall McLuhan noted about media invention in general, the strongest tendencies are to first oppose a new medium and then to only gradually accept it by assimilating mostly old forms for content. The real media revolution often requires several generations of fuddy-duddies to die off before the children gradually work their way into understanding the real powers of the medium. Unfortunately the innovators, who very often did understand what the new idea was good for, also die off and never get to see the real fruits of their ideas.

The real-time enterprise requires true innovation. By studying the works of the innovators discussed in this chapter and by funding research into human-computer interaction, companies can help drive innovation forward.

20

Escaping the Asylum through Interaction Design

As the father of Visual Basic, Alan Cooper's contribution to Microsoft Windows was far-reaching and profound, so much so that in 1994 he received a Windows Pioneer Award. In the process of inventing and developing software-based products, Cooper was bedeviled by just how difficult it was to use software. He ceased programming to devote himself full-time to the goal of making software user-friendly. For over 10 years his firm, Cooper, has created groundbreaking interaction product designs for such clients as 3M, IBM, Microsoft, Sony, and SAP. In 1995 Cooper codified his thoughts in About Face: The Essentials of User Interface Design. In 1999 he counseled no less than a complete overthrow of the software development process in The Inmates Are Running the Asylum, laying out the challenges to achieving the real-time enterprise, while offering new metaphors to describe human-computer interaction. Alan Cooper has become a global guru in interaction design because his practice embodies what he preaches.

Alan Cooper

The real-time enterprise is a bold vision. It is an opportunity, even a call to arms, to make the user central to the enterprise application. Today's exponential increase in computational power is like a runaway train. There are innumerable applications for bleeding-edge technologies, but we at Cooper are worried that in the rush to exploit the potential of wireless, handheld devices, and web services, the lesson of building user interfaces, something that we call interaction design, is being shunted aside in favor of expediency. It *is* possible to show the real-time enterprise to users in a way that doesn't confound but enhances their lives.

The exigencies of software design, which first drew my attention three decades ago, still demand our attention. For the promise of the real-time enterprise to be realized, we must take from the past that which works, while being daring enough to discard obsolete methodologies.

Hasso Plattner is a kindred spirit in our journey to restore the user to the central position in software development for enterprise applications. As I will explain, he invited Cooper to join the EnjoySAP initiative with the goal of making SAP applications more usable. Through his support we managed to question conventional wisdom. Engineers were persuaded to take themselves out of the problem and to become aware of the user's presence throughout the process. Ultimately, we came to see that solving problems with interaction design is only the first step in realizing the real-time enterprise. We have to reinvent the software development process itself.

In the past, an interface was considered "front end." It was created as a superficial shell often just before shipping. We do so today at our peril. While the Digerati endlessly tout the march of technology, all our efforts will be squandered unless we realize that if we don't get it right, we're in for a Tower of Techno-Babel. We don't have to look far for examples of such a future; we can glean them from today's headlines.

FEAR OF FLYING

In the last few years the airline industry has had a tumultuous ride. Apart from the obvious after-effects of 9/11, in-flight entertainment (IFE) systems can now deliver à la carte movies and music to each and every passenger — be they first class or coach inclined. A perfect example of the real-time enterprise in action? Or not.

Local area networks (LANs) connect these IFEs, which are used for longer, transoceanic routes. For one carrier, so perplexing was the IFE that flight attendants were bidding for shorter routes — all to circumvent flights offering IFE. These tools were so bad that they hastened a staff morale problem as well as dampening customer loyalty — the very opposite of the desired effect. A rival airline had an even more infuriating IFE. Its system linked movie delivery with a cash collection function. Before the IFE went online, flight attendants provided goods and services when convenient; cash was accepted in a *laissez-faire* fashion. With this "upgrade," cash had to be tendered first and the attendant's password had to be entered on a console. Passengers could enjoy the latest Disney feature or Top 10 single, but only if the transaction was complete before the plane made its final approach. Over time, flight attendants took matters into their own hands — tripping the circuit breakers on the IFE system as the planes were taxiing down the runway. They would then announce that there would be no movies on *this* flight due to a computer malfunction.

The in-flight entertainment system illustrates the goal of the real-time enterprise: helping users achieve their goals by eliminating intermediate steps. Before the IFE, a flight attendant provided headsets for movies and took money at her discretion. The IFE forced the attendant to *literally* add steps, walking from the passenger's seat to the head end of the cabin to enter a transaction and then back to provide the passenger with change. The IFE also demonstrates that no matter how well software functions — and this system worked like a top — it's a non-starter if the user isn't taken into account. The two airlines meant well. They invested millions of dollars to develop a new system at a time when their industry was just barely holding on.

Whether or not we are discussing IFE, CRM, or ERP, the issues are fundamentally the same. It is mission critical to recognize that while technology has the capacity to improve the quality of our lives, it can also drive a wedge between us and our goals.

FOCUS *AWAY* FROM THE ENGINEERING

While SAP's mission is to enable automation and communication in support of the real-time enterprise, our calling at Cooper has been to make software products easier, even pleasurable, to use. When Hasso Plattner initiated EnjoySAP, a usability program, we were recruited to help them improve their enterprise applications. SAP recognized that at one level, the job was done. It had every reason to be confident that its software was powerful, but it was also self-aware that the user experience — as the project name clearly indicated — could be more pleasurable.

SAP provided us with a playground to leverage its powerful enterprise applications in the service of the customer. This partnership in learning advanced the cause of both the real-time enterprise and the discipline of interaction design.

Engineers think about engineering. This is natural. Our core idea was to focus *away* from engineering and to think about the users. Rather than consider what task was required to achieve a given goal, we simply asked, "What's the goal?" Instead of thinking, "How am I the engineer going to solve this problem?," the focus became, "How is the user going to solve this problem?"

The staff responded (of course, not in the way we expected). One of the engineers proclaimed, "There's rightness here." The software engineers accepted the approach, but not blindly. Ultimately, it was adopted broadly and successfully at SAP, in ways compatible with the culture. Even in our absence, developers asked, "How is the user going to solve this problem?" The engineers were aware of the user's presence at every step of the process. This was a real change and a real accomplishment for both of our organizations.

One area where we made an impact was in the complex materials management procurement (MMP) process in SAP® R/3®. This process was very implementation model-based, addressing interaction in the terms of how the software is constructed rather than looking at interaction in the terms in which it is used. Implementation model interfaces deliver up a screen per function and divide things up on a function-by-function basis.

> " [T]he procurement interaction involved a huge number of screens, between 30 and 40. We reduced it to four screens, a radical change. "

This approach is like building a ten-room house as ten separate buildings. A house, be it colonial or Bauhaus, is one building, with halls and doors and transitions between the various rooms. There was a dawning awareness within the organization that it's not an advantage to the user to be given one screen or one menu per function. From an engineering point of view, it's a very good thing. But for a user, this is not a good thing.

A user has his *goal* in mind, not what task is to be performed to achieve that goal. It's very natural for a programmer to think in a task-centric way because that's the nature of programming: codifying tasks. This is a new kind of thinking: to think in terms of an ensemble of functions that brings a human to a goal, as opposed to thinking about the discrete functions themselves.

In terms of quantifying changes to a process, the procurement interaction involved a huge number of screens, between 30 and 40. We reduced it to four screens, a radical change. After some initial skepticism, our approach was adopted.

CHALLENGES FOR THE REAL-TIME ENTERPRISE

The challenges facing the real-time enterprise come at a time when the entire industry is in an uproar. How has the relationship between business and technology changed? What is innovation? How can we ensure that the real-time enterprise is a reality?

Within the industry, there's a lot of talk these days that technology is at a crossroads. Nicholas Carr's article, "IT Doesn't Matter" (*Harvard Business School Review*, May 2003) caused a tsunami. Whatever the failings (or merits) of the piece, it led to a long overdue discussion about technology's relationship to business. The value of your business, regardless of industry, is based on the quality of your information and your information systems. Whether or not you're an old-line industrial age manufacturer and even if you have a lot of money sunk into hard assets what allows you to differentiate yourself, to establish your brand, and to generate a profit is the quality of your information. It's no longer your ability to deliver a product or a service. What differentiates you today is your ability to deliver the *right* product and service to the *right* person at the *right* time. That's a complete information management issue. People who create ERP software are therefore more vital than ever to every aspect of a business. SAP is more important, its products are more important, and its customers rely on SAP more for the fundamental profitability of their business.

While technology itself is no longer a differentiator, innovation is and always will be. But we're living in a curious time where there's no consensus about innovation. Some people view innovation in negative terms. To such people, innovative software is something you clamor to have back — *when it's taken away*. At SAP, innovation fulfills a felt need, whether or not that need has yet been consciously identified. This response to innovation would be closer to "Yes, yes. I want that!" Perhaps this manifests the difference between cultures at SAP and other companies and reveals what kind of environment can best foster innovation.

WHEN TECHNOLOGY OUTSMARTS ITS USERS (COGNITIVE FRICTION RESULTS)

Today's wireless devices are more powerful than yesterday's mainframes. This has often contributed to interface design that's device-inappropriate. Interactions can be rich or fleeting. In some cases, complex interfaces are shoehorned into a device the size of a domino. Exploiting the functionality of these myriad devices to achieve the real-time enterprise presents both challenges and opportunities. Companies tend to bundle wireless phones or PDAs with powerful applications. The problem you run into is the limitations of the communications bandwidth between the person and the device. If you have a Pentium computer, take away its keyboard and replace it with twelve keys; trade its high-resolution VGA screen for a 1"×1" screen with a few thousand pixels. It's like trying to have a conversation through a keyhole. The solution is to not have a conversation through a keyhole. These devices can be used for simple computational issues. A wireless phone, for example, is perfect for holding a cell phone conversation; it's inappropriate for decision-support analysis.

Many folks are getting carried away in their enthusiasm for the new portable technologies. But the desktop computer is not going away. True, more and more people will use handhelds, even eyeglass-mounted devices. Yet this won't take away from desktop computing; it will augment it. When it's time for thoughtful analysis, communication, or planning, you'll see even bigger screens and more sophisticated keyboards on desks. Beyond that, thanks to radio frequency ID (RFID), a new generation of devices will be, to some extent, intelligent and autonomous. These physical objects inside organizations will have Internet addresses and communicate with one another.

These powerful and increasingly complex devices present software engineers and users with unimagined challenges. *Cognitive friction* is a concept that shows how we think about technology and software. We behave differently toward humans than we do toward inanimate objects. During the machine age, it didn't matter how complex things were — they were still objects. When things began to exhibit complex behavior, we started to treat them differently. Software has achieved a sufficiently interactive threshold that it actually triggers in the human mind that kind of cognitive thinking that one normally associates with other human beings. How many of us rail at our desktops when our OS crashes? We have emotional reactions to software that we don't have to manufactured things. This has everything to do with the complexity of the interaction as well as the unpredictability.

To illustrate, think of a house. You enter a room, and there are a pair of light switches on the wall. You flip the first switch; it doesn't do anything, least of all generate an emotional reaction. You immediately try the second. Let there be light!

You then enter a second room and are met with 100 switches. This would be complex, but without cognitive friction. But imagine this scenario. You flip the first switch, and it randomizes the behavior of the remaining 99. This might keep you in the dark or at least have you reaching for a match.

The behavior of the light switches triggers cognitive friction. They have become sufficiently complex that they simulate human emotion. This is the nature of software today; you push one button, and it essentially randomizes the behavior of all other buttons.

The closer you can get users to their goals without intermediate steps, the more successful you are going to be. This concept is implied in the whole idea of real-time enterprise. The opposite of real time is an entity taking time to do something — an unnecessary task mechanically required but not part of the user's goal. We want to get end users closer to their goals by eliminating intermediate steps

> " *If I want to drive from here to there, I don't want to stop to put gas in my car. The essence of the real-time enterprise is getting rid of intermediate steps.* "

or an "excise tax." If I want to drive from here to there, I don't want to stop to put gas in my car. The essence of the real-time enterprise is getting rid of intermediate steps.

Will the real-time enterprise be a swamp of cognitive friction that ratchets up our anger? Our fear at Cooper is that unless we retrain engineers that's exactly what will happen.

INTRODUCING *HOMO LOGICUS*

While the concept of *cognitive friction* helps us to understand human-computer interaction on a deeper level, the psychology of the software builder provides valuable insight on how programmers can be motivated to create interaction that is good for users. *Homo logicus* (the software builder) behaves fundamentally different from *Homo sapiens* (the user). *Homo logicus* trades simplicity for control; he or she exchanges success for understanding, and he or she considers the possible to the exclusion of the probable. These distinctions might sound negligible, but we have ignored them at our own peril.

Let's return to the friendly skies. Why? A disproportionate number of *Homo logicus* are avocational pilots. While passengers routinely place their faith in the tenants of the cockpit, the programmer/pilot cannot surrender control. He or she is undaunted by, and even embraces, the difficult learning curve involved in aviation. It's no wonder that in software projects this need for control is embodied in the software design and, literally, in the features programmers project that the user desires. Take a robust "Find File" function. A programmer wants options to allow him or her to partition a search and the latitude to set parameters. *Homo sapiens* wants simplicity — not an array of choices.

Rather than create a program that mirrors user goals, *Homo logicus* creates an interaction that follows the contours of the mechanism within, making the mistake of believing that when the user understands how the software works, he or she will understand how to use it. We know this as the "implementation model."

While *Homo sapiens* are routinely indifferent to long odds (the threat of a nuclear attack, an earthquake in Queens), *Homo logicus* is trained to plan for every contingency. Jack User deploys probability each and every day of his life: "What are the chances that I'll be fired if I ask for a salary increase?" Even though the odds might be 1 in 100, he accepts the conditions and schedules a meeting with his supervisor. Jill Programmer, on the other hand, is more concerned with what is *possible* — even if it is remote. If the odds are 1 in 10 *million* that a system error will occur, she steels herself to write code that we might otherwise think of as unnecessary. For *Homo logicus* this code will be timely, be it tomorrow or in a millennium. This need for advance preparation explains a behavioral trait of such people that author Po Bronson characterizes as being "generous in their selfishness."

Finally, *Homo logicus* possesses the worst traits of both the nerd and the jock. Both are given to bullying, intense competitiveness, and immaturity. But while the jock is soon benched in adulthood (unless he or she is drafted for pro ball), the nerd flourishes. His or her mental acuity is recognized and rewarded in the halls of business. Do not confuse *Homo logicus* for a deferential wallflower just because he or she knows Pi to 100 places.

REINVENTING THE WHEEL

Even as we negotiate human-computer interaction and familiarize ourselves with species *Homo logicus*, without rethinking the software interaction process itself we cannot hope to achieve the real-time enterprise.

Commonly, people think that the roles of the engineer and the programmer are the same in software construction. In fact, they are quite different. Add to these two another important role: the architect. In recent years, we've blurred the functions of engineer and programmer, while excluding the software architect from the process. Here's how to tell them apart. Simply put:

- Architecture is design from the human side.
- Engineering is the design from the technical side.
- Programming is the construction of a shippable and usable product.

SAP really adopted this idea of architecture (or interaction design). This is design of software through the lens of the user.

A major issue in software construction is the idea that engineering is problem–solving, *not* a production discipline. Many people say that engineers build software and that engineers build bridges. Actually they don't; *ironworkers* build bridges. Engineers draw pictures of bridges. Engineers solve stress and manufacturing problems. They work in a world of pencil and paper, rulers and mathematical models. They don't actually go out there and rivet or weld steel together.

> " *[E]ngineering is problem-solving, not a production discipline.* "

This distinction — in software construction — is long past due. Engineers need to solve technical problems — "How will this software be built?" — but not build it. A second group should create shippable software. Why? The demands on the programmers who build software for actual use and distribution are dramatically different from the pressures placed on those engineers who are determining the engineering *structure* of software. Design and engineering will become design, engineering, and production programming. Managing this process remains the scarcest of commodities. We now have a generation of trained software construction managers — and they've learned it old school — doing engineering and programming at the same time. This approach will have to be supplanted by a new methodology. First, you do the architectural design for humans, then the engineering for technical aspects, and then you do the construction for shipping out the door.

PERSONAS KEEP THE USER IN MIND

In the service of the EnjoySAP project, employing the Goal-Directed® process we use at Cooper, we tried to create an objective mechanism for knowing the user. *Personas* are the wedge for breaking that open. Personas are hypothetical archetypes, fictional persons who accurately represent real users. In the world of software design, users are discussed in vague terms. Without a real user to focus on, it's only natural that programmers put themselves in the position of a user. They make the fatal mistake of thinking that if they can figure out a problem, so can the user. Even when we go out into the field to interview users, their opinions can be red herrings. After observing and talking with users, you have to go back and build a hypothetical construct that you can control. The specificity of this construct holds your focus — it's a powerful tool. Let's call our persona "Danny." Danny has this set of skills and wants to accomplish these goals. What would happen to Danny under the following conditions? All of a sudden you become focused. This allows you to make coherent decisions that are really powerful for designing software. Personas allow you to omit code that won't be necessary, saving time in the construction phase. In fact, personas are a focal point for the whole construction process. So many details are involved when building commercial quality software that it's easy to lose sight of what you're trying to do. Having a single, specific persona allows you to maintain focus: this is what the user is trying to accomplish. Personas have been a remarkably effective tool.

A bevy of chorus girls ushered in SAPPHIRE 1999 in Nice, France. As they finished their routine, Hasso Plattner took center stage and delivered that year's keynote speech: "How SAP Must Change in Order to Grow." To our surprise our 4 screens — yes, the screens from procurement that we had streamlined from 30 to 4 — shone on the wall.

Proudly, Hasso explained their significance and, fixing them in everyone's minds, called out, "Look what we've done!" For those of us in the audience, this was a signal moment. Hasso got it. He understood our credo: Less is more in interaction design.

21

Data and Documents in the Real-Time Enterprise

Bruce Chizen, president and CEO of Adobe, has transformed Adobe from a product company to a technology platform provider, particularly by pushing Adobe's Portable Document Format (PDF) into new arenas, including mission-critical integration with XML.

Bruce Chizen

L ong before terms like *open systems* and *real-time computing* were standard, SAP promoted these benefits to customers. The company realized early on that integrated, rapid processing of core business data was key to an organization's success. By focusing on the potential of computing technologies — powerful, highly adaptable systems that work across platforms, borders, and currencies — and not on perceived limitations, SAP revolutionized how companies operate.

Vital business data now resides in transactional systems that communicate in real time with other core applications, improving enterprise processes at every level. These integrated systems deliver numerous benefits, from enhanced customer and partner services to greatly reduced operating costs. With the widespread use of high-powered Internet and wireless applications, organizations have further eliminated barriers to real-time computing, bringing people closer to the information and services they need.

Yet even with advances in enterprise systems and the popularity of the web, mobile computing, and handheld devices, organizations still rely extensively on slow, costly paper processes for key tasks, such as handling customer orders, collaborating with business partners, and developing new products. This is in part because paper is familiar and widely available. It is also because the costs traditionally associated with extending enterprise applications to end users have been prohibitive.

Fortunately, new technologies are enabling organizations to rethink paper processes in terms of real-time computing — and helping to realize Hasso Plattner's vision of reliable processing of data and documents across an extended enterprise. By combining web and wireless applications with electronic documents that contain intelligence for computing business logic and for transporting XML data, organizations are extending the power of enterprise systems to employees as well as to partners and customers outside corporate firewalls.

> " Fortunately, new technologies are enabling organizations to rethink paper processes in terms of real-time computing . . . "

These "intelligent documents" provide a crucial link to achieving real-time enterprise computing by securely connecting all end users with core applications. In essence, the documents bridge the gap between people's comfort and familiarity with paper and the power and flexibility of web, wireless, and enterprise technologies. With built-in intelligence for automating document creation, security, content validation, and other functions, electronic documents can support rapid transactions and on-demand information delivery, reaching end users at anytime on any device.

For example, applications for government programs or loan applications for financial services that previously could take weeks to deliver, complete, and process can now be handled electronically in minutes with far greater accuracy. The electronic documents can be tailored to an individual's needs and can be completed online or offline before being digitally signed and returned for automated data capture and processing by back-end systems.

CONNECTING EMPLOYEES, PARTNERS, AND CUSTOMERS

Adobe Systems shares the vision of the real-time enterprise conceived by Hasso Plattner and other SAP founders. As one of the world's largest software companies and a leader in helping businesses and people communicate better, Adobe is providing the platform to move organizations from disconnected manual document workflows to integrated digital document services.

In 1985, the company forever changed the quality of printed pages by developing Adobe® PostScript®, a language for describing how text and graphics are printed on paper and film. With the introduction of Adobe Acrobat® software in 1993, Adobe further eliminated barriers to high-fidelity, professional communications by allowing people to digitally distribute materials exactly as intended in platform- and application-independent Adobe Portable Document Format (PDF) files. Today, with the Adobe Intelligent Document Platform, the company is delivering enterprise and desktop applications that enable organizations to securely and reliably connect employees, partners, and customers with core systems.

Leveraging the flexibility of Adobe PDF and the ubiquity of Adobe Reader® software, organizations are linking core applications to front-end processes for secure, digital document generation, collaboration, and process management. The results: reduced operating costs, improved quality and accuracy of enterprise information, and faster, more personalized delivery of customer services.

SMARTER WAYS OF WORKING

Dealing with documents is second nature to us in our professional and personal lives. We complete paper forms to apply for jobs, purchase homes, or register for government services, and in return receive even more documents as follow up to the processes we initiated. At the same time, corporations and government agencies manage huge volumes of paper daily, whether bringing new products or services to market, billing customers, or responding to constituents. Because of this, the opportunities for business process improvements are tremendous and so are the returns.

Document services support key activities, including automated creation and delivery of customized documents, complex internal and external collaboration, and the reliable capture of data and transactions.

CREATING AND DISTRIBUTING QUALITY DOCUMENTS

Enterprises need quality documents to communicate business information. To be effective, documents must include current data and incorporate images essential to conveying a company's brand. In some industries, materials must also comply with regulations governing document content and appearance. Unfortunately, many core business systems produce only rudimentary documents, preventing organizations from repurposing these materials for delivery to customers or even for distribution to employees. Document generation problems are further compounded when data comes from multiple sources.

Document services overcome these obstacles by merging content from enterprise applications with flexible electronic templates to create personalized, intelligent documents. For example, large financial institutions with branch offices worldwide can automate the creation of regional marketing collateral documents customized to each location's services and business requirements. The same system can then be used to allow branch employees to instantly generate loan applications, financial statements, and other materials tailored to a customer's needs.

Everyone benefits from these automated processes — corporate executives know that remote locations are using consistent, branded, and professional communications; branch employees spend less time on administrative tasks and more time focusing on customers; and customers enjoy efficient, personalized services.

IMPROVING COLLABORATION

Effective collaboration among employees and between employees and partners is at the center of any successful enterprise. When done on paper, collaborative processes can bog down as people wait for materials to arrive by mail, sift through dozens of document versions, try to decipher team members' handwritten comments, and manually track materials across reviewers. Collaboration processes done electronically can also present problems if participants lack the same applications or system configurations to support proprietary or specialized document formats.

In contrast, intelligent documents integrated with enterprise applications enable collaboration across diverse user groups by providing a universally accessible format for digitally viewing, commenting on, and approving materials. From legal contracts to complex engineering drawings, review teams can comment electronically on documents, applying feedback and approving them with digital signatures. Electronic comments can be tracked separately throughout the review cycle for auditing purposes. All the while, the integrity of materials is protected.

CAPTURING BUSINESS DATA

Data and information from employees, customers, and partners drive core business processes. To ensure success, data must be securely captured, validated, and then reliably stored in enterprise systems. This can be particularly challenging given the variety of channels, operating systems, and client devices used to submit data.

A common approach to capturing data uses paper forms, such as those for tracking employee expenses, applying for bank loans, or interacting with government agencies. While seemingly simple at first, paper presents problems every step of the way, from difficulties ensuring that people put the right information on the right forms to problems processing forms

> " *[I]ntelligent documents integrated with enterprise applications enable collaboration across diverse user groups by providing a universally accessible format for digitally viewing, commenting on, and approving materials.* "

because staff incorrectly keyed data from forms into back-end systems. To effectively capture data, electronic forms must be used that incorporate business logic to validate information, integrate easily with enterprise systems, and convey the look and feel of familiar paper forms.

For example, pharmaceutical companies can use document services to enable thousands of physicians to complete and submit clinical trial forms in Adobe PDF via the web. Previously, this paper-based process required company researchers and physicians to manually exchange volumes of clinical forms daily. Now, built-in validation features in intelligent documents verify that physicians enter the correct type of data, minimizing errors and improving the accuracy of submitted information. Because data goes directly into back-end systems, tracking research results is faster and more reliable. Moreover, assembling compliance reports for federal regulators is easier than ever.

BUILDING ON OPEN INDUSTRY STANDARDS

Three components are central to the successful implementation of the Adobe Intelligent Document Platform:

- Intelligent documents
- Universal clients
- A set of document services that provide the underlying technologies for creating and integrating documents into enterprise processes

Intelligent documents leverage the visual fidelity of Adobe PDF to retain layout, typography, and graphics, regardless of the device on which documents appear. In addition, the documents contain powerful business logic and support XML data transport and user-defined schemas to quickly move data into and out of enterprise applications.

Universal Access to Documents

As access points to intelligent documents, universal client applications such as Adobe Reader software and web browsers enable anyone to reliably interact with enterprise applications. Data can move securely from core applications to intelligent documents and out to employees, customers, and partners for review and completion online or offline. Completed materials can be rerouted, submitted and processed, with new information saved automatically to enterprise systems. The seamless exchange of information enables companies to link highly structured transaction data in enterprise applications with unstructured, document-centric processes.

DOCUMENT SERVICES

In addition to automated document creation, electronic collaboration, and data capture, document services need to address security and control, critical issues as organizations move from paper to electronic documents. Digital signatures add important security by helping to certify and authorize transactions. Integrated document controls, such as password protection and encryption, further protect sensitive information by restricting who can view, modify, repurpose, or print materials.

REAL-TIME RESULTS

The advantages of document services are evident in all sectors. Manufacturers are reducing costs and improving customer service by automatically generating customized product documents — purchase orders, packing slips, product guides, and other materials — from electronic templates populated with data from enterprise applications. Government organizations can permit constituents and partner agencies to access, complete, and submit forms online, greatly reducing administrative costs and enhancing citizen services. In the competitive financial services industry, on-demand delivery of personalized investment information and loan packets can make or break deals.

And this is only the beginning. The proliferation of powerful handheld devices and the greater use of high-bandwidth Internet connections support the delivery of more interactive, complex intelligent documents. Increasingly, once-inaccessible enterprise systems are yielding to the secure, successful exchange of

> " *For organizations, these advances deliver on the promise of the real-time enterprise as reliable, high-quality business data and documents move effortlessly, where and when they are needed.* "

information between core applications and employees, partners, and customers. For end users, intelligent documents are reminiscent of paper, except much faster and more convenient than ever. For organizations, these advances deliver on the promise of the real-time enterprise as reliable, high-quality business data and documents move effortlessly, where and when they are needed.

22

Ubiquitous Devices in an Interconnected World: From the Desktop to the Mobile Device

Nokia President Pekka Ala-Pietilä leads Customer and Market Operations, the part of Nokia responsible for sales and marketing, manufacturing, logistics, and sourcing for the full range of Nokia's mobile phones and other mobile terminals. Before starting in this role at the beginning of 2004, he focused on the strategic direction of the company and headed Nokia Ventures Organization, which develops new businesses to contribute to Nokia's renewal. Prior to that, he was in charge of Nokia's mobile phone business during its groundbreaking years in the mid-1990s. He is also a member of SAP's Supervisory Board.

Pekka Ala-Pietilä

I t is estimated that about 30 percent of today's workforce is mobile, spending at least one day a week out of the office on average. In Europe, an average of 40 percent of workers spend more than 8 hours a week away from their company's work sites. These same people are critical resources for daily business — 34 percent of them have a field sales role, 28 percent are field technicians/engineers, 22 percent are executive level, and 16 percent are in other roles.

Increasingly, the workforce is mobile not only on local or long-distance travel, but simply away from their desks. Whether at a customer site or in a conference room in their own office building, employees are expected to remain in touch with coworkers, partners, and customers. To achieve this goal, mobile workers need mobile communications and mobile access to business-critical information simply, securely, and reliably. In short, the real-time enterprise needs to be in constant contact with all required information in real time.

The need for "access to any content at any time from anywhere using any device" has become a business imperative. Seamless and secure access to information has transformed from a barrier into an enabler, and a comprehensive mobile connectivity strategy is the best way to successfully leverage this important trend.

But mobility presents new challenges to enterprises. The very definition of work has changed: Work is no longer tied to a place. This concept brings about parallel developments in the customers' minds. Customers demand that enterprises and their employees are reachable and ever more responsive to their needs. Employees' expectations have also changed. While mobility helps them to be more efficient and accessible, it also increases employee satisfaction through the flexibility it offers. Mobile voice and messaging have already changed the workplace; mobile data will churn up the next wave of change.

In the world of enterprises, mobility is already achieved with a variety of devices: mobile phones, smartphones, laptops, PDAs, and numerous variations on these themes. One device already holds a unique position in the pockets of businesspeople around the world — the mobile phone. It is the one device that is always with the user and contains the user's content and services. With more than one billion users worldwide, mobile phones really are ubiquitous.

THE EARLY DAYS OF MOBILE WORKERS

The idea of putting the office in your pocket and making the office worker mobile made its debut in 1996 with mobile phones that combined a digital phone, organizer, and messaging device for fax and SMS (Short Message Service) as well as web browsing capability. Since then, new generations of mobile phones have added features and have been complemented by innovative business-enabled mobile devices and smartphones.

Mobile phones have already proven their value for the mobile worker by facilitating efficient client communication while away from the workplace. The progress of mobile device penetration and use is anticipated to be rapid — it is expected that more than half of enterprise users will have mobile access to email and personal information management by 2007. The future use of mobile devices in businesses is expected to evolve in three phases: horizontal applications for all mobile staff, vertical niche applications for selected groups of personnel, and core business processes extended to mobile devices.

Vertical applications for field service, delivery personnel, field sales, or field inspectors will be custom-built and targeted at certain user groups. The business justification for these applications can be estimated from the improved accuracy of data collected in the field, being able to check the level of stock for a product on the spot, or getting an acknowledgment from a customer for a task and passing it to invoicing right away.

High-value IT systems that manage core business processes such as Customer Relationship Management, Sales Force Automation, or Enterprise Resource Planning will soon be extended to mobile users. Enterprise IT architecture must support scalable, portable technology to be able to extend from the Internet to end-to-end mobile solutions.

EMAIL: A BUSINESS-CRITICAL APPLICATION

A natural starting point for mobilized information and services has been corporate email, a necessary tool. There are 176 million business email accounts in Europe today, with the average employee receiving about 30 emails per day. In many companies, email is the preferred method of communication even between people that sit relatively near to each other. Mobile workers who are cut off from email risk missing valuable business opportunities when unable to check their inbox.

Accessing email when mobile has many benefits. Idle time becomes productive time. You can read and respond to email while waiting for a meeting, sitting on a train, or waiting to board a flight. It can be used quickly — no need to wait for a laptop to boot and connect to the network. A mobile handset can be open most of the time and connected to the network so checking email while on the move is quick and pain-less. Faster response time is another benefit — email alerts inform the user immediately when an important email arrives, allowing a rapid response. Freedom and quality of life improve — no more sitting by the computer waiting for that last email before going home. You can stay abreast of developments within the company through email correspondence.

While early email applications and services were among the first to move to the mobile device, it showed employers and employees the potential for mobile access to corporate information and applications. Both have begun to demand more sophisticated devices and services to support their mobile working needs.

THE RISE OF THE SMARTPHONE

The demand for mobile business phones is increasing. As a result, the smartphone market is expected to grow rapidly. Smartphones are devices that bring mobile phone and handheld computer functionality together in a small, pocket-sized package.

After smartphones were established for use in multimedia messag-ing, content downloading, and mobile browsing, business software ven-dors realized that the software platform could also offer everything needed for enterprise applications, such as email, intranet access, and vertical applications.

A few examples highlight the expanding variety of software appli-cations already available for mobile business users:

- Sales force automation tools update and share information in real time.
- Customer Relationship Management tools synchronize account and prospect data.
- Barcode scanners provide transportation, logistics, and inventory tracking.

THE ROLE OF DESIGN IN MOBILE DEVICES

Before falling in love with the technological possibilities, the mobile phone industry must always keep technology in balance with two other elements: user acceptance and business models. When this triangle of fundamentals is skewed in any direction, the solution will not be successful and sustainable.

To achieve high user acceptance, services must be appealing, but they must also be easy to discover and use. In this way, mobile devices themselves play a role in service adoption. The design and layout of functional keys and the user interface determine the ease of use. These in turn impact how frequently and willingly users will utilize the device. No matter how compelling the content or the usefulness of mobile business applications, if the device to access them is not intuitive and comfortable, employees will not use them.

A product creation philosophy that is design-focused should encompass three pillars: reliability, ease of use, and beauty. Each pillar is essential for creating products that are high quality, suited to the task, and esthetically pleasing. For a successful marriage between the physical phone and its software, this philosophy must be applied to both.

In the mobile phone industry, graphical user interfaces with icons that are clicked are becoming standard in smartphones. These graphical user interfaces make increasingly complex software easier to use. Considering the screen size and keypad requirements of mobile phones, a mobile phone–specific user interface is compulsory. Developing intuitive user interfaces requires a deep understanding of the end user, the applications, and end-to-end service system. To ensure a positive user experience, the interface should be easy, effective, and enjoyable to use. The basics of clear typography, consistent language, and intuitive navigation are critical for mobile devices.

Mobile phones come in a variety of shapes and sizes to allow for the individual users' preferences. There are classic designs, folding phones, and even models with full QWERTY keypads, just to mention a few. Design must also consider local and cultural aspects. For example, in the Asia-Pacific region, mobile devices must make allowances for character-based text input so users can most intuitively communicate.

The future will bring a wide range of specially designed mobile devices to meet the varied needs of professionals. Mobile workers will select the device optimized for their particular tasks and working mode. Some will opt for a voice-centric phone, while others will require heightened messaging capabilities and still others will demand integrated connectivity with business processes.

MOBILE CONNECTIVITY AS A STRATEGY AND COMPETITIVE ADVANTAGE

Extending the desktop involves more than just mobilizing email and content. To truly harness the power of mobility and the Internet, companies should develop and implement a mobile connectivity strategy. Those enterprises that do will most notably improve productivity, make or save money, reach new markets, serve customers better, achieve greater economies of scale, and bolster competitiveness.

The mobile workers of today do not need cookie-cutter solutions. Different types of workers use different devices — PCs, mobile phones, handheld communicators, PDAs, and home PCs or laptops — based on what is most practical and convenient when and where they need access to information.

Regardless of the device, any enterprise can get much more value from its investment in virtually all business applications with a comprehensive mobile connectivity strategy. The enterprise stands to benefit from mobile connectivity for many other existing applications, including the following:

- Intranets that help increase productivity and reduce costs by facilitating better communications among all employees
- Extranets with customers and business partners that can streamline business processes and increase both revenues and profits
- Customer Relationship Management (CRM) and similar systems, especially for large field service or sales organizations, that can enhance a company's competitive advantage by enabling constant online access to customer information from anywhere in the world

A comprehensive mobile connectivity strategy also supports full- and part-time telecommuting arrangements, which can accommodate employees with special needs or those desiring flexible work conditions. Empowering workers results in greater job satisfaction and employee loyalty, which inevitably leads to improved productivity and one other cost-saving advantage: reduced recruitment and training costs.

Mobility adds another dimension as enterprises must also account for the variety of wireless networks and locations employees may connect from. In essence, mobile connectivity must be available for the at-home worker, the commuter in his car, the sales representative at a customer site, the executive in the airport lounge, and the team member sitting in a conference room down the hall.

INTEROPERABILITY AMONG ENTERPRISE DEVICES AND SERVICES

The vision for the future is a world where business users do not have to think about interoperability among their mobile devices, services, and business applications — it is a given. Interoperability increases the utility and value of investments into a mobile connectivity strategy. When mobile users are able to move freely yet remain connected to business-critical information and services, they will be able to truly take advantage of the benefits of enterprise mobility.

Imagine a manager who accesses her company email and Enterprise Resource Planning (ERP) system on her mobile phone from a customer site. After creating an email with an attachment and adding order data to the ERP system, she must update two different applications either when she returns to the office or while still on the go. The challenge to enterprises is finding ways to accommodate connections to and between a multitude of mobile and fixed devices and the equally numerous applications and databases. Devices and applications must become agnostic in terms of ability to connect and communicate regardless of manufacturer or technology.

A full implementation of interoperability applies to three areas:

- Interoperability among mobile and fixed devices, for example, mobile phone to mobile phone or PDA or desktop computer
- Interoperability between mobile devices and applications and services, for example, mobile phone and enterprise email and other personal information management systems
- Interoperability between mobile devices and back-end systems, for example, mobile phone to network security systems or proprietary database systems

Whether the connection is established via Bluetooth, wireless local area network (LAN), cellular networks, or another technology, the important point is that the ability to connect and sync is not limited. Business users will demand full interoperability so they can cut the cords to the physical office and work when and where it is most effective for them.

SECURE, RELIABLE ACCESS

As the number of mobile employees, applications, and access points increases, the importance of maintaining secure, reliable access to an enterprise network in a way that is easily managed cannot be overstated. A management challenge arises when an enterprise has a large number of mobile users whose security must be kept up-to-date. A well-designed deployment system can significantly alleviate administrative burden and contribute to providing mobile users (employees and customers of an enterprise alike) with uninterrupted secure, reliable service.

Security in the mobile enterprise is as critical as ever and remains a multifaceted issue covering areas such as email, content, viruses, and networks. Mobile phones differ from other corporate mobile devices (PCs and laptops) with respect to the capabilities of the phones and the mobile environment they operate in. They are also often utilized for both business and personal use, which presents challenges for managing multiple identities and security domains on phones. Requirements for security applications on mobile phones and management of them are specific and complex.

EMAIL SECURITY

Email security is increasingly important for a number of reasons. For the end user, a good number of messages that are received or sent might contain private, sensitive, or proprietary information. When an email is related to or originating from a business, that firm also has an interest in both the content and transport security of the mail traffic. For an entirely different reason, the enterprise has another reason for concern with respect to the security of the email system. Local security administrators may view email traffic as a hole in the enterprise firewall system.

CONTENT SECURITY

Content security is a complex subject in that it, like the content itself, is constantly evolving. In the past, the focus has often been on controlling and validating access to the enterprise. However, many of the problems of today actually arise from the content received. This content may be received from a perfectly legitimate source and therefore would not be blocked by access security methods.

Email scanning may bring to mind monitoring or restrictions imposed upon the individual. This is a perfectly valid practice and one that has been adopted in some cases by organizations as well as by national governments. What may be scanned and how it will be scanned must be determined by the each company to ensure compliance with the law as well as with company policy.

Apart from individual privacy concerns, there is an equally valid case for implementing content scanning from a security standpoint. The enterprise, in taking on the task of retransmitting traffic on behalf of its employees, partners, and customers, is opening itself up to potential security threats and liability.

FILTERING FOR VIRUSES AND NUISANCE MAIL (SPAM)

Both virus and nuisance mail scanning are important issues in the mobile environment. In addition to the desktop issues relating to unwanted mail, the user faces additional hassles when the content is mobile. Since mobile devices are by nature smaller than desktop systems, they have less processing power and are battery operated. Viruses and spam consume valuable power from both these limited resources, not to mention consuming the most valuable resource of all: the worker's time.

The first level of content security, virus scanning, has existed for some time. Unfortunately, the sophistication of exploits also increased over time, and most companies have found themselves dealing with at least occasional reinfection of the network. Companies are gradually shifting to preventing and eradicating viruses by filtering at Internet gateways.

A common abuse of the mail system is the generation of spam traffic. In the early days of the Internet, the volume of nuisance mail was proportionally quite low, but the amount has grown significantly in recent years. Stopping illegitimate email traffic is a difficult task, but one that must be tackled for mobile email users.

REAL-TIME ENTERPRISES REQUIRE END-TO-END SOLUTIONS

Even though challenges exist for enterprises that want to extend the desktop to the mobile device, they are surmountable. The issues require attention and investments from companies, but the returns from what mobility can offer more than justify the expenditures. Mobile communication has changed, and will continue to change, the face of the workplace.

Today, the idea of connecting people extends beyond just personal communication. People want to be connected in their professional lives as well. They want to be connected not just to the people that matter but also to the data and processes that matter. By bringing mobility to enterprises, the mobile phone industry can help enable enterprises to mobilize business processes to increase productivity and competitiveness while reducing costs, providing a critical enabling technology for the real-time enterprise.

23

Real-Time Case Study: A Portal for Worldwide Integration at Siemens AG

Founded over 150 years ago, Siemens AG is a world leader in communications, automation, power, medical solutions, transportation, and lighting. Siemens and its subsidiaries employ 417,000 people in 192 countries and report worldwide sales of $80.3 billion. Friedrich Fröschl joined Siemens in 1995 as president of the business services division. Today Fröschl is Corporate Vice President of Corporate Information and Operations (CIO).

Friedrich Fröschl

The Siemens global group is a wide-ranging group of businesses, encompassing the construction of power plants, medical technology, lighting, consumer electronics, financing, and real estate services. We have product-based businesses, like cell phones, service-based businesses, like medical CT scanner maintenance, system-based businesses, like software, and plant engineering businesses, like the construction of the Transrapid rail system. We are represented in more than

190 countries worldwide, the largest being the U.S., which accounts for around 26 percent of our entire business with over 77,000 employees.

It is vital that all our employees are able to access their task areas, no matter where they are in the world. They must be able to navigate quickly and easily to their user-specific roles in the system environment, finding the tools, guidelines, and workflow that they need to work efficiently and interact with colleagues.

Because of the worldwide reach of the company and the diversity of industries in which we play a part, portals that facilitate a broad range of views are of great interest to us — not only for our employees but for our customers as well. The flexibility to map the processes of a given industry, energy transmission and supply for example, is desirable. Another vital functionality is the ability to create a regional view for the customer, showcasing all the Siemens activities in a given country.

Siemens companies operate in their own fields and face different challenges. Until now they have had the freedom to structure their own information technology to meet their own requirements, resulting in a multitude of business systems. Over the years, we have built more than 250 different SAP systems, investing heavily in SAP's software.

ENTER THE PORTAL

To protect this investment in SAP and to leverage its capabilities to support our employees in the future, we decided to implement the SAP® Enterprise Portal solution on a global scale. We were confident that this solution would integrate easily with our old software applications and would provide an efficient universal solution to link our employees with customers, partners, and suppliers.

Last year, we began building a system using SAP Enterprise Portal 5.0. Each month we added a Siemens operating company, and today we have some 36,000 U.S. employees using this portal. We started with a few of the most important applications, such as travel planning and travel expenses, and then we incorporated some human resources activities, such as payroll, medical provision, and stock options for employees. Standard applications are gradually being introduced to the portal, too, because we have a shared services department that relies on such applications.

Parallel to our U.S. rollout, in Europe we are running a major change management project, and construction of a new SAP Enterprise Portal version 6.0 system is underway. We intend to perform a mass transfer of 80,000 employees to the new portal on April 1, 2004. Primarily, this will be a project portal supplying the relevant tools and processes required by our employees in all phases of project management — from business development, team creation, and proposal management through to project implementation. Project work is at the top of our list of priorities because it accounts for more than half of our business.

Our aim is to provide our account managers with real-time access to information from a variety of sources — something that would not have been possible in the past. Marketing and sales activities can be carried out much more efficiently with the portal. Individual activities concerning multinational accounts can be consolidated, enabling the global account director to identify new opportunities or offer support to another country if required.

Of course, the new systems have met with some opposition. Every company was used to structuring its own business processes and designing its own web site. Additionally, users had a familiarity with the areas of the old system, which are mapped differently in the new portal. Now we have standard functionality and require that corporate standards be put into effect.

PORTAL ADVANTAGES

In spite of some inconvenience, the portal provides many advantages. In the old systems, an employee would have to log on and enter a password for every different activity. Now only a single sign-on is required. The portal also offers a standardized search environment connected to a knowledge management system, where we store information and results from a variety of business areas. Employees on one continent can now help their colleagues on another continent process customer queries. Problems that would previously have taken days to solve are now rectified within hours. Employees can compare cost calculations and review histories to determine risk areas and potential problems. This improves the quality of our offerings, with fewer errors and a shorter time to production.

We believe that the portal will facilitate the complete transformation of our businesses into a real-time process organization. The organization of our group is, to a small extent, already process-oriented, with monitoring of process cost calculations and key business-based performance indicators. And, of course, a unified workflow connecting all the live systems will undoubtedly leverage this process orientation. But I believe that this is only a first step. I can imagine much more across-the-board assimilation.

- First, we need better integration of the Microsoft Office products. We have MS Office installed on 328,000 desktops worldwide and have standardized our businesses around it. We must link it efficiently with SAP Enterprise Portal.
- Second, we must ensure that employees can access their information all the time, in all locations, with every device. Employees in customer services want to work with PDAs or smartphones and be able to process information, not just read it.

The future holds more interfaces than the ones we currently use, and I think that voice processing will become more prominent, too.

We are not quite there yet, but we're working toward it. I think that with intensively integrated modeling, and the "click-and-use" configuration of web services, our vision of a real-time enterprise will ultimately become a reality.

24

Multi-Modality: Interfaces for the Real-Time Enterprise

Realizing the full potential of the real-time enterprise will demand a better user interface than the one we've had for the past 20 years — a keyboard, a mouse, and a screen. The rise of mobile computing has created new possibilities and challenges with interfaces based on sound — the speech of the user and the voice of software agents. SAP Global Research & Innovation is leading the charge to invent new interfaces for the enterprise — harnessing sight, sound, and touch.

SAP Global Research & Innovation

As humans, we communicate with each other using at least three of our five senses — sight, sound, and touch. Usually, we use some combination of the three to send a particularly nuanced message. So why do we limit ourselves to just one sense, sight, when using our computers?

We've borrowed the term *modality* from psychology to replace the word *sense* in our description of our ongoing research to evolve computer interfaces beyond just the screen. A *multi-modal* interface allows users to access and alter data through a combination of devices and techniques in tandem — a traditional keyboard and mouse might be combined with voice recognition and a touch pad to elicit a response that might include sound and video as well as text. A full-scale multi-modal system will be able to receive and interpret our input as it arrives simultaneously via different media, and then respond accordingly, also through multiple media, using whatever combination the user prefers. Compared to the single-mode methods we're accustomed to, multi-modal applications promise to be much easier and more intuitive to use.

Research in multi-modality began in earnest in the early 1990s, when new handheld devices like the Palm Pilot were coming to market at about the same time as telephony-based services like interactive voice responses (IVR) were emerging. In the past few years, while mobile phones and PDA melded, data formats supporting both converged, leading to an alphabet soup of markup languages created to link them to traditional applications. Suddenly there was VoiceXML, XHTML, XHTML+Voice Profile (X+V), and the Speech Application Language Tags (SALT), just to name a few. While an industry standard has yet to emerge, all enable a multi-modal approach through voice and sound to reach information and web services through any telephone or wireless device. But these proposals are just a start.

Taking the next step forward has been complicated by the inability of Human-Computer Interaction (HCI) specialists to implement their findings in code. HCI experts have tended to deliver their research to software engineers in human-readable but (mostly) machine-unreadable terms. Transforming their findings into functional software has proved to be an error-prone process.

> " At SAP, we've launched a number of research projects aimed at addressing the pain points a future real-time interface will need to have solved. "

At SAP, we've launched a number of research projects aimed at addressing the pain points a future real-time interface will need to have solved. We developed a voice interface for the SAP portal as a way to refine our approaches to voice-based navigation and parsing natural language commands. With our partners, we have also been working extensively with artificial intelligence software to create the most effective way for applications to talk back to users, so to speak, leading to our work with social agents and the invention of the

Talking Assistant intelligent headset at the Technical University of Darmstadt. While space constraints preclude me from going too deeply into detail, even a glimpse of these technologies will illuminate some of the challenges ahead.

THE VOICE-ENABLED PORTAL

Our first goal in voice-enabling the SAP portal was creating an efficient way to navigate it. Even on screen, the portal has a very complex interface. Users typically launch several "channels" at a time, and each channel may have several frames nested within it. The ability to quickly select and launch a channel was vital, but how was the user supposed to specify the focus of a command, particularly if there were multiple entries with the same name? (This is also a problem when web browsing by voice, where multiple links might say, "click here.") So our first challenge was providing "command focus" for users — a way for them to keep track of where the system was currently focused to help reduce ambiguity in their voice commands. This becomes even more complicated when limited visual cues come into play. Consider the case of users speaking commands to mobile devices with small screens.

In traditional navigation, anyone clicking a mouse is specifying exactly what link or application he or she would like opened. When two items have the same name, the physical act of clicking resolves any ambiguity. The person speaking commands has no such luxury.

In our testing, we developed two different voice interfaces to the portal.

- One, called *rigid scoping*, requires users to navigate up and down the portal hierarchy when selecting commands. To reach an item nested within the "Roles" area, a user must drill down to it one step at a time, by saying "focus on LaunchPad," then "focus on Roles," then "Travel Agent," "Airlines," and so on. This answered questions about ambiguity by adapting the screen-based interface for the voice.
- Testing revealed that users preferred our other approach, which we called *relaxed scoping*. This method doesn't require direct navigation; it recognizes commands for any channel at any time. As a result, it takes less time to issue commands and fewer commands to complete a task, although it still has trouble in situations where multiple commands have similar names. In those cases, the system opts for the default choice with no recourse for selecting other, less obvious options.

In trying to fix this problem, we developed what we called *implicit scoping*, which kept the best parts of relaxed scoping but invisibly tracked a user's place in the portal hierarchy. Ambiguous commands are resolved according to wherever the user is at that moment rather than just selecting the default. Other rules dictate the handling of commands for items outside the hierarchy, and if a command is still too ambiguous (and assuming the user was also looking at a screen), numbered icons appear next to the likeliest targets of the command, giving the user one more choice to make and leaving no doubts. Testing implicit scoping against relaxed scoping confirmed our opinion of its potential effectiveness.

Still to be determined is a way to effectively handle data input by voice alone. Translating speech into text is one thing, but addressing interface elements such as radio buttons, check boxes, pop-up lists, and so on requires further investigation. Asking users to speak their choice from a list but not giving them a chance to review their selection could become complicated. Voice input for text fields is another issue. Dictating to a phone number field, for example, should sound significantly different from a zip code field, even though both expect numerical input. Generic voice dictation software may be able to handle it, but such software is currently prone to errors. New, specialized grammars may need to evolve to handle such data. Another idea involves using nonspeech audio cues to signal, for example, how much work the user has to do to finish completing a particular form. While such sounds could potentially be useful, it remains to be seen how they would be used, or even what they should be.

SOCIAL AGENTS

Research in HCI reveals that users prefer to interact with computers using the same modality. If they are speaking commands, they like it best when the system speaks back. Taking this idea to its extreme, the ideal interface would be an avatar that understands natural language commands and appears to emote. Our Virtual Human project incorporates AI software such as a conversation engine to create a software agent capable of natural-sounding speech. Our Social Agents project similarly uses human-sounding characters to keep up user interest during prolonged interface sessions (such as a web-based sales transaction) with context-appropriate conversation. For now, the social agents use prerecorded speech that plays when users provide appropriate cues and therefore isn't truly interactive. But by someday combining the two, we could eventually create an agent that communicates effectively, intuitively, and seemingly naturally.

THE TALKING ASSISTANT

The Talking Assistant (TA) is a very intelligent headset that consists of a processor, memory, wireless connection, and special audio software (an MP3 decoder and speech recognizer) that is continually aware of its location, its user, and the direction its user's head is pointed. Developed by SAP's research partners in the Tele-Cooperation group at the Technical University of Darmstadt, the TA is a prototype of the fully multi-modal devices about to be born.

Designed for any situation where hands-free/eyes-free mobile work is important (for example, factory floors, warehouses, and hospitals), the TA accepts speech input and is meant to be used as a giant browser of "structured audio" documents — sort of an audio-based Internet Explorer for large documents like online manuals. Users can automatically drill down through the use of context-aware software of the kind outlined previously in this chapter. Voice over IP could make conversations with local colleagues or back-office operations seamless.

The TA's location awareness would come into play when a user moved into the vicinity of RFID-tagged goods or machinery, which the TA would recognize over the local wireless network. Knowing its user's identity would prove useful for authentication, privacy, and even mobile commerce operations such as timesheet automation.

Such applications are still off in the distance. The consensus among researchers is that true multi-modality is an elusive goal. We have yet to establish the industry standards, create the software toolkits for development and simulation, refine natural language speech and recognition, and determine how to debug it all.

Doing so will require the help of gifted individuals from a broad spectrum of disciplines, including computer science, electrical engineering, linguistics, psychology, signal processing, pattern recognition, and statistics.

In the end, though, it will likely all be worth it. According to Allied Business Intelligence, the number of multi-modal users worldwide will number more than a quarter of a billion, and there will be close to a billion wireless portal users at the same time. Our challenge is to make what will soon be an almost-universal experience into an enjoyable and efficient one. The real-time enterprise requires interfaces that users perceive as natural and easy to use, and we are making progress toward that goal, making such interfaces enabling technology for the real-time enterprise.

> " *Our challenge is to make what will soon be an almost-universal experience into an enjoyable and efficient one. The real-time enterprise requires interfaces that users perceive as natural and easy to use . . .* "

PART V

BUILDING BLOCKS FOR THE ENTERPRISE NERVOUS SYSTEM

As the real-time enterprise evolves, it will begin to shed its remaining similarities to its client/server ancestor. The desktop as we know it will be left behind, as the enterprise migrates first to the successors of the mobile devices we have now and then to screens, objects, and environments in which computing has never been present. Up to this point, the contributors to this *Festschrift* have focused entirely on the monumental task of bringing the real-time enterprise to fruition through infrastructure, applications, and interfaces.

If the essence of real time is forging a final, direct link between users, information, and process, the next steps are to multiply that link and strengthen it by bringing its components closer.

Interfaces will proliferate, freeing themselves from the keyboard and screen and extending to the other senses. Experiments in voice recognition and art, which has harnessed the body and movement as interface, suggest possible implementations. They will eventually be combined with and camouflaged by real-world objects. As the interface becomes less obvious (or at least less screen-dependent), the need for metaphors disappears: It blends in with the thing it would have borrowed from.

Those formerly dumb things will be imbued with their own intelligence through embedded processors and radio frequency ID tags (RFIDs) that promise to transform every store or warehouse into a latent wireless network. Imagine both the challenges and possibilities of every item in every one of its stores being connected to a global chain of suppliers able to monitor not only how much of any one thing is in stock, but also where it is on the floor, how it's being sold, what competing brands are in proximity, and so on. Intelligent software agents will analyze this information and then shuttle and share it with many more corporate chains spread across multiple borders, all happening in an instant.

Now consider what real time means for manufacturing and automation — if the real-time enterprise is one where executive impulses metaphorically become actions in the body of the business, assume it will happen literally as well. Robotic factories will receive orders, monitor output, and track material supplies in a single, continuous feedback loop, with humans quite possibly absent.

These are just ideas. Making them real is another matter. Even after we complete the first version of our goal, successive iterations will only grow more complex. Discovering new best practices, creating ever more elegant architectures, and teaching tomorrow's software engineers to confront these problems are more next steps.

And after that, what's next? Perhaps we'll incorporate nanotechnology, cybernetics (will a brain/machine interface literally incorporate us into the enterprise?), biotechnology, and artificial intelligence into a digital nervous system that will literally grow smarter every day.

CONTRIBUTORS TO PART V

- **Craig R. Barrett** is the architect of Intel's manufacturing systems and the principal driver behind the company's management methods and culture. Formerly COO and president, he became Intel's Chief Executive Officer in 1998. Prior to joining Intel, Barrett was an Associate Professor at Stanford University in the Department of Materials Science and Engineering.
- **Esther Dyson** is chairman of EDventure Holdings, which publishes the influential technology-industry newsletter *Release 1.0* and sponsors the annual PC Forum conference. She is an author and *New York Times* columnist and was founding chairman of the Internet Corporation for Assigned Names and Numbers (ICANN), the international agency responsible for setting policy for the Internet's infrastructure.
- **Michael Fleisher** is chairman and CEO of Gartner, Inc., a leading technology research corporation. Since joining Gartner in 1993, Fleisher has been a key player in Gartner's rise to prominence as the leading technology advisor to business and government. In 1993, Fleisher led the company's Initial Public Offering as well as the company's later move to the New York Stock Exchange. In addition, Fleisher completed over 30 acquisitions and investments that have made critical contributions to Gartner's research capability and geographical expansion. For the past 5 years, Gartner has been performing ongoing research into the real-time enterprise and its implications for business.
- **SAP Executive Board**
- **SAP Global Research & Innovation**

25

Enterprise Services Architecture

SAP Executive Board

A simple analogy to an automobile provides a quick road to the essence of Enterprise Services Architecture. Think of a car in two parts:

- The first part is the machines under the hood: the engine, brakes, transmission, and all of the other components that make the car work. This part is the domain of the mechanics and engineers.
- The second part is the controls on and around the dashboard: the brake, accelerator, steering wheel, speedometer, and so on, which provide the driver the control and information needed to drive the car safely. This part is the domain of the drivers.

At its most fundamental level, Enterprise Services Architecture is an explanation to the mechanics and engineers of how to build the machines under the hood so that the best possible dashboard can be created for the drivers at the lowest possible cost.

This analogy may be a gross oversimplification, but keeping it in mind will help you navigate the complexities and maintain a clear focus during this explanation of Enterprise Services Architecture.

This chapter expands on this analogy and connects it to the moving parts of modern information technology (IT) so that, in the end, Enterprise Services Architecture emerges as what it is: a set of fundamental principles and guidelines for creating a flexible computing environment with the greatest business value at the lowest possible cost.

Two groups of readers are served in different ways by this chapter. For those who are new to the concept of Enterprise Services Architecture, it provides a step-by-step explanation of all of the concepts involved using the engine and dashboard metaphor just introduced. In this way, even those who don't live and breathe IT can get a clear idea of what Enterprise Services Architecture is and what it means for business. For the IT cognoscenti, we break open the metaphor at various points and explain in greater detail what is going on under the hood, so to speak. At the end of the chapter, after the basic ideas have been communicated, advanced examples are analyzed.

ENTERPRISE SERVICE ARCHITECTURE AND THE REAL-TIME ENTERPRISE

The real-time enterprise raises the level of integration required both within a company and across company boundaries. To remove artificial barriers to automation and rapid response, connections between applications must be inexpensive to create and easy to maintain. Processes must be configurable, and the services supporting those processes must be found and incorporated into the process without great difficulty or delay. Meeting these demands requires a new architecture.

> " *The real-time enterprise raises the level of integration required both within a company and across company boundaries.* "

Enterprise Services Architecture is the roadmap for the real-time enterprise. It creates an infrastructure that meets these demands. It provides the ability to evolve rapidly from the current state of affairs into one that unlocks the real-time potential of technology.

WHY IS ENTERPRISE SERVICES ARCHITECTURE NEEDED?

The simplest answer to the question of why Enterprise Services Architecture is needed is as follows: Enterprise Services Architecture is a comprehensive plan to help businesses take advantage of the incredible possibilities created by the invention and adoption of web services.

Web services are revolutionary because they are becoming the standard way for one application to talk to another. Absolutely every technology vendor has jumped on board the web services bandwagon.

The vast importance of the rise of web services can be seen by looking at the transformation of online services by the web. During the late 1980s and early 1990s, before the rise of the Internet, CompuServe, Prodigy, and AOL dominated the market, and each had its own custom technology. If you wanted to see information from all three services, you had to dial up, connect to a private network, log on to three different accounts, and use three custom programs that worked differently.

After the web arrived, the online world became simpler. People could access information from any place using one standard program, a browser. The web used the Internet, a public network with standard ways of formatting and transmitting information to and from a browser — HTML and HTTP, respectively. Broad acceptance of open standards led to phenomenal growth.

Web services have the revolutionary potential of the web and present a huge opportunity for companies seeking a competitive edge. Enterprise Services Architecture is the roadmap for taking advantage of web services to gain flexibility and reduce costs for IT.

How Do Web Services Work?

Everyone has used a standard plug that allows computers, TVs, refrigerators, and everything else to receive power from electrical sockets. An easy way to understand web services is as a flexible and configurable plug and socket for applications.

Like HTML and HTTP, web services are based on a standard definition that is not controlled by any one company. That's one of the reasons that web services became so popular so quickly. Another reason is that web services connections between applications are much cheaper to create and maintain than earlier ways of making such connections. Unlike some of those earlier ways of building connections, web services are reusable. One web service can be used by any number of other applications. One application can provide many different web services.

This revolution is already underway. Web services exist for all sorts of reasons. Federal Express and UPS publish web services for package tracking. Google and Amazon provide web service interfaces to create front ends to their sites. These are just the first few drops in a deluge.

The power of web services to connect one application to another also opens up the door for abuse. How many connections are really needed? Why bother connecting applications at all? Should there be any rules for how one application connects to another? How will all of this happen with the appropriate level of security and reliability?

Web services standards will help address issues of security and guaranteed delivery of messages, but on many of these questions, standards will be silent. It is up to those using this powerful technology to do so correctly. When web services standards need to be applied to create a scalable, robust enterprise-wide solution that can adapt to any usage model, many more questions need to be resolved. Enterprise Services Architecture builds on the base web services standards and adds to them a blueprint for how to use these standards within a reference implementation to meet the needs of the enterprise.

WHAT WILL BUSINESSES DO WITH WEB SERVICES?

Businesses are becoming increasingly attracted to web services because they open the door to flexibility if used properly. But to understand fully why businesses care about web services, we must step back a bit and look at the IT infrastructure at most companies.

The story of the evolution of IT at most firms goes like this. Starting in the late 1980s, mainframe applications gave way to more modern client/server applications. First, large systems like Enterprise Resource Planning (ERP) were implemented to automate and control financial and administrative processes. Then, based on the efficiency and productivity created in successful ERP implementations, the scope of automation naturally expanded. Every vice president got his or her own application that was identified with a Three-Letter Acronym (TLA). The VP of Sales got Customer Relationship Management (CRM). The VP of Manufacturing got Supply Chain Management (SCM). The VP of Product Development got Product Lifecycle Management (PLM). The VP of Purchasing got Supplier Relationship Management (SRM).

For a while, everyone was happy because all these new applications automated previously manual functions. But it didn't take long for people to realize that sometimes an important business process started in CRM, moved to ERP, and ended up in SCM. Few of these enterprise applications could easily share data with each other, and almost none were able to support the idea of managing a cross-application, cross-functional process.

Companies did the best they could to bridge the gap between these applications and used expensive techniques to connect one application to another. A partial solution to this problem appeared in the form of human integration, as shown in Figure 25-1. The brains of people who had access to all of the information from different systems became the *de facto* hubs for the cross-application integration of processes.

Enterprise Services Architecture - Situation Today
Example: Make-To-Order Process in Automotive

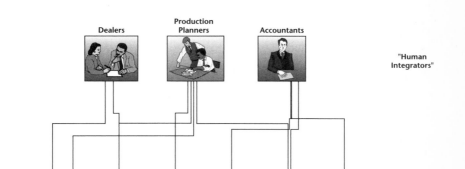

Figure 25-1. Human Integrators

Enterprise Application Integration (EAI) products also emerged to help with making application-to-application connections, but even with such products, making connections remained expensive and difficult. EAI, as it turned out, provided only a fraction of what was needed to connect applications. Specifically, the focus of EAI on sending, receiving, and routing messages and mapping one format to another meant that it lacked the ability to solve the top-to-bottom application integration problem including the user interface, process innovation and optimization, information integration, and collaborative functionality.

The fact that companies frequently had enterprise applications from different vendors, either by choice or because of mergers, exacerbated this problem. At many companies, many different installations of the same application, such as ERP, were in place.

With this situation, companies often had a significant investment in technology that extended automation from one end of the enterprise to the other, but it was quite difficult to make the applications talk to one another.

PROCESS OPTIMIZATION AND THE HUB

At the same time, competitive forces in every industry have been heating up. Even when a company gets some sort of advantage, it doesn't last as long as it used to. Companies are feeling brutal pressure from both customers and investors to cut costs but at the same time increase market share.

> " [I]t is seldom the case that the ideal process fits neatly within one enterprise application. More often, the ideal process crosses application and functional boundaries. "

Due to the increasingly popular use of component outsourcing, product innovations provide less differentiation. As a result, companies have started to analyze and optimize the processes by which they run their businesses as the key pathway to success. But it is seldom the case that the ideal process fits neatly within one enterprise application. More often, the ideal process crosses application and functional boundaries. When asked to implement such processes, the IT department frequently has to explain that it will be expensive and take a long time.

The emphasis on processes has also created a desire to change the way applications appear to users and work inside. Let's go back to our automobile analogy to understand this.

Right now each enterprise application is like its own car. It has an engine that does the work and a dashboard, the user interface, that lets the businesspeople drive it around.

What businesspeople want is one dashboard per role that shows how that role is helping to carry out a process, not one dashboard per application. That means that a single dashboard might have to show what is happening in the engine of one enterprise application at the beginning of a process, another in the middle, and another at the end. Businesspeople want to see a dashboard that helps them drive a process from beginning to end, regardless of how many different engines have to get involved.

Businesses also increasingly want to extend their processes across company boundaries so that the engines running at other companies can be brought into the process. Such connections can be used to make processes run more smoothly or to outsource context activities that used to take place inside a company.

To make this happen requires creating lots of connections between applications and between applications and dashboards. Before web services, the cost of creating and maintaining all of these connections made reaching the full potential of cross-application integration so expensive that it became practically impossible. But now companies will increasingly use web services as a way to make their existing architecture more process-centric and to extend automation across application and company boundaries.

But there is a huge danger lurking in these possibilities. Most IT professionals remember the early days of BASIC programming when programs frequently had little structure, lots of GOTOs, and a large amount of complexity. Such programs are impossible to maintain. Changing one line could have an unintended effect and break the entire program.

Breaking a program is one thing. Breaking an entire complex of integrated enterprise applications is a much more costly mistake and can severely damage a company.

To understand how unstructured complexity will be avoided in favor of a design that allows efficient and reliable management of many-to-many application connections, we must dive a bit deeper into our metaphor. An enterprise application can be thought of in two parts, as an engine, the guts of the application that does the work, and the dashboard, the user interface that allows the user to drive the application. But this leaves the question of where all of the work of the managing the cross-application processes will happen. The user interface layer is not normally considered such a place.

Actually, to really represent how Enterprise Services Architecture works, a layer must be added to the dashboard in addition to the user interface. This layer is the hub. It is the layer that manages all of the connections to the engine portion of the enterprise application. The engine portion can be thought of as the part accessible through web services. The hub portion uses these web services to connect many engines to user interfaces as needed. This is very similar to the way modern cars are designed to "drive by wire" instead of by a direct mechanical connection between the steering wheel, brake pedal, and dashboard and their respective wheels, brakes, and various components being measured and displayed by the dashboard instruments.

Figure 25-2 illustrates this structure quite clearly. The boxes marked "enterprise systems" are unified by two horizontal layers that make up what we have been calling the dashboard. One of those horizontal layers is the portal, which handles the user interface. The other layer is the hub — the integration broker and master data management layer, which we will explain later — that connects all of the enterprise systems together.

Many companies that recognize the potential of web services are hesitant to undertake an ambitious program until someone presents a comprehensive theory of how web services will be implemented on top of existing programs and how the new dashboards will be created without turning the entire infrastructure into a mass of unmaintainable complexity. The hub just mentioned is the first step in understanding how Enterprise Services Architecture solves the problem. Enterprise Services Architecture describes what each element and each layer in the world of IT must do to make web services a powerful force for creating business value.

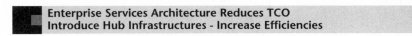

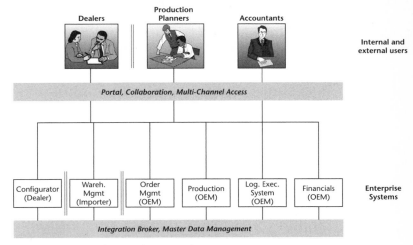

Figure 25-2. Hub–Based Integration

WHAT WILL SAP DO WITH WEB SERVICES?

For a company like SAP, web services represent the key to allowing customers to enjoy the applications they have purchased over the past 10 years and gradually make a transition to a better architecture.

The problem facing SAP is that applications like ERP used to be the center of the universe. Business processes were automated within these applications. Now corporate strategy and related business processes are the center of the universe, and they frequently cross application boundaries. In Enterprise Services Architecture, processes will be managed increasingly in the hub. It is now the job of each application to provide the hub with help to manage processes as they pass from application to application. This means the hub will be making connections between lots of applications. Integration is another name for making all these connections.

All of the changes that SAP is making to adapt to the possibilities of web services can be summarized in the following statements:

- Make every application ready to provide and consume web services.
- Base integration on web services and provide all the supporting tools needed.
- Change the way applications are created to take advantage of web services.
- Prepackage the connections between applications, between tools, and between applications and tools so that as much integration as possible is available out of the box.
- Use a hub and supporting services to manage cross-application processes and the many-to-many connections based on web services.
- In making all of these changes, reduce the cost of owning applications and changing them to adapt to new strategies and operational processes.

Web services solve many different problems for SAP.

- First, web services allow the existing set of applications, including legacy, SAP, and third-party applications, to more easily and cheaply participate in cross-application and cross-enterprise processes using either adapters or native support.
- Second, web services make it much easier for SAP to extend existing enterprise applications with new functionality.
- Third, web services make it easier to create versions of enterprise applications for specific industries.
- Fourth, web services make it easier to create new applications to implement innovative ways of doing business that automate processes beyond the scope of existing applications.

At the beginning of 2003, Hasso Plattner addressed a company meeting and explained the workings and the significance of Enterprise Services Architecture.

"We developed the technology to build applications which predominantly sit on services. They do not have their own database. They use services," Hasso said to the group. "Many applications are providing services, and we can now reuse these services and build new applications." Hasso pointed out that banks and credit card companies were among the first to offer services to other applications.

"We have our strengths, we maintain our strengths, and we add new capabilities. This is why I believe Enterprise Services Architecture is more important or probably at least as important as our invention in the early 1990s of the three-tier client/server architecture," Hasso concluded.

What makes all of this possible is the dashboard that has been permanently separated from the engine and the hub that allows a dashboard to connect to many different engines. Now the needs of the driver, the business users, to execute, monitor, and control processes are the major factors in designing a new dashboard, not how one particular engine works.

Web services are not enough by themselves. The key to making this work in practice is to have the best set of tools for taking advantage of web services to

> **" . . . I believe Enterprise Services Architecture is more important or probably at least as important as our invention in the early 1990s of the three-tier client/server architecture . . . "**

create great dashboards. Enterprise Services Architecture explains the structure of how great dashboards are created. SAP NetWeaver™ is the set of tools used to create both the hub and the user interface portions of the dashboard. Both are explained in the next section.

HOW DOES ENTERPRISE SERVICES ARCHITECTURE WORK?

With all of the decks cleared, Enterprise Services Architecture is actually a pretty simple concept. Let's return to our analogy of the car to complete the explanation.

APPLICATION VERSUS ENTERPRISE SERVICES

The engine of the car is the functionality of the enterprise application. Inside the engine is all of the programming language code that does the work of automating business processes. What web services do is allow these engines to present any externalized capabilities of the engine without exposing the internals of how that functionality is being executed. That externalized functionality is presented as a guaranteed contract that other dashboards and applications can rely on and leverage for their needs. *Application services* is the name for the web services that expose services from an engine or an enterprise application.

While application services perform some useful task, such as canceling an order in the CRM system, they are usually too low level to be shown on a dashboard for a business user. To display application services on a dashboard would be like showing the workings of each spark plug to the driver of a car. The driver just does not need to know that much information.

Enterprise services are the kind of services that are shown on a dashboard. These services are meaningful to the driver, the business user, and reflect how the company thinks of its business. For example, an enterprise service for canceling an order would invoke the application service to cancel the order in the CRM system but would also check the SCM system to see if any parts had been ordered, the financial system to see if an invoice had been created, and any other system that had been involved in the creation of the order. An enterprise service is a higher level service that may use many application services to do its job. When a business user presses the cancel order button on the dashboard, the enterprise service manages the complexity of that activity and doesn't leave it to the business user to figure out what else needs to be done.

So, application services are lower level services to perform needed functions and enterprise services are higher level services created from application services that are aware of the larger business process. Another way to think of this is that application services are created on top of the engine and enterprise services are composed in support of the dashboard. It is possible that sometimes an application service has such general applicability that it is used as an enterprise service.

THE STRUCTURE OF COMPOSITE APPLICATIONS

Two important points must be discussed before we move on. First, it is important to note that an engine, or enterprise application, can provide application services and still work the same way it always has with the dashboard that was provided with the original application. This point is key to understanding why Enterprise Services Architecture is not disruptive and allows for incremental creation of new services.

The second point is that the dashboard as it has been discussed so far has been assigned three jobs: creating the user interface, implementing cross-application processes, and managing the many-to-many web services connections between applications. These last two functions have been called the integration hub, but the integration hub is actually much more than that. The hub also allows for the creation of enterprise services from application services and for orchestrating all of the application and enterprise services into new applications that manage a process that flows through many different engines using many different powerful tools. This dashboard layer provides quite a lot of functionality and power, which will be described in the later section on SAP NetWeaver and dashboard development. For now, however, it is important to keep in mind that the dashboard actually enables the creation of a new kind of application called a composite application.

Composite applications are applications that are constructed using web services as building blocks. Composite applications make sense because existing enterprise applications have so much useful functionality. Many of the natural objects that we discussed exist in the current collection of enterprise applications. It doesn't profit a new application to replicate existing functionality. Most companies have too many repositories for basic customer information already. It doesn't make sense to create another one. Figure 25-3 shows how enterprise services exist in the hub layer and use application services.

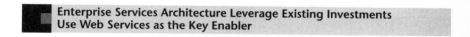

Enterprise Services Architecture Leverage Existing Investments Use Web Services as the Key Enabler

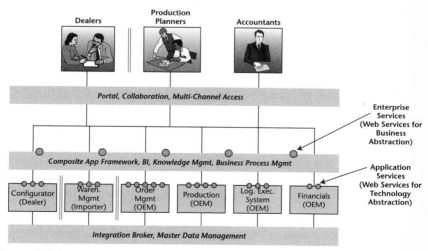

Figure 25-3. Enterprise Services and Application Services

This figure introduces a new layer to the hub that contains a bunch of tools starting with the Composite Application Framework. We will explain those tools in the section on SAP NetWeaver. The important point to take away is that a composite application may use the services from many existing engines — that is, enterprise applications. The hub may first aggregate different application services into an enterprise service, and then the composite application can use those enterprise services to do the intended work. If new custom web services are needed, they are created in the dashboard layer. A new composite application is born using a combination of application and enterprise services along with other services and capabilities provided by all of the rest of SAP NetWeaver functionality for creating portal interfaces, managing business processes, and many other tasks that will be described shortly.

> " . . . [A]t all levels, SAP's application and tools are ready to integrate with web services from any source. This is a key requirement for success in a world in which most companies are awash in technology from many different vendors. "

Note the efficiency here. A new application is created leveraging as much as possible of the existing enterprise applications. Note also that the composite application is free to span as many enterprise applications and be as process-oriented as it needs to be. The dashboard is not tightly bound to one engine.

HETEROGENEOUS INTEGRATION

SAP is dedicated to making sure that Enterprise Services Architecture serves to lower total cost of ownership by delivering SAP NetWeaver and all of its enterprise applications with prepackaged integration at all levels.

This message should not be seen as a declaration that only SAP tools and applications can participate in Enterprise Services Architecture. Web services are universally accepted, and at all levels, SAP's application and tools are ready to integrate with web services from any source. This is a key requirement for success in a world in which most companies are awash in technology from many different vendors.

We can now be more specific about the explanation we want to give to the mechanics and engineers about how to build the engines under the hood to enable the creation of the best possible dashboards. Here are some guidelines:

- Expose useful functionality from engines, enterprise applications, as application services.
- Use the integration hub and the dashboard to aggregate those application services into enterprise services.
- Create an environment for composite application development based on application and enterprise services, using as much additional existing functionality as possible to create new applications to support process innovation and optimization at all levels.

The next section dives more deeply into how SAP NetWeaver helps create composite applications. The following section then outlines the business benefits of Enterprise Services Architecture.

SAP NETWEAVER AND DASHBOARD DEVELOPMENT

Up until now, we have strongly hinted that quite a bit goes on inside the dashboard. At first, the dashboard was presented as the controls for the engine of an application. Then, we added the idea of a hub for implementing cross-application processes and managing many-to-many connections. The last addition was the idea of using the hub layer of the dashboard as a place to create enterprise services from application services and develop composite applications.

The notion of the dashboard has become more and more complex. Now the innards of dashboard will be revealed, and we will explain how SAP NetWeaver is the key enabler for creating the kind of dashboards we have described so far and therefore the key enabler of Enterprise Services Architecture.

In terms of Enterprise Services Architecture, the way to think of SAP NetWeaver is as a platform for building what we have been calling dashboards. Now that we have identified all the moving parts, we can be a little more precise. SAP NetWeaver is a platform for integrating enterprise applications and building composite applications. It is important to point out that SAP NetWeaver is one way to build software that follows the recommended structure of Enterprise Services Architecture. SAP NetWeaver is not equal to Enterprise Services Architecture.

SAP NetWeaver has components that help with integration that fall roughly into the following groups:

- **People integration** is about making sure dashboards have the ability to allow employees to collaborate and work together and is accomplished using the following capabilities of SAP NetWeaver:
  - Portals provide a unifying layer that can bring information and functionality from many different sources to a user in a form that increases productivity.
  - Collaboration features connect users to each other through instant messaging, chat rooms, web presentations, discussion forums, email lists, and other means presented in context to an application.
  - Multi-channel access brings the application to the users wherever they are through support for a wide range of mobile devices.
- **Information integration** is about bringing together information into one unified form and making it accessible to the right people at the right time. The portal helps with this on the front end, but the information comes together in the following capabilities:
  - Business Intelligence is an environment for bringing together information from many different sources, making it consistent, analyzing it using advanced tools, and then distributing it as needed.
  - Knowledge Management allows indexing and searching of unstructured documents in many different locations along with a repository for such documents.
  - Master Data Management is an advanced capability for unifying, synchronizing, and managing data that is distributed across many different applications. Master data is data about key objects, such as customers and products, that is used for many different purposes.
- **Process integration** is about coordinating the workings of various programs to manage process across applications. The following capabilities help with this task:
  - Integration Broker features connect one application to another through capabilities for sending XML messages back and forth between applications, mapping between different message formats, providing a way to build adapters to allow applications to send and receive messages, and describing in a repository web services that communicate using messages.
  - Business Process Management capabilities allow for implementation of advanced business processes and complex synchronization and routing of messages between applications.

- The **Application Platform** provides the foundation for building all of these layers, including the ability to write programs in Java and ABAP, SAP's programming language that is used to write mySAP Business Suite applications. Using the database and operating system abstraction layers, programs can run on any platform, including Unix and Microsoft Windows.
- Advanced capabilities of SAP NetWeaver include the **Composite Application Framework**, a development environment for composite applications, and **Solution Life Cycle Management**, services and tools for managing the process of packaging components together into a program that can be installed, configured, maintained with bug fixes, and upgraded.

All of these capabilities are delivered through a single unified platform called SAP NetWeaver, delivered as a product, not just an architecture or a concept. SAP NetWeaver comes with a unified installation and management environment. The environment includes the SAP NetWeaver Development Studio, an integrated development environment for developing Java and ABAP applications.

With all of this functionality, SAP NetWeaver provides a massive leg up to companies seeking to integrate their IT infrastructure at the lowest possible cost. As mentioned earlier, SAP lowers costs for integration by provided prepackaged integration between all the SAP NetWeaver tools and all of the mySAP Business Suite Enterprise Applications. Of course, with SAP NetWeaver, SAP includes the required tools and connectors to integrate non–SAP applications as well.

The key benefits of SAP NetWeaver are that it creates an environment that allows the

> *" By adopting Enterprise Services Architecture and using SAP NetWeaver to implement it, companies gain unprecedented flexibility while keeping costs under control. "*

power of web services to be unleashed and the complexity inherent in using them to be managed, all according to the structure dictated by Enterprise Services Architecture. Composite applications lend themselves to rapid improvement because web services by their nature can be easily reused. By adopting Enterprise Services Architecture and using SAP NetWeaver to implement it, companies gain unprecedented flexibility while keeping costs under control.

A NEW WAY OF PROGRAMMING

Enterprise Services Architecture is a new way of designing applications. SAP NetWeaver is a new set of tools for building applications. In order to bring them together, SAP has created a new programming model, the fundamental approach and basic building blocks that programmers use to create programs. The new model bridges Enterprise Services Architecture and SAP NetWeaver so that programmers have a ready-made paradigm for achieving the former with the latter.

Using web services based on existing applications, both application services and enterprise services, is a big part of this new model. But the complete model goes way beyond that. The ultimate goal of this new model is to lower the costs of developing and owning software. SAP will use this new model to build its products, and customers will use the new model to extend and customize SAP products and to create custom applications of their own.

Goals of this programming model include:

- Increasing the use of modeling in application development to express relationships between services so that more of an application can be generated automatically instead of programmed by hand. This speeds development and makes programs easier to change.
- Increasing the number of reusable components used in an application. One set of tools would be used to manage master data in all applications. A tax engine might be created to perform tax calculations. Commonly used functions would be carried out with shared components and standard approaches.
- Making SAP NetWeaver and the tools it provides the foundation of all SAP products.
- Using the portal as the user interface for all products.
- Accelerating user interface development through the use of patterns.
- Employing business process management tools to control and customize the behavior of programs, ensuring a clear separation between process control and business logic.
- Using a consistent approach across all applications to such challenges as reporting, integration of desktop applications, and data access.
- Adopting a single approach to storing all different kinds of data that takes into account the different needs for transactional data, replicated master data, and unstructured data like documents.

At its heart, this new programming model maximizes the amount of each program that is composed of reusable components, anticipates as many potential problems as possible, and provides a standard method of solving them. The result of such a model is a new kind of software that is far easier to change and far less costly to develop and maintain.

This programming model will show up on the desks of programmers as new libraries and tools for the Composite Application Framework and SAP NetWeaver Developer Studio.

INCREMENTAL ADOPTION

One common mistake when considering adoption of Enterprise Services Architecture is thinking in terms of a big bang approach. While Enterprise Services Architecture is a comprehensive theory that offers suggestions about how to improve every corner of a company's infrastructure, the nature of web services and SAP NetWeaver allows the changes to occur gradually.

For example, here is one approach to incremental adoption:

- Start small by using the SAP Enterprise Portal to implement a role-specific user interface that assembles all the information from different enterprise applications to help automate a cross-functional process.
- Provide more power for such portal interfaces by creating custom web services with the SAP Web Application Server.
- Using SAP Exchange Infrastructure, create a platform of reusable web services that extend the power of many different applications to new audiences.
- Combine the web services created with those from existing enterprise applications to create a comprehensive composite application that automates an end-to-end process using the Composite Application Framework.

This is just one path forward that shows how Enterprise Services Architecture can be achieved in a series of small steps.

THE BUSINESS BENEFITS OF ENTERPRISE SERVICES ARCHITECTURE

Another way to look at Enterprise Services Architecture is as a new paradigm of IT infrastructure. As Figure 25-4 shows, the transition from the mainframe era to the client/server era was largely a matter of replacement. The transition to a services-oriented architecture, by contrast, will leave current systems in place. This architecture extends the current infrastructure and adds a new level of flexibility at the same time.

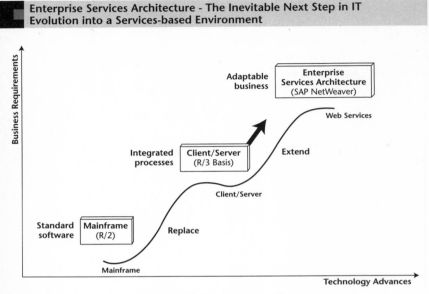

Figure 25-4. The Stages of IT Infrastructure Development

Of course, Enterprise Services Architecture really means little if it doesn't help companies succeed. When you combine the general principles of Enterprise Services Architecture with the technical power of the SAP NetWeaver components, IT architects have the ability to build flexible solutions that can be rapidly evolved to meet business needs. IT is transformed from a bottleneck to an enabler of change, and therein lies the greatest value of Enterprise Services Architecture and SAP NetWeaver.

Using this approach, businesses now have framework in which to define business processes, support them with process-centric composite applications, and rapidly improve them. Optimizing business processes in real time is the key to creating a sustainable competitive advantage.

By its very nature, Enterprise Services Architecture allows for leveraging the investment in existing systems. The flexible nature of web services also enables incremental progress in which the most valuable composite applications can be built first, with a gradual implementation of less urgently needed applications. The process-centric nature of composite applications dramatically increases usability by providing business users just what they need to get a particular job done. The prepackaged integration and powerful development tools drive down total cost of ownership and the cost of building and integrating solutions.

Enterprise Services Architecture enables the real-time enterprise by enabling real-time change. In doing so, it provides the most future-proof approach to IT infrastructure yet defined.

" [T]he transition from the mainframe era to the client/server era was largely a matter of replacement. The transition to a services-oriented architecture, by contrast, will leave current systems in place. "

26

Real-Time Hardware

Craig R. Barrett became Intel's fourth President in May 1997 and Chief Executive Officer in 1998. He was elected to Intel Corporation's Board of Directors in 1992. He served as Chief Operating Officer from 1993 to 1997. He began his tenure at Intel as a Technology Development manager in 1974. Prior to joining Intel, Barrett was an Associate Professor at Stanford University in the Department of Materials Science and Engineering.

Craig R. Barrett

A t Intel Corporation, we spend every day thinking about the real-time enterprise. Every digital transaction, every digital decision starts with silicon and moves to action with software. Thousands of Intel architects, software designers, and consultants are dedicated to ensuring that SAP and a multitude of other technology companies work hand in hand so that all businesses can rely on our industry to provide some of the world's most powerful, flexible, and reliable computing and communications solutions.

Having learned how to invest their money and resources in technology, corporations now understand that IT provides a competitive strategic advantage. Intel has invested heavily in manufacturing technology and product research and development over the past 3 years to deliver innovative silicon technologies and products that underpin today's leading-edge IT solutions. Examples of these efforts include two pioneering Intel architectures: Intel® Centrino® mobile technology for wireless computing and Intel® Itanium® architecture for mission-critical servers. We've also added new features to our platforms, such as

Intel Hyper-Threading technology, which allows software to view a single processor as if it were two, thus increasing client and server performance and multitasking abilities. Still, many more exciting innovations are on the horizon.

Together, ever better silicon and software innovation bring greater power and flexibility and ultimately greater value and lower cost of ownership to businesses. The challenge we share is to deliver a truly "anywhere, anytime" computing and communications experience. Top IT companies such as Intel and SAP are leading the way in providing these solutions. We look forward to continuing our work with Hasso Plattner and his SAP team in making IT ever more important in determining the competitiveness of real-time enterprises around the world.

27

Cultural Change in the Real-Time Enterprise

Esther Dyson is a global Internet visionary. Since 1983, as chairman of EDventure Holdings, she has focused on cutting-edge technologies and business models as a newsletter writer, active investor, New York Times columnist, and policymaker. In her best-selling book, Release 2.0: A Design for Living in the Digital Age, she shared a sophisticated yet succinct overview of the Internet's implications for individuals. Ms. Dyson was founding chairman of ICANN, the Internet Corporation for Assigned Names and Numbers, the international agency responsible for setting policy for the Internet's infrastructure. Dyson's early thinking on software products turning into online services, nearly a decade ago, anticipated the current discussions over intellectual property and web services business models. Release 1.0, her monthly newsletter, is an indispensable first look at emerging technologies and timely policy debates. In this chapter, Dyson focuses on how the real-time enterprise will change the role of the employee from a cog in a machine to an autonomous actor in a corporate immune system.

Esther Dyson

From the industrial revolution until the recent past, the classical business model was based on a command-control hierarchy and the division of labor. In this context, a manager dictated a set of tasks to his division. Unless employees were in sales, they might not have any idea who the customer was. Only if they were in marketing, might they have a sense of what the ultimate product could do.

Thirty years ago when SAP's business software was in its infancy, it allowed the enterprise to become a process organization. Tasks were still distributed across people and departments, but each department manager now had software from ERP to CRM to HR. Managers obtained access to interdepartmental data, but workers remained in the dark. In time, SAP's business software evolved, unifying departments across the enterprise. The dream of the real-time enterprise is at last beginning to take shape. But at this point, the role of the manager will be deemphasized, and the worker will take center stage. Without doubt, IT matters. But the last mile towards the real-time enterprise is no longer about zeros and ones. It's about flesh and blood.

The metaphor of choice for the enterprise is currently the Digital Nervous System. This made sense when the business model dictated a command-control organization. This top-down notion, however, with everything stemming from the brain, is no longer valid. More appropriate is a company-wide immune system. Each worker knows his identity as part of that company, and the corporate culture knows how to react instinctively; workers don't need to ask the nervous system what to do. For the nervous system with its explicit instructions to work well, you must also have an implicit corporate identity that encourages all the components to work together within a common culture. This corporate identity is the medium, a chemical environment. In theory at least, everyone on staff is working together, sharing profits, and working toward the same goals.

> " [T]he last mile towards the real-time enterprise is no longer about zeros and ones. It's about flesh and blood. "

While CEOs and CIOs agree that "business as usual" is dead, beyond touting radio frequency ID (RFID), web services, and other nifty tools, next steps require a commitment by management to empower staff and distribute responsibility from managers to workers. Culture is the key to this transition. As always but more so, the enterprise must be responsive to the customer and flexible enough to accommodate rapid change. This requires agility, innovation, and autonomous decision-making. Software should support such adaptation rather than cast current practices in stone. The challenge here is making each and every worker accountable — and in effect, her own boss. Just as a chain — be it supply or demand — is only as strong as its weakest link, each and every worker embodies the organization.

It's fashionable to note how the real-time enterprise has moved us from a command control structure to a flattened hierarchy, but once all of the routines have been automated, what's your differentiator? Your competitive advantage beyond IT becomes how your people behave — their interactions with other people — their peers, your partners, your customers.

Ideally, web services allow the enterprise to manage context (undifferentiated business processes required by the market) while nourishing core (whatever gives a sustainable competitive advantage). (Core versus context is discussed further in Chapter 16.) To ensure this, we'll need a system that allows for reaction, measuring privileges, and defining rights and responsibilities. Since services — billing, core reputation, and allocation of resources — won't reside in any one place, we'll need a system that permits distributed allocation of activities. Most visions of web services lack details on the rules of the game, how companies will supply all the context required to use web services to create business relationships on the fly. Management consultant John Hagel (a contributor to *Release 1.0*) has dubbed this missing social, legal, business, and technical infrastructure the *service grid*. It includes things such as performance monitoring and management, billing and pricing, allocation of resources, dispute resolution, and liability for problems.

REALIZING THE SERVICE GRID

Managers are quick to suggest a raft of new policies for the new corporate culture. But the whole point is to have principles and then let employees figure out the policies on the fly. If they have the right immune system, they will make the right decisions by themselves.

What we will need then are meta-policies. While the customer isn't always right, we still aim to please him. Internally, we nurture our employees. We won't fire them over a first mistake, unless it's a matter of ethical transgression. It's not a question of policy; it's a question of personality. The difference is *doing* your policy (and in the process, respecting staff and customers). Think of your mission statement. What was a lofty statement of principles, often in a vacuum, can actually describe our best business practices and act as a sustainable competitive advantage.

GIRDING FOR THE GRID

Conceiving of, organizing, and managing IT resources as a set of well-defined services promises to be a dominant theme in thinking about corporate IT for some time to come. It is the latest way of abstracting software function and data and thereby hiding complexity. The so-called services-oriented IT architecture will enable a more accurate internal pricing of IT resources, better alignment of IT and business objectives, cleaner interfaces between disparate software, a new level of flexibility in applications, and more. The service grid concept described here by Dyson is also explored at length in Chapter 25, which focuses on SAP's own Enterprise Services Architecture.

This change will destabilize and unsettle bosses. Managers will have to trust their employees' judgment. Technology is no longer a differentiator if everything is automated. Competitive advantage lies with the people skills of the front-line workers and managers as they interact with one another and with the public as well as their creativity and adaptability to change internally.

> " Technology is no longer a differentiator if everything is automated. Competitive advantage lies with the people skills of the front-line workers and managers as they interact with one another and with the public as well as their creativity and adaptability to change internally. "

In addition to creativity and adaptability, we will need courage. Having real-time information is not enough. Cisco's huge inventory write-downs weren't due to a lack of information; they were due to a lack of *attention* to information — the courage to ask uncomfortable questions. Had they asked whether the same customers were ordering from five different distributors, they would have adjusted their backlog accordingly. The advent of web services isn't just about technical prowess. We must have the fortitude to look at the available information and make a decision on that basis. This will be the competitive advantage — not simply having the information but looking at it with clear eyes.

THE EXCEPTION IS THE RULE

In essence, software is all about finding something that used to be an exception and automating it. In the old, old days, when you asked for a special airline meal, someone wrote it down for special handling. Now that you can check off the request on a web form, that exception is routine. Likewise, in a supply chain, it's all about taking everything that was an exception and making it into a routine. The challenge is the 1 percent that remains. Because it's not routine, it requires decision-making or at least a reaction from a person. It requires learning: "Going forward, this is how we'll handle it." By definition, you can't have specific policies for exceptions; you must have good people.

An exception is not anticipated, but guidelines and rules can be created. To be good at exception handling, you need people with personality who react viscerally, who are stakeholders, who are apprentices rather than blind followers. They learn from *managers*, not a manual. How does my manager react when a problem arises? Does she: Perform triage? Fix it this time and then ignore it? Postpone it until next quarter? Or get more information and jump head first into it?

> **" The real-time enterprise relies on real-time decision-making, not on canned policies. It learns, iterates, and adapts in response to what happens. "**

The enterprise must bring people into the corporate personality and have them understand the principles beyond it. It must empower them to use their intelligence to further its goals. The real-time enterprise relies on real-time decision-making, not on canned policies. It learns, iterates, and adapts in response to what happens.

BARRIERS TO CHANGE

John Hagel writes that human resource managers can act as talent arbitrageurs, looking out for the corporation's long-term needs. They can also recognize what he terms *pivotal jobs* — those positions that are crucial in facilitating end-to-end processes and in enabling web services. Right now there *is* a shortage of "good people." That is not to say that there is dead weight but that you need to train your staff if you ever expect to place the company's trust in their hands. Think about your personal network. Would you trust your dry cleaner? To clean your clothes, yes, but not to manage your plant. Your health club owner? Your mailman? Your secretary or your plant manager? Would you put your future in their hands? Not necessarily. It's no secret that most managers aren't comfortable giving up control. They don't trust their employees. This is understandable. But management implies delegation. Managers can't take care of everything all the time. They must relinquish some control and become coaches to their empowered workers.

You need to create a corporate culture where mistakes are acceptable as long as you learn from them. Once you've screened for strength and capacity, help employees gain confidence. Hand in hand with automating what's possible, you infuse a company's people with the corporate vision and train them to be intelligent about customer satisfaction.

BUILDING RELATIONSHIPS BEYOND THE ENTERPRISE

The same automation that serves your company can facilitate relationships with your partners. As your competitors develop flexible architectures, these relationships become the start of the service grid. But there's no express train to the service grid. It's hard to achieve for the following reasons. Having your partner manage your inventory requires trust, which must be earned. If you think it's hard to trust and empower your own people, it's certainly difficult to trust a third party. The fact that you can assign responsibility to them and sue them later might be convenient, but it doesn't generate trust. It's a last resort. You want to use contracts and legal agreements only if everything breaks down. It's a sign of failure. This is an exception you don't want. You begin to trust your partner when you can say, "Everyone that I've met at Acme.com is smart and responsive. They get things done. I'm going to trust them to work with my customers." That's the kind of system you want to create. If it were easy we'd have done it already. There would be no competitive advantage to doing it. If it were easy we'd all be living in a much better world. But it will be easier with automation and incremental trust building.

For this reason, you won't see an explosion of intercompany automation. It will happen in pockets. For example, you could see Federal Express start to do so and then Airborne or UPS could follow suit. But not always. FedEx has bought rather than just partnered with Kinko's. There will not be a smooth rollout of trust everywhere. It will be lumpy and sporadic. It's going to pop up here and there. Let's look at Wal-Mart. While others in the retail industry have tried to copy Wal-Mart because they have to compete with it, they haven't all become as smart as Wal-Mart.

The enterprise will need to know if it can trust a particular third party and have enforceable contracts as well as ways of assigning responsibility for any mistakes. This mechanism will manage and evaluate who's in charge. It will reflect pricing, allocate resources, and run markets and bids across interacting parts — you can call it the service grid. In any case, it will be a distributed mechanism for everything from monitoring performance to managing billing to deciding if there are free web services that can perform a function that an enterprise is currently paying for.

You aren't born with a good reputation; you earn it, and so it will be in the service grid. If you are new to the service grid, you'll need someone to vouch for you. Or you could post a bond for performance, in effect paying someone to vouch for you. While this might be perceived as gatekeeping, the infrastructure of the service grid in fact *helps* the little guy. Without the grid, companies would deal only with those they know and trust. If the mechanism isn't closed, it will permit midsize enterprises (if not the tiny guy) to compete by creating a structure within which they can operate and prove themselves.

To be a success, web services will have to reflect or embody what underlies the communities they support. It's the public market where people publish prices, where they discuss reputations. It's where they go to articulate needs, where you have agreements with other parties. It's also a technical means for handling accountability and allocation of resources and pricing. In the end, when you get into exceptions, you call in the people. You say, "This vendor didn't perform. I lost a customer." People will judge the dispute and adapt the rules to handle new situations going forward if necessary.

CHANGES INSIDE THE ENTERPRISE

As CEOs and CIOs ramp up for the real-time enterprise, they must devote far more resources to motivating and recruiting good people. They should let their employees move around the company so that they understand the different parts and operations. They should also move them around the world to other offices so that they understand the company and don't view some offices as secondary. Since more people will have access to information, management will also need to worry about security issues. You'll have to be very careful about your data and your customer's data.

At the strategy level, you'll need to grasp where your competitive advantage is, think about outsourcing what isn't core function, and con-sider how much can be auto-mated (understanding that doing so fixes routines in place). You want to build a system that is flexible, allowing you to change and adapt. For the most part, the conversations between CIOs and CEOs will be industry-specific. They will need to know how to operate in context of a given industry with its customers and competitors.

> " As CEOs and CIOs ramp up for the real-time enterprise, they must devote far more resources to motivating and recruiting good people. "

Leveraging specific differences between themselves and their competition will be key.

WANTED: NEW TOOLS

In the process of handing over a degree of control to the worker — imbuing him with the flexibility to turn data into knowledge — col-laboration across the enterprise demands new software applications. While enterprise software gives us access to vast amounts of data, dynamic workflow tools are needed. For instance, we currently handle email in an almost ad hoc manner. Email could be used as a collabora-tive tool, permitting people to organize, handle, and manage their email.

In the future, new enterprise applications with new three-letter acronyms will arise alongside ERP, CRM, and so on to embrace industry- or function-specific tasks. We'll need employee relationship management software. We'll need better support for social networks through management of people's contacts — the frequency and quality of their interactions. While the mechanisms for this (including monitoring of employee email and phone logs) might be considered intrusive — and they will require consent — they will be helpful. Empowered workers must be accountable for results. Their results are visible — both good and bad. Workers should benefit and learn from mistakes.

ONLY HUMAN

The enterprise must be especially wary of focusing on the technical side while ignoring these human factors. These mechanisms for accountability can be helpful or they can paralyze. It's all about tone. Rather than being punitive, you want to create an atmosphere that makes it easier to learn from watching the results of what you do. You can have all the collaborative software in the world, but it's all for naught if people don't want to share ideas.

> *" The enterprise must be especially wary of focusing on the technical side while ignoring these human factors. "*

For the most part, the technology to realize the real-time enterprise and the service grid is already in place. The real issue is making it work. We have to learn to work together in a distributed world. We have to behave differently while realizing that human nature will not change. In short, culture counts.

28

Maximizing Value from a Real-Time Enterprise

Michael Fleisher is chairman and CEO of Gartner, Inc., a leading technology research corporation. Since joining Gartner in 1993, Fleisher has been a key player in Gartner's rise to prominence as the leading technology advisor to business and government. In 1993, he led the company's Initial Public Offering as well as the company's later move to the New York Stock Exchange. In addition, Fleisher completed over 30 acquisitions and investments that have made critical contributions to Gartner's research capability and geographical expansion. For the past 5 years, Gartner has been performing ongoing research into the real-time enterprise and its implications for business.

Michael Fleisher

Although the idea of creating a real-time enterprise (RTE) has been around for more than two decades, only recently have we seen broad interest and focus on this concept within the business community. Yet despite the welcome attention to this important and powerful idea, many RTE efforts suffer from a flawed vision of what RTE really means and an incomplete appreciation of the value that its methodologies can actually deliver. Most people involved with RTE believe that becoming an RTE simply means *responding* to business issues much faster than ever before. For the past 5 years, Gartner analysts have been conducting research into this emerging area and have identified an important deficiency in this "response-dominated" vision of RTE.

To profit most from becoming an RTE, executives must initially focus on the instantaneous *detection* of "material" events, and only then concentrate on delivering far more rapid *responses* to those events. This critical distinction is often overlooked, resulting in many RTE initiatives that deliver far less than optimal results. Executives must direct their RTE efforts to three critical areas to receive maximum value:

1. Instantaneous detection
2. More effective responses
3. Critical technology prerequisites

INSTANTANEOUS DETECTION: THERE'S ALWAYS WARNING

A real-time enterprise monitors, captures, and analyzes root cause and overt events that are critical to the success of a company the moment those events occur. RTEs will then exploit that real-time information to progressively remove delays in managing and executing its critical detection, reporting, decision making, and response business processes.

The vital importance of monitoring, capturing, and analyzing certain critical events in real time was highlighted by our examination of scores of positive and negative events that have occurred both in daily society and in business. We analyzed numerous situations to determine if manmade episodes arrive with prior warning. We studied the circumstances that preceded plane crashes, Three Mile Island, the Challenger and Columbia shuttle disasters, and, most disturbing of all, September 11th. We also studied the findings of special commissions and formal investigations that followed each manmade disaster. We consistently found that there was warning prior to each and every event.

> " A real-time enterprise monitors, captures, and analyzes root cause and overt events that are critical to the success of a company the moment those events occur. "

We then turned our primary attention to the world of business to identify whether sufficient warning existed in advance of business mishaps or business opportunities. After reviewing circumstances leading up to negative earnings reports, positive earnings reports, bankruptcies, failed business mergers and acquisitions, SEC investigations, and other so-called business "surprises," we concluded that there is no such thing as a legitimate surprise. Prior to every business "surprise," there was always warning.

We then investigated how anyone could perform real-time monitoring of all the information available needed to avert disaster or to pursue genuine opportunities. After reanalyzing dozens of business case studies, we created a pair of complementary tools, an identification model and a justification model, so that executives could ascertain the information they truly needed to avoid mishaps and pursue the right business opportunity. Once a selection of candidates for real-time information monitoring passes through the two models, the results invariably reveal "materially important information." "Material" information became a key factor in our research and is borrowed from the disciplines of law and especially accounting. In each endeavor, information is considered material if upon receipt of such information a reasonable person would have changed her judgment or course of action.

> " *The results of this information-filtering exercise led us to a critically important conclusion: to avoid mishaps or pursue opportunity, you need to monitor only a very, very small amount of information in real time.* "

The results of this information-filtering exercise led us to a critically important conclusion: to avoid mishaps or pursue opportunity, you need to monitor only a very, very small amount of information in real time.

During the course of our research, we asked numerous CEOs whether there was real-time information that they believed could enable them to run their enterprises far more effectively. Every time we asked this question of CEOs, they *always* answered "yes." We then asked what specific information they would like to receive in real time. They *always* had an answer and *always* provided it quickly. These affirmative, resolute, and specific answers clearly show that CEOs already appreciate the value of real-time information. As companies continue their search for new ways to compete and improve growth performance, we advise CIOs to determine where monitoring, capturing, and analyzing real-time information fits into their CEO's wish list. The way to do this is to ask them. The time to do it is now.

MORE EFFECTIVE RESPONSES

So far, we have explained how the path towards becoming a real-time enterprise begins with the instantaneous detection of important events. We now turn our attention to combining detection with effective response.

SIX REAL-TIME ENTERPRISE IMPERATIVES

We recommend adopting six key imperatives that will enable enterprise executives to realize the greatest value from becoming a real-time enterprise. Undertaking an RTE endeavor is not a trivial exercise — the stakes and risks are substantial. Senior executives must come to the conclusion that deep change is required to improve competitiveness and that a focus on end-to-end, elapsed-cycle time reduction is more likely to deliver substantive change than yet another round of cost-cutting. They must also understand that the technology of the Internet era can enable substantial process time-lag reductions.

However, even with senior-level commitment, time-based transformation is likely to fail if business units and the IT organization don't get off to the right start. These six top-line imperatives — three for business units and three for the IT organization — will help enterprise leaders focus on critical issues from the beginning of the RTE endeavor.

Three Business Imperatives

The three business imperatives can be reduced to simple phrases:

1. Simplify and select
2. Slash and stabilize
3. Set and sell

The focus of these imperatives is to ensure that there is a clear objective and that everyone involved with the change process knows what it is. This sounds like common sense, but it is in marked contrast to many of the technology-enabled change initiatives of recent years that often evolved organically, such as e-commerce, corporate portals, and customer relationship management. In contrast, to succeed, RTE initiatives require coherent messages and enterprise-wide discipline from the start.

1. Simplify the View and Select Critical Cycles

RTE principles of change can be applied to any of an enterprise's major process areas including its supplier and customer processes. However, the RTE approach can't be applied to all of the major processes simultaneously. Attempting too much parallel business change will lead to confusion, interference, and slow progress — or possibly no real progress at all.

2. Slash Some Processes and Stabilize Others

Within the selected cycles, there likely will be many large and complex processes. Changing all of the processes simultaneously is not possible without unacceptable risks to current operations. Enterprise leadership must identify the process areas that they want to alter significantly and those that will remain constant to maintain stability. For example, if the order-to-cash cycle is selected for change, the enterprise can change the timing and delivery mechanisms for billing as it moves to 24/7 direct selling, but it might leave the pricing model intact during the first wave of change.

The objective must be to trim or cut the selected processes, not merely to improve them minimally. The term *real time* should serve to remind everyone involved that they must seek drastic change. Only a goal of radical improvement will generate a level of creative thought sufficient to mitigate the forces that will try to maintain the status quo. Managers must understand from the beginning of the RTE endeavor that radical, end-to-end cycle time reduction is the objective.

> " Only a goal of radical improvement will generate a level of creative thought sufficient to mitigate the forces that will try to maintain the status quo. "

3. Set Time-Reduction Goals and Sell Them to Employees Enterprise-wide

A significant attribute of the RTE approach is that elapsed time is an easy concept to understand and is easy to measure, which in turn allows hard targets to be set. Enterprise leadership should begin the RTE endeavor by widely communicating specific and easily measurable targets for time reduction. For example:

- Marketing director: "Today, it takes 20 months on average to design and introduce a new product. By November 2005, we will reduce this to 10 months."
- Finance director: "This company has a clear, long-term strategy of growth by acquisition. However, it takes nearly a year to assimilate an acquired company with our accounting methods and human resources management controls. By year end 2004, we will reduce this to 3 months."

Setting hard, visible, simply articulated, public targets clarifies the intent to change. The elapsed time of processes can be readily measured and independently verified if necessary. Elapsed-time targets should be made the basis for at least a portion of senior management's performance-based compensation.

Three IT Imperatives

The three IT imperatives can also be reduced to simple phrases:

4. Map and measure
5. Mobilize and reskill
6. Architect for agility

IT leaders and architects should understand these imperatives from the beginning of the RTE project. Following these imperatives will help ensure that the IT organization can respond quickly and appropriately to a business-led RTE initiative.

4. Map Enterprise Application Latencies and Measure the Cost of Change

A decade ago, it was wise to batch-base many back-end processes because the cost and complexity of a transactional or event-driven alternative significantly outweighed the advantages. Even during the client/server era, network traffic costs frequently prevented an IT architect from deploying a solution where applications were set up to poll each other frequently. Because of this mixed provenance, current enterprise architectures contain various latencies. Some applications respond to input in seconds. Others may take minutes. Batch processes may run hourly, daily, weekly, monthly, or even quarterly.

IT architects should create an enterprise-wide map of applications that represents their latencies as the key dimension. This enables easy identification of slow points in business processes as well as in the systems that support them.

Simply creating a map is not enough, however. As business managers work to radically transform the elapsed time of a process, they must rapidly assess the costs of various options. As architects map the latency of key elements, they should also ascribe expense numbers for upgrading speed of response. For example, what is the cost of upgrading from a monthly to a weekly batch feed of billing transaction data? What is the cost to make it daily? Can it be made into an immediate, live response to ensure that the customer's bill is updated every few minutes?

Business planners will require a cost estimate for these various levels of upgrading. The IT organization should carefully examine the map in advance of these requests because only by considering the whole picture can optimal solutions for broad architecture and infrastructure changes be devised.

5. Mobilize Staff to Work on Latency Reductions, and Reskill Appropriately

As the RTE endeavor progresses, the changes that must be made to established business processes and their supporting applications will require considerable integration work. Conversely, the demand for understanding and implementing new, packaged applications from external service providers will decrease. Core infrastructure elements — particularly in middleware and messaging — must be added and extended, and up-to-date skills in these areas must be obtained. These shifts in emphasis will be the same regardless of whether the systems development and operation work is done internally or externally.

Skills in demand will include systems integration staff who can cross over between old and new technology sets and who understand the reality of the business process details within the enterprise and its industry value chain. This implies less demand for new Java programmers and more demand for 5- to 15-year IT veterans from the enterprise's industry.

Great value will be obtained by bringing previously underinvested administrative processes online, which reduces cycle times by enabling direct access to information. However, this requires more than web browser client resurfacing of old systems. As the underlying business processes are simplified and expedited, the interaction dialogues, data models, access rights, directories, and system support methods must also change. Training and coaching that transfer industry knowledge into data modelers or communication infrastructure planners, for example, will be beneficial. It will be more important to ensure that cost-saving and downsizing initiatives do not lead enterprises to lay off older, knowledgeable staff, only to discover belatedly that they need those employees' industry-specific system and process knowledge.

> " As the RTE endeavor progresses, the changes that must be made to established business processes and their supporting applications will require considerable integration work. "

6. Architect for Agility for a Fast and Flexible Response to Business Change

Modularity in enterprise architecture to lower levels of granularity will be key to the ongoing development of the RTE endeavor. The IT organization must support modularity by breaking apart and remodeling end-to-end business processes — especially those that span multiple departments and business units. The simplification and expediting of processes most likely will apply to partners and suppliers as well. Therefore, architectures must enable repeated change to applications, change that must be implemented quickly and economically. Structural links between elements in the architecture that rely on the continued existence of a particular business model or process sequence will become more fragile. An architecture model that relies on components that can be used and reused in various contexts is a better approach.

The rate of change will be high and continuous. For example, consider how consumer banking has changed during the past 5 years: bank account access via the web; 24/7 systems availability, which improves convenience; account access via mobile devices; and account updates processed in seconds rather than days.

The IT organization must work toward an "enterprise nervous system" architecture and consider how the enterprise nervous system interacts with the broader multi-enterprise technology grid. This grid view is the IT reflection of the business strategists' industry value chain or value network perspective, which is critical to consider when process changes involve outsourced and partner-sourced business services. These process changes require:

- Migrating the enterprise architecture to an Internet infrastructure base
- Developing web services capabilities and a service-oriented-architecture conceptual approach
- Applying application integration middleware

CRITICAL TECHNOLOGY PREREQUISITES

A real-time infrastructure (RTI) is required for an enterprise to be an RTE. A real-time infrastructure represents the future of managing the distributed computing environment. It is a critical prerequisite to achieving RTE business goals. Within RTI, resources — servers, storage, databases, networks, middleware, and applications — used for the delivery of IT services will be standardized and shared across business processes (an insourced model) and businesses (an outsourced model). Unlike today's static computing islands, business priorities and Service Level Agreements (SLAs) will determine resource allocation across end-to-end IT services. IT services will dynamically consume the appropriate level of resources to meet service goals at the lowest price. IT service owners will pay for resource use, like a utility model. The potential future benefits of RTI are dramatic — significantly lowered capital and labor costs, higher IT service quality and increased agility for the infrastructure to respond to changes in business priorities and demand for IT services.

The RTI vision has been made possible in part through base resource markets' maturation, consolidation, and standardization. Just 5 years ago, most data centers were deploying applications built on 5 to 10 application development environments, 5 to 7 databases, and 6 to 9 operating system variants and associated hardware architectures. These markets have consolidated dramatically. At the same time, the underpinnings for a more standardized application architecture — that is, web services — have emerged. With fewer application and technology architecture variants, each supplier has a vested interest in making its offering more manageable. The vision of a more automated, dynamic data center realizing the goals of cost reduction, improved service levels, and increased agility is possible.

CONCLUSION

For many enterprises, investments in information technology over the past 50 years were largely motivated by desires to improve the productivity of various job functions and enterprise processes as well as the efficiency and timeliness of many back-office procedures. These efforts were commonly based upon the need for managers and executives to gain insight into the operational and financial status of the organization. However, all too often the results of those information compilation efforts revealed difficulties that either already occurred or that lay ahead but were too late to avoid. Captains of ships have the ability to determine their location, course, speed, and progress toward their goal, all in real time. Captains of industry deserve nothing less. We strongly urge IT professionals to lead efforts within their enterprises that will specifically detect the events that could lead an enterprise to harm or toward lucrative opportunities and to monitor those events in real time. They should then examine the processes employed to respond to these detected events and alter them to achieve optimal productivity and profitability. To accomplish these detection and response efforts, the appropriate real-time infrastructure must be planned, designed, implemented, and operated to yield maximum results. When all these steps are in operation, you will have truly transformed your organization from a backward-looking environment into the exciting realm of the real-time enterprise.

29

Real-Time Case Study: Item-Level Tracking and Auto-ID

From May through August 2003, SAP, along with the Massachusetts Institute of Technology, International Paper, Inc., and a leading consumer goods company, participated in a unique test of a remarkable possibility for adaptive logistics and supply chain management: complete manufacturer–to–retail shelf-space RFID inventory tracking. In this chapter, SAP Global Research gives us a nuts-and-bolts look at this leading-edge deployment.

SAP Global Research & Innovation

Radio frequency identification (RFID) is perhaps the most exciting emerging technology in supply chain management since the barcode. Inventory control at the product level is the holy grail of supply chain management. SAP has been examining its possible impact for years. In September 2002, the company began internal development on an MIT-hosted pilot program to test a unique end-to-end logistics program. SAP also partnered with a number of equipment suppliers and consumer goods marketing companies to launch a large-scale pilot that began in the spring of 2003. This program created a prototype software and hardware system for a new network that would allow companies to track goods using low-cost RFID tags. In theory, the system could enable wide-scale vendor-managed inventory at some future date. With such a system in place, a company could eliminate spot inventory shortages and ensure that store shelves are always stocked with products, generating millions in additional sales every year.

This deployment was a pilot of the SAP® Auto-ID Infrastructure, a Java-based application that uses RFID to create a corporate nervous system that communicates with SAP® R/3®. The most important goal was to test this technology at the per-item level without disrupting existing inventory control methods. Previous tests have been conducted at the shipping container level and in distribution centers, but no one had used RFIDs to track the item level, all the way to the store shelf. We also had to maintain Planogram compliance, ensuring that each product is stocked at the right shelf location. Planogramming is a widely used inventory control and display system.

Smart shelves, manufactured by International Paper, Inc., figured prominently in this deployment. These retail shelving units are capable of recognizing RFID codes and communicating wirelessly with a server. On March 27, 2003, we installed smart shelves in selected retail stores. The SAP Auto-ID Infrastructure went live in May, and all SAP systems were operational on June 11. Shortly after, the first successful planned order was created by our supply and demand planning module, SAP® APO. We created the first Event Handler using Supply Chain Event Management (SCEM).

The pilot program ran successfully until the first week in August when, based on privacy concerns, the retail shelving portion was curtailed. Consumer privacy concerns stem from the impression that RFID tags would not be disabled at purchase and the unscrupulous could use the technology for surveillance or profiling. After the retail program was curtailed, distribution-level research continued until the end of the program on September 1.

THE PHYSICAL LANDSCAPE

The system assembled by SAP and its partners consisted of equipment at four distinct locations, two distribution centers and two in-store locations — one in the storeroom and one at the shelf. At the first location, the tote room, in this case a regional distribution center, a

Philips, Inc. 13.56-MHz I–Code radio frequency identification (RFID) tag was attached to every product. The tag contains a unique Electronic Product Code (EPC) that is used throughout the supply chain for tracking. Tag readers are connected to a network hub communicating with Savant, MIT's data management/monitoring and task management software. Once Savant receives the EPCs, it sends a query over the Internet to an Object Name Service (ONS) database that matches the EPC number to the address of a server with extensive product information.

Once logged into the system, the products were packed into RFID-tagged cases, loaded onto RFID-tagged palettes, and put into shipping containers with Matrics ultra-high frequency (UHF) RFID container tags attached. After container-to-item associations are sent from Savant to the Auto-ID Infrastructure, the containers are taken to the cross-dock (in this case, the retail store's distribution center). Loading dock RFID readers record the containers leaving the center. Upon arrival at the retail store's distribution center, the container tags are read and the product's current status data is migrated into the system.

From the cross-dock, the products are sent to the retail store where they are stored in the stockroom prior to being displayed on the shelf. Upon arrival at the retail store, the shipping container is automatically logged into the system at several points within the store, including the loading dock and the impact door. When shelf restocking is necessary, the individual products are unpacked and placed on a smart shelf that monitors tagged items at each slot on the shelf and sends add/remove events wirelessly to a server and then into the system via Savant.

THE SYSTEM LANDSCAPE

Each location had commercially available job-specific hardware tied to individual installations of Savant through network hubs. The individual Savant installations communicated with a master Savant installation at MIT over a dial-up connection. In this scenario, the regional distribution center contained a terminal; Feig Electronic, Inc., tote readers; item readers; tag writers; and barcode readers. The retail distribution center used a conveyor reader. The retail store had Matrics, Inc., container readers at the receiving dock door and the impact door. On the store's show floor, the smart shelf communicated via wireless with a local server that was connected over dial-up with a global server and terminal for web reports. As the information was tabulated through the master Savant installation at MIT, the data was sent over the Internet using web services to the SAP Auto-ID Infrastructure.

SAP SYSTEM LANDSCAPE

The system consists of an installation of the SAP Auto-ID Infrastructure, R/3, SCEM, APO, SAP® Enterprise Portal, and SAP® Business Information Warehouse (BW) communicating globally. Authorized personnel view the information through a web portal.

The Auto-ID Infrastructure (AII) stores a model of tracked items for each site and its associated storage methods (that is, containers, docks, and smart shelf). AII sends periodic inventory updates to the APO planning system to generate sales forecasts and recommended weekly orders. AII sends handling unit/container updates to the SCEM execution system to track the entire lifecycle of each shipment.

The object elements in the data model in this scenario are very simple. Each element represents a tagged product, case, palette, or container. Each tag is uniquely identified by a 96-bit EPC number. The EPC provides unique identifiers for 268 million companies with 16 million object classes and 68 billion serial numbers in each class, more than enough serial numbers for years to come. Each element can have both parent and children associations to tie a product to a case, a case to a palette, a palette to a container, and so on.

The structural elements are also straightforward: each structural element represents either a physical location (for example, in a distribution center or on a smart shelf) or a transit state (for example, outbound from a distribution center, being moved from the storeroom to the shelf). Each element also has a hierarchical relationship; structural elements may be parents to object elements. Other data elements include business status (transaction state, approvals, shipments), which, unlike object and structural elements, do not persist throughout the life of the product.

LESSONS LEARNED

Every section of the study — human factors, physical factors, system factors, structural factors — yielded important findings. Of course, in almost any enterprise-level study, the most enlightening and helpful lessons are often those relating to people.

Participants in this kind of study often demonstrate flights of creativity that show researchers new ways systems can be used or reveal flaws that seem self-evident in retrospect. In this study, most of the research's value came from the system's ability to track individual items from start to finish. However, applying item tags in this scenario was not automated — and in some cases it was not performed. It became immediately apparent that the system needed exception management tools to provide that flexibility in dealing with untagged items, items not associated with cases, cases not associated with palettes, and so on.

Timestamps were another important issue. When events come from multiple sources and multiple sites, the system must be updated based on a timestamp. Add and remove events must be time-stamped to correctly reflect the current inventory on the shelf. For a distributed system, this requires synchronizing timestamps across multiple time zones and locations.

The study also helped us formulate operational rules. The shipment lifecycle does not end when the container is received by the store but when the item from the shipment appears on the shelf. When the system receives an event from the smart shelf, it checks to see if the item is the first item from a particular shipment. If this operational condition is met, this triggers the end of the shipment, and an event is dispatched to SCEM.

On the physical location level, we learned that a thorough site inspection and survey must be conducted both before and after deploying the system. Installation problems can be anticipated. Once the system is in place, hardware and software testing should be conducted. Tag readers must be operational and must communicate with network hubs and servers. Radio interference must be detected and avoided. Shielding must be in place. Tag readers are purposely designed to have a short range, and deployment patterns must take this into account. Obstacles in storerooms can also prevent accurate record-keeping. Local Savant installations must communicate with the master installation over dial-up connections. All these elements need to be tested and confirmed operational. Like any mission-critical function, Auto-ID systems rely on electricity, so power management and backup systems must be in place to ensure continuity.

Configuration rules are required. Derived or implied information must be configurable. Employees have to learn that a beep at the loading dock door is different from a beep at the smart shelf. Events from different locations should trigger different actions and processes.

This pilot demonstrated the power of RFID in creating a corporate nervous system. It showed us some of the real-world issues that must be handled and helped SAP, along with its partners, continue their leadership in making the vision of the real-time enterprise a reality.

Conclusion

In its quest to lay a wreath before the accomplishments of Hasso Plattner's first 60 years, this book has covered a lot of ground. The origins of the real-time enterprise in the founding minds of SAP discussed in Part I led to an analysis of the expanding landscape of computing power in Part II. Leading business and technology thinkers explained in Part III how all this would and should be put to work. The user interface in all its forms was the center of Part IV, and the book ends in Part V with a look at how the digital nervous system of the enterprise will emerge and grow.

With so many voices and so many ideas, spanning so many careers, it is hard to distill it all into one simple message. Nevertheless, we identified several themes that do provide a workable summary of some of the arguments in this book. These themes may not solve the urgent problems of implementing the real-time enterprise, but they categorize them in a useful manner for those on the battlefield.

- **Design and Abstraction** — Many contributors told the story of how the real-time enterprise must first exist in a coherent design, one that has proper separation of layers and uses abstraction to manage complexity. The history of SAP pointed out how disciplined design leads to practical business benefits. Many of the contributors emphasize the need for good design to support evolvability, outsourcing, and compelling user interfaces.
- **Standards** — The growth of both XML and web services illustrates the profound impact of simple standards with the right governance structure

at the right time. Every layer of the enterprise and the application needs more standards. Both companies and vendors must find a way to meet the challenge of cooperating to create standards to drive down the cost of creating new technology to automate business relationships.

- **Human Factors** — The real-time enterprise is held back in some ways because the user interface exposes too little or too much of the complexity of a process. The contributors stressed that understanding the goals of the user, the role played in a process, and the nature of the user interface tools are all key to providing the right controls so that the ultimate real-time processing engine, the human brain, can have the proper effect on a business.

- **New Demands on Applications** — A major part of realizing the real-time enterprise will be getting existing applications to do what they do better, faster, cheaper, and with more flexibility. But it is also clear that new challenges are on the way unlike any experienced until now. Radio frequency IDs (RFIDs) and the expansion of automation threaten to drown the corporation in data. The explosion of mobile devices will not only create the demand to support many new and profoundly different types of user interfaces but will also change the way many fundamental business processes work. Applications must become always on and always aware. It will be impossible to anticipate every new demand. The only refuge will be found in conscious design, elegant abstraction, and continuous improvement.

- **Rise of Process** — Perhaps the single most important lesson in these pages is the emphasis on proper understanding and design of process as a key enabler of the real-time enterprise. Process is the membrane between the world of business and technology. Process is the container for the innovations of businesspeople that can be implemented by technologists, enabling end-to-end support for business scenarios that represent the whole value chain. Creating the necessary skills and systems for business process evolution to rapidly improve performance and adaptability based on experience may well become the only sustainable competitive advantage.

- **Cultural Change** — The real-time enterprise will provide more information and capabilities from the top to the bottom of the organization. Managing empowered employees will become a challenge to organizational structures and traditional corporate culture. Innovation in creating culture, finding the right employees to embody the culture, transmitting it through training, and embedding it in software may become a key point of differentiation.

When this project was first conceived, the SAP Executive Board hoped that it would become a fitting tribute to the energetic mind of Hasso Plattner, a man of relentless focus and drive. We believe that the wisdom contained in the many insights and recommendations from this elite collection of contributors is just the right way to honor a man who has helped so many to achieve so much.

The SAP Executive Board